The Unofficial Legend of Zelda Cookbook

The Unofficial Legend of Zelda Cookbook

By Aimee Wood

Standard Edition

This book is unofficial and unauthorized.

This publication is designed to provide accurate and authoritative information with regard to the subject matter covered. It is sold with the understanding that the publisher is not engaged in rendering legal, accounting, or other professional advice. If legal advice or other expert assistance is required, the services of a competent professional person should be sought.
---From a *Declaration of Principles* jointly adopted by a committee of the American Bar Association and a Committee of Publishers and Associations.

Many names and phrases used by corporations to set apart their product are claimed as trademarks. Where those names appear in this cookbook, and I was aware of a trademark claim, the names have been printed with initial capital letters.

This book is unofficial and unauthorized. It is not authorized, approved, licensed, or endorsed by Nintendo, The Legend of Zelda, or any of their developers, creators, distributors, or publishers.

Recipes, cover, and interior design by Aimee Wood.

Signature page illustration by Brittney Weiland.
www.brittneyweiland.com

The Standard Edition of this book is available at quantity discounts for bulk purchases.

The Master Edition includes an exclusive Master Chapter with an additional 7 Master Recipes in a faux leather bound, rounded spine, foil stamped, author signed and foil numbered tome, with ribbon book marks and luxury paper. Limited Availability.

For more information, please visit:
aimeewoodworks.com
theunofficiallegendofzeldacookbook.com

For Link

And for all those who find courage when stepping into Link's shoes.

I hope these recipes help to transport you back to Hyrule, with an ocarina in one hand, a trusty sword in the other, and a kingdom worth saving.

Contents

Foreword

This book exists thanks to The Legend of Zelda fans all over the world.

*"If more of us valued food and cheer and song above hoarded gold,
it would be a merrier world." - JRR Tolkien*

The recipes in this cookbook lay in the intersection between love for food and love for Zelda, and at that crossroad I've found a community who is making the world merrier with their food and cheer and song. I hope these recipes will inspire you to cook, and to share good food with good friends, old and new.

For years, I wrote this cookbook alone. Upon completing it, I found that I could not publish it alone. I didn't have the capital to bring this book to life physically, in a way that would do it justice. When I launched the Kickstarter, I hoped enough people might meet me in the crossroads to order a small print run of 100 copies. Instead, over 2000 copies were reserved.

You've unlocked over one hundred extra pages for everyone, bonus chapters, dozens of bonus recipes, and an exclusive Master Edition print run. As promised, those who wished to be are forever listed in the back of this cookbook, starting on page 310! Thank you!!!

We've laughed together, cried together, and now, finally, it's time to cook together! Thank you for your patience and your incredible encouragement as I both finished this cookbook and navigated the world of independent publishing. I'm so glad it is, at long last, in your hands. No matter what happens now, I'll still be here!

For those of you who have just found this cookbook, welcome to the cooking adventure!

Thank you, all of you.

Aimee ♥ ♥ ♥

Introduction

Hey! Listen! Here are 8 things to know before starting your adventure.

1. *These recipes are yours.* They are meant to be adjusted to your taste! Feel free to add more or less of anything, skip or substitute, season to your heart container's content, and experiment! You're now an adventurer in the kitchen, this cookbook is just your trusty guide. Be like Link, and don't be afraid of making dubious food!

2. *Special Instructions.* You will find special instructions and guides in each chapter introduction. If you ever feel lost, please consult these chapter guides! This is especially important for the Salt Grilling, Leaf Steaming, and Chu Jelly Preserves chapters.

3. *Oil.* Use your favorite oil, or if it's a small amount, go without by using a splash of water instead. Many recipes will not indicate what kind of oil, as people have their own preferences. I use a light olive oil, or go without. Please use what you prefer!

4. *Alternatives.* When a recipe calls for butter, milk, or another potential allergen, feel free to use vegan or allergen free alternatives. I've tried to include many suggestions to help make the majority of these recipes accessible to everyone.

5. *Ingredient size.* If it says '2 Swift Carrots' and you aren't sure how large they should be, it's up to you! If you love carrots, go large. If they are not your favorite, go small. If you hate carrots, take it up with Steen. If you're a garlic fiend, add more garlic.

6. *Game Accuracy.* Recipe ingredients don't always match game ingredients. In recreating these dishes, my priorities were game accurate appearances, deliciousness, and compatibility with a majority of dietary habits! With this strategy, some recipes will use different ingredients than they do in game. I hope you don't mind that Rock Sirloin isn't made of rocks. A few recipes are absent due to official versions already existing; if you are looking for Yeto's Soup; a pumpkin, fish, and goat cheese recipe, there is already an official recipe available!

7. *Hygiene.* Wash your hands, wash your ingredients, wash your tools!

8. *Community.* You can still join our cooking adventure on the next page!

Community

A cookbook is just a cookbook. It's the people that bring the food to life!
An online community has grown around this cookbook, and you're invited!

Ingredients:
1 Discord Server*
Taste Testing, to taste
Copious Recipe Discussion
Copious Food Galleries
3 more Zelda Channels; Games, Memes, and Music
750+ Zelda and Cooking fans
Cat Photos, as a garnish

Directions:
1. Find an invite to our Discord at theunofficiallegendofzeldacookbook.com!
2. Discord will walk you through the process to join our server if you haven't done it before.
3. Explore the recipe photo galleries, comment, review, and post your own photos! I plan to compile a gallery of real and in game photos on the official website.
4. If you ever get stuck on a recipe, this is where you can go to get your questions answered quickly! You can also message me there directly if you ever need to, and you can connect with Zelda and cooking fans from all over the world.
5. Enjoy! We're all looking forward to meeting you!

The Unofficial Legend of Zelda Cookbook Website:
theunofficiallegendofzeldacookbook.com

*Discord is basically a large, organized group text and picture forum, like Slack. On our server, you'll find discussions, recipe experiments, alternatives, Zelda memes, and cat pictures. It's where we kick back, chit chat, and snick snack!

Conversions

As a thank you to international backers, this book has been translated into metric, and now includes both US and metric measuring systems in each recipe! Below, you will find charts for additional common conversions, in approximation for rounding purposes.

US	Metric
1 teaspoon	5 ml
1 tablespoon	15 ml
1/4 cup	60 ml
1/3 cup	75 ml
1/2 cup	120 ml
2/3 cup	150 ml
3/4 cup	175 ml
1 cup	240 ml
1/2 ounce	15 grams
1 ounce	30 grams
3 ounces	90 grams
4 ounces	115 grams
8 ounces	225 grams
12 ounces	350 grams
16 oz / 1 pound	450 grams
2 1/4 pounds	1 kilogram
1 inch	2.5 centimeters
2 inch	5 centimeters
12 in / 1 foot	30 centimeters
3 ft / 1 yard	91 centimeters

US	Metric
250 Fahrenheit	120 Celsius
300 Fahrenheit	150 Celsius
325 Fahrenheit	160 Celsius
350 Fahrenheit	180 Celsius
375 Fahrenheit	190 Celsius
400 Fahrenheit	200 Celsius
425 Fahrenheit	220 Celsius
450 Fahrenheit	230 Celsius
500 Fahrenheit	260 Celsius

US

3 teaspoons = 1 tablespoon

2 tablespoons = 1/8 cup

4 tablespoons = 1/4 cup

5 tbs + 1 teaspoon = 1/3 cup

8 tablespoons = 1/2 cup

2 cups = 1 pint / 16 ounces

2 pints = 1 quart / 32 ounces

4 quarts = 1 gallon / 128 ounces

1 pound = 16 ounces

Themed Menus and Recipes

From the themed Hylian Royal Menu, to the Fairy Forest Feast, the menus in this chapter each include a selection of complementary dishes, a suggested drink, and a bonus theme recipe on the following page! This chapter can serve as your inspiration to create delicious formal five course Yiga Clan dinners, Termina Tea spreads, or Lon Lon Ranch Brunches!

Thank You

This chapter was brought to life by over 1500 Zelda and cooking fans. Every hundred new people helped to unlock an additional menu and recipe for this chapter! With your overwhelming help, this chapter has grown to 15 sets of menus and mystery recipes!

Chapter Guide

Each set in this chapter includes two parts; a menu of compatible recipes from this cookbook with page numbers, and a new themed recipe. Whether you need ideas for a fancy Deku Royal Family dinner, a kid friendly New Player Menu, or a Goron Rock-Hard party buffet, this chapter helps you to choose compatible dishes for delicious meals!

Yiga Clan Menu

Start with hors d'ouvre banana coin fritters, cleanse with chilled Creamy Heart Soup, follow with banana leaf Steamed Meat, Vegetables, and Mushrooms, finish with Roasted Mighty Banana sundaes; and sip your Yiga Pursuit all while cursing Link's name.

5 Courses	Dinner Menu

Beverage:
Yiga Pursuit, next page

Appetizer:
Fried Bananas,* page 150

Soup Course:
Creamy Heart Soup, page 76

Main Courses:
Banana Leaf Steamed
Meat or Vegetables, page 204
Banana Leaf Steamed
Steamed Mushrooms, page 203

Dessert:
Roasted Mighty Bananas, page 249

*Coin the bananas instead of halving them, serve in small stacks of 2 to 3 banana coins, speared with a toothpick through the center, and lightly dust with powdered sugar.
Serve on a platter as a light appetizer before dinner.

Yiga Pursuit

A Yigan spin on The Noble Canteen's famed Noble Pursuit, here's the ignoble alternative. Filled with icy mighty bananas and resolve, surely this will please the boss.

2 servings	10 oz glasses	Vegan	Gluten free

Standard:

1 cup cream of coconut *(8 oz or 240 ml)*

3 ripe bananas, halved

1/4 teaspoon ground cinnamon *(.6 g)*

1 teaspoon vanilla extract *(5 ml)*

2 to 3 cups cubed ice *(480 ml to 720 ml)*

6 maraschino cherries or raspberries, for garnish

2 toothpicks, particularly the ones that look like swords

2 bendy straws and umbrellas

Alcoholic:

Add before blending:

2 tablespoons dark rum *(1 oz or 30 ml)*

Directions:

1. Blend coconut cream, bananas, cinnamon, vanilla extract, and ice together until creamy and smooth.

2. Pour into two fancy glasses.

3. Garnish with 3 cherries or raspberries speared onto each toothpick, and an umbrella. Extra points for red or white umbrellas adorned with the Yiga clan symbol. Serve with a bendy straw, and enjoy!

Sheikah Clan Menu

A menu inspired by Koko, the Sheikah Clan's budding chef! Locally sourced Cucco Quiche, Veggie Cream Soup, Stuffed Pumpkins, and choose-your-apple dessert will have you nostalgic for Kakariko village.

4 Courses   Dinner Menu

Beverage:
Guardian Potion, page 286

Appetizer:
Cucco Quiche, next page

Soup Course:
Veggie Cream Soup, page 92

Main Course:
Meat or Veggie Stuffed Pumpkins,
page 122

Dessert:
Hot Butter Apple, page 165
or
Honeyed Apple, page 156

Cucco Quiche

These bite sized Cucco egg canapes are an ideal appetizer for dinner or brunch!
Cocorico is French for the sound a rooster makes, making it likely that Kakariko village is
partially named after the feathery cucco friends that are found in the Sheikah town.

12 servings	40 minutes

Ingredients:

2 large eggs
1/4 cup milk *(60 ml)*
1/8 teaspoon salt *(.7 g)*
1 teaspoon minced garlic *(3 g)*
1/4 small onion, very finely chopped
1 large portobello mushroom, very finely chopped
1 baby red bell pepper, very finely chopped
Shredded pepper jack cheese, to taste
Pie crust dough, if desired*
Non-stick mini muffin pan

Directions:

1. If using pie crust dough, let it warm to room temperature, and then cut into circles and press into your non-stick mini muffin pan.
2. Preheat the oven to 375 degrees Fahrenheit *(190 degrees Celsius)*.
3. Whisk together eggs, milk, salt, and garlic in a large glass measuring cup.
4. Pour a small amount of egg mixture into each muffin cavity, then follow with a sprinkle of onion, mushroom, bell pepper, and shredded cheese, into each.
5. Whisk the egg mixture again, then pour atop the ingredients in your muffin tin. They should each be filled most of the way, not full or over flowing.
6. Bake for 25 to 30 minutes, until the egg is gently browned and done all the way through.
7. Let cool, but serve still warm from the oven. Enjoy!

*I enjoy these mini quiche without crust, but they are delicious with crust as well!
  1 pie crust should be enough for 12 quiche.

Hylian Royal Menu

This royally luxurious six course dinner begins with Red Chu Jelly Canapés and finishes with a dreamy Fruitcake dessert! Serve each course in small portions, and accompany with red or blue Water of Life potions for a dazzling occasion.

6 courses	Dinner Menu

Beverage:
Water of Life Potions, page 280

Hors D'oeuvre:
Red Chu Jelly Canapés,* page 132

Soup Course:
Elixir Soup, page 73

Fish Course:
Blue Shell Escargot, page 208

Main Course:
Meat or Veggie Pies,** page 114

Sorbet:
Royal Apple Sorbet, next page

Dessert:
Fruitcake, page 152

*Prepare Red Chu Jelly. On pita crackers, spread cream cheese or vegan cream cheese, add red chu jelly, and garnish each with a sprig of parsley. Serve canapés on a platter before dinner.

**Be sure to make individual sized hand pies.

Royal Apple Sorbet

This apple lemon palette cleanser is ideally served after the Royal dinner, but before dessert! Naturally sweet, and so simple to make!

4 servings	Overnight	Vegan	Gluten free

Ingredients:

1 cup water *(240 ml)*
1 cup sugar *(225 g)*
1 tablespoon honey or maple syrup *(15 ml)*
1 pound granny smith apples, cored and thinly sliced
2 small lemons, 1 juiced, 1 thinly wedged for garnish
Ice cube tray

Directions:

1. In a sauce pan, mix water, sugar, and honey until dissolved, then bring to a boil.
2. Allow to cool, then pour into an ice tray, and freeze over night. At the same time, freeze apple slices in a sealed bag or container over night.
3. Blend sweetened ice, frozen apples, and 1 lemon's juice until smooth, try to avoid over blending, as you do not want the blade to melt your sorbet.
4. Serve right away, or store in a sealed container in the freezer.
5. To serve, scoop a small sphere onto a tiny rounded dish, to prevent it from sliding around. Garnish each with a lemon wedge, and enjoy!

Monster Mask Menu

This monstrously purple banquet is ideal for your Blood Moon Celebration!
From appetizer to soup and main course, to cleanser and dessert, each of these recipes
utilize monster extract; sure to shock your guests while delighting their stomachs!

5 courses	Dinner Menu

Beverage:
Monster Extract Drink, page 298

Appetizer:
Mini Monster Rice Balls, page 182

Soup Course:
Monster Soup, page 86
or
Monster Stew, page 88

Main Course:
Monster Curry and Rice, page 191

Cleanser:
Wildberry Monster Sorbet, next page

Dessert:
Monster Cake, page 162

*I highly recommend purple *gel* food coloring, for the most shocking pop of color in all of these recipes. If you prefer natural dyes, I have also prepared a couple of natural food coloring recipes, see the Monster Extract Dye on page 173.

Wildberry Monster Sorbet

Cleanse your palette with this icy purple sorbet while basking in the glow of the rising Blood Moon!

4 servings*	10 minutes	Vegan	Gluten free

Ingredients:
1 1/2 cups mixed raspberries and blackberries, frozen *(225 g)*
3 tablespoons honey or maple syrup *(45 ml)*
Fresh mint leaves, for garnish

Directions:
1. Pulse blend the raspberries and honey or maple syrup until smooth, try to avoid over blending, as you do not want the blade to melt your sorbet.
2. Serve right away, or store in a sealed container in the freezer.
3. To serve, scoop a small sphere onto a tiny rounded dish, to prevent it from sliding around. Garnish each with a mint leave, and enjoy!

*This assumes a very small, ~2 ounce, serving size, to be used as a palette cleanser. To serve larger scoops, please double this recipe!

New Player Menu

This menu is full of easy to make, kid friendly food! Have a lovely time planning and cooking dinner with little ones, and get your hands messy!

4 courses	Dinner Menu

Beverage:
Red Potions, served in bottles, page 277

Appetizer:
Veggie Rice Balls,* page 176

Main Courses:
Skewer Adventure,** page 49

Dessert:
Rock Hard Food, page 170

Experiment:
Star Fragment Candy, next page

Cooking Guide

Preparation:
-Make Veggie Rice mix and cool.
-Set out skewer ingredients in bowls.
-Age dependent: prepare the potion bottles yourself, or set out supplies.
-Measure out ingredients for dessert.

Cooking:
-Make Skewers first, then while they are cooking:
-Make potions and Rice Balls, eat.
-When skewers are done and cooled, eat.
-Wait a bit for dessert, then make and eat Rock Hard Food.

*Leave out the green onions, ginger, and garlic, to appeal to children's taste. Make sure the rice mix is properly cooled so little ones can touch it safely to roll their own rice balls, and feel free to add corn or other vegetables.

**Kids can have a lot of fun designing their own skewers if you prepare chopped ingredients before hand! Do make sure to prepare any non-vegetable skewers yourself, to prevent contamination.

Star Fragment Candy

Grow your own creamsicle flavored Star Fragment with this week long experiment!
This recipe is for 2 candy sticks, please duplicate for more!

2 servings	1 week	Vegan	Gluten free

Ingredients:

4 cups sugar *(900 g)*
2 cups water *(480 ml)*
1/2 teaspoon vanilla extract *(2.5 ml)*
1/2 teaspoon orange flavor or extract *(2.5 ml)*
Yellow food coloring
2 wooden cake pop sticks
2 glass jars, 12 ounces each *(350 ml each)*
2 clothes pins or clips, to hang sticks inside jars

Game Guide

The Legend of Zelda: Breath of the Wild.

Star Fragment

Day 1:

1. Soak your wooden sticks in water for half an hour.
2. Roll wooden sticks in sugar until they are coated, then lay them carefully on a tray to dry.

Day 2:

3. An adult should boil the water, then sift in sugar while stirring. Mix until sugar is completely dissolved, then bring back to a light boil for 5 minutes.
4. Allow sugar syrup to cool for 10 minutes, then stir in yellow food dye, 2 drops at a time, until the syrup is bright yellow. Continue to cool until safe for children.
5. Carefully pour syrup into jars.
6. Hang a dried sugar stick in the center of each jar, and leave at least an inch of space at the bottom, otherwise a stalagmite may grow from the bottom of the jar to your stick, trapping it there.
7. Store in a cool and dry space, with no direct sunlight for 5 days. You can monitor the progress each day, draw what you see, and keep a log of the crystal growth!

Day 7:

8. Carefully lift the sticks, gently shake off any excess moisture, and hang to dry in a sunny place. When dry, discuss the experiment, the color, the crystals, and what you might do next time for a new color, flavor, or shape! Enjoy!

Rito Celebration Menu

Bring traditional Rito Village cuisine to your next dinner party! Start with vegetable nest Swallow's Roosts appetizers, follow with a spicy soup course, then enjoy the classic Hearty Salmon Meunière paired with a Sunshroom sauté, and finish with one of Misa's specialties!

5 courses	Dinner Menu

Beverage:
The Spicy Elixir, page 289

Appetizer:
Swallow's Roosts, next page

Soup Course:
Spicy Meat or Vegetable Stew,*
page 84

Main Courses:
Hearty Salmon Meunière, page 216
Mushroom Sauté,** page 119

Dessert:***
Nutcake, page 166
or Apple Pie, page 140

*Be sure to use the Spicy variation, you can find the recipe poster in Rito Stable!

**Drop by the Slippery Falcon to purchase Sunshrooms for this dish!

***Both of these recipes can be found in Misa's recipe book in Rito Village!

Swallow's Roosts

These miniature vegetable nests are a delicious novelty appetizer!

4 servings	30 minutes	Vegan

Ingredients:

1 carrot, finely julienned
1 small zucchini, finely julienned
1/2 cup shredded baby spinach *(15 g)*
1 egg or 1 flax egg*
1 tablespoon bread crumbs *(7 g)*
1 tablespoon all purpose flour *(10 g)*
1 tablespoon soy sauce *(15 ml)*
1 teaspoon brown sugar *(4 g)*
8 small pearl onions
A vegetable spiralizer or vegetable spaghetti maker, optional**

Game Guide

The Legend of Zelda: Breath of the Wild.

Swallow's Roost is the name of the Rito Village inn.

Directions:

1. Preheat oven to 350 degrees Fahrenheit *(175 degrees Celsius)*, and line a baking tray with aluminum foil.
2. In a large bowl, add all ingredients except for pearl onions. Mix until well combined, and then stir clockwise until ingredients have straightened out in that direction. This makes it easier to pick up a bundle of vegetables to shape into a nest.
3. Using your hands, pick a bundle of vegetables, about 1/4 of the mixture, and curl it into a small circle. Set it onto your baking tray, and add more vegetables if necessary to make it look like a nest. Make a small divot, and add 2 pearl onions as 'eggs'.
4. Repeat for the remaining nests.
5. Bake for about 18 minutes. They are done when crispy on the edges and bottom. Check with a spatula, they're ready when they keep together instead of falling apart!
6. Serve immediately, or make these in advance and reheat before serving. Enjoy!

*1 tablespoon ground flax seed, plus 3 tablespoons boiling water, mixed and left to sit for 5 minutes. *(15 ml per tablespoon)*
   **This makes julienning the vegetables much easier, but you can do it by hand pretty easily too!

Zora Banquet Menu

Start with bite sized crab cakes, follow with a clam chowder soup course, crispy individual fish pies and seafood paella! End this seafood themed banquet with Zora Taiyaki dessert; scrumptious fish shaped pancakes with a red bean filling.

5 Courses	Dinner Menu

Beverage:
The Electro Elixir, page 287

Appetizer:
Salt Grilled Crab Cakes,* page 98

Soup Course:
Hearty Clam Chowder, page 82

Main Courses:
Fish Pies,** page 214
Seafood Paella, page 228

Dessert:
Zora Taiyaki, next page

*Make these in bite size miniatures, to be served as hors d'oeuvre before dinner.
**Make individually sized pies, one for each person.

Zora Taiyaki

These Japanese Taiyaki inspired desserts are fluffy fish shaped pancakes filled with traditional sweetened red bean paste!

~5 servings	1 day	Vegan

Ingredients:

Red Bean Paste Filling:*
1 cup dry Azuki beans** *(210 g)*
Water
1 cup granulated sugar *(225 g)*
1/8 teaspoon salt *(.7 g)*

Taiyaki Cake:
Taiyaki pan
1 cup all purpose flour *(150 g)*
2 tablespoons sugar *(25 g)*
2 teaspoon baking powder *(10 g)*
1/3 cup water *(80 ml)*
1/3 cup milk, sweetened almond milk works well *(80 ml)*
1 egg or 1 flax egg***

*You are welcome to buy premade filling! You can find red bean paste, or alternatively fill your taiyaki with nutella, chocolate mousse, cream, pudding, anything!

**This is a particular type of red bean, used in many Japanese confections! This recipe uses a chunky red bean paste, that includes the whole bean. If you prefer smooth, you'll need to strain the mixture to remove the bean skins.

***1 tablespoon ground flax seed, 3 tablespoons boiling water, mix and let sit for 5 minutes.

Red Bean Filling Directions:

1. Rinse the Azuki beans in water, and soak them overnight. Rinse again and strain.
2. Add the Azuki beans to a very large pot, then add water about 1.5 inches *(3.8 cm)* over than the beans.
3. Cook on high and uncovered until boiling. Once it's reached a full boil, take it off the heat, cover, and let it stand for 5 minutes. Strain the beans, toss out the water, and add the beans back to the pot.
4. Add water until it just covers the beans, then cook on high until boiling. Once it's reached a full boil, turn it to medium low.
5. Continue cooking, adding water to just cover the beans as it evaporates, for about an hour. The azuki beans are done when you can squish one all the way through with your fingers.
6. Add the sugar and pinch of salt, turn heat to medium high. Stir and mash constantly until it thickens. It's done when you can see the bottom of the pot for a couple seconds after each stir.
7. Remove from heat, and pour beans into a cooling container. I like to use a glass casserole dish. The beans will continue to thicken as they cool, when they are room temperature, use immediately, or cover in plastic wrap and keep chilled.

Taiyaki Cake Directions:

8. Run the flour through a sieve into a large bowl, then mix in the baking powder and sugar. Scoop a small well in the center of the mix
9. In a separate container, whisk the water, milk, and egg together, then pour it into the flour well.
10. Mix just enough to combine, then cover and rest in the refrigerator for an hour, then transfer to a container you can easily pour from.
11. Grease the taiyaki pan, and put on medium to medium low heat. Add batter to each fish, just over half way. Be sure to cover all of the fish.
12. While it begins to cook, add your filling to the center of each fish, then pour batter on top to finish filling the mold.
13. Immediately close, and flip. Cook for 2 to 3 additional minutes on each side. Check the fish, when they are golden throughout, they are finished!
14. Let cool for a few minutes, then enjoy!

Goron Rock Hard Menu

This themed buffet will inspire guests with Goron delicacies! Spiced Roasted Lotus Seeds, hot Rock Salt Grilled Greens, and Curry Rice made with Goron Spice! Quench thirst with muddy milkshakes and fireproof elixirs, then dessert with Rock Hard Food and Rock Roast!

5 Courses	Dinner or Buffet Menu

Beverages:
Death Mountain Muddy Milkshakes,
page 296
The Fireproof Elixir, page 282

Appetizer:
Roasted Lotus Seeds, page 248

Main Courses:
Rock Salt Grilled Greens, page 101
Curry Rice, page 190
Made with Goron Spice, page 188

Dessert:
Rock Hard Food, page 170
Rock Roast, next page

Rock Roast

These miniaturized Rock Roasts, also known as Rock Sirloin and similar in looks to Monster Bait, are adorable and delectable. This is a no bake fudge, rolled in walnuts for a rocky coating, and skewered so they can be eaten off the bone. Best of all, you don't have to hike to Gortram Cliff to get one!

| 10 servings | 1 hour | Vegan | Gluten free |

Ingredients:

10 bones, 3 to 5 inches long* *(8 to 12 cm)*
1 cup your favorite chocolate chips, *(8 oz or 225 g)*
1/2 cup unsalted creamy almond butter** *(125 g)*
1/2 teaspoon vanilla extract *(2.5 ml)*
1 1/2 cups walnuts, mixed chopped and whole *(175 g)*
Hot chocolate powder or powdered sugar for dusting

Game Guide

Rock Roast, also known as Rock Sirloin and Rock Brisket, is a Goron delicacy! They can be found on Gortram Cliff in *The Legend of Zelda: Breath of the Wild*, in Dodongo's Cavern in *The Legend of Zelda: Ocarina of Time*, or once, on Rolling Ridge in *The Legend of Zelda: Oracle of Ages*.
You can only find Rock Roast thus far, not make it yourself. However, you can cook a Rock Roast using a cooking pot in The Legend of Zelda: Breath of the Wild to create Grilled Rock Roast!
Monster Bait is another similar looking dish served on the bone, used to attract enemies for a quick getaway. Call this dish whichever you want to!

*Bones! To make your own white chocolate bones with raspberry marrow filling, refer to the Dubious Food recipe on page 144! Or you can use real bones, plastic bones, or anything you have on hand!

**Or any nut butter will work! Unless nut butter doesn't work, in which case sunflower seed butter is wonderful here, or another no nut alternative.

Rock Roast

Directions:

1. Line a large baking sheet with baking paper, and place in the freezer.

2. In a saucepan on low heat, or using a double boiler method, slowly melt the chocolate chips, almond butter, and vanilla extract while stirring until the chocolate is just melted and softly liquid. Try not to heat it too much!

3. Retrieve the baking sheet from the freezer. Carefully pour the melted fudge onto the center of the baking sheet, try not to let it touch the edges of the pan. Your goal is a thin layer of fudge you can later cut into strips and roll onto your bones!

4. Freeze the fudge for around 20 minutes. It should be cool and malleable, not frozen.

5. Remove from the freezer, and with a butter knife, cut the fudge into strips. You want the width of the strips to be smaller than the length of your bones, so they can roll up comfortably and leave bone visible on either end. As tightly as you can, roll the fudge strips onto your bones.

6. Next, prepare a plate of mixed chopped and whole walnuts. Pick up each roast, and roll them in the walnuts. Firmly press the walnuts into each roast, covering all sides.

7. Dust each roast with chocolate powder or powdered sugar to prevent stickiness. Return to the freezer for an additional 30 minutes until completely firm. Serve or store in the refrigerator until serving. Enjoy!

Korok Treat Menu

Finally, enjoy delicious lemon meringue Korok seeds, Hestu's Gift, Deku nuts, and more in this nutty dessert spread!

4 Courses	Dessert Buffet

Treats:

Hestu's Gift and Korok Seeds,
next page

Nutcake, page 166

Honey Candy, page 158

Roasted Acorn, page 241

Deku Sautéed Nuts, page 125

Roasted Lotus Seeds, page 248

The following recipe was inspired by two backers of this cookbook. Teegan and Sarah, enjoy Hestu's gift and Korok Seeds! Thank you!

Hestu's Gift and Korok Seeds

These delicious lemon meringue cookies, shaped like Korok Seeds, might help you forget about the hours you spent collecting all 900 of them. Multiply recipe by 37 for 900 servings.

24+ servings	4 hours	Gluten free

Ingredients:

4 large egg whites, room temperature
1/2 teaspoon cream of tartar (1.7 g)
1/8 teaspoon salt *(.7 g)*
1 cup superfine sugar *(125 g)*
1/2 teaspoon vanilla extract *(2.5 ml)*
Yellow gel food coloring
1/2 teaspoon lemon extract, or finely grated lemon zest *(2.5 ml)*
Pastry or frosting bag with 1/2 inch *(1.25 cm)* round tip

Game Guide

The Legend of Zelda: Breath of the Wild.

Hestu's Gift

Korok Seeds

Directions:

1. Preheat oven to 225 degrees Fahrenheit *(110 degrees Celsius)*. Line 2 cookie sheets with baking paper.
2. In a perfectly clean and dry bowl, whisk together egg whites, cream of tartar and salt. You can do the next part with a standing mixer, or by hand. Mix until foamy, about 3 to 4 minutes by hand.
3. Add 1 spoonful of sugar at a time, mix until fully dissolved, and repeat until all sugar is incorporated. This should take about 10 minutes of constant mixing.
4. When the sugar is fully incorporated, continue mixing and monitor the texture. You are waiting until it all turns shiny and thick. When you pick up your whisk it should leave a stiff peak behind, one that stands up on its own.
5. Add vanilla extract, lemon extract or lemon zest, and food coloring to desired color. Mix until uniform, then scrape into your pastry bag with round tip.
6. Pipe the cookies close together on cookie sheets, go for a Hershey's kiss type shape and size for Korok Seeds, and a larger stacked swirl for Hestu's gifts.
7. Bake for 1 hour, do not open the oven. Turn the heat off, and leave closed for an additional 2 hours, until it is fully cool.
8. Serve immediately or keep in a sealed bag. Enjoy!

Gerudo Warrior Menu

Keep cool with icy drinks and satisfying foods inspired by the shops, poster recipes, and food near Gerudo Town!

5 Courses	Dinner Menu

Beverages:
Ice Chu Jelly, page 307
The Chilly Elixir, page 284

Appetizer:
Speared Hydromelon, next page

Soup Course:
Hearty Clam Chowder, page 82

Main Courses:
Mushroom Risotto, page 118
Seared Steak, page 255

Dessert:
Baked Palm Fruit, page 236

Speared Hydromelon

Harvest your hydromelon from the Gerudo Desert, and enjoy it in this caprese style appetizer! Fresh, juicy, delectable, this will whet your appetite!

| 8 servings | 10 minutes | Vegetarian | Gluten free |

Ingredients:

8 small watermelon balls
8 small mozzarella balls
Fresh basil
3 tablespoons balsamic vinegar *(45 ml)*
2 tablespoons olive oil, optional *(30 ml)*
Freshly ground black pepper
Toothpicks, or miniature swords or spears

Game Guide

The Legend of Zelda: Breath of the Wild.

Hydromelon

Directions:

1. Assemble each appetizer with 1 watermelon ball, 1 mozzarella ball, 1 small and folded leaf of basil.
2. Arrange on a platter, then drizzle with vinegar, and olive oil if you desire. Top with a sprinkling of freshly ground black pepper.
3. Serve immediately, and enjoy!

Vegan- Skip the mozzarella balls, or replace them with baby tomatoes!

Fairy Forest Feast

This vegan Forest Feast is inspired by the Kokiri and the Great Fairies! Enjoy fresh greens, pumpkin stew, refreshingly pink and glittery drinks, and finish with Blupee Pudding!

5 Courses	Dinner Menu

Beverages:
Great Fairy's Tears, page 294
Fairy Tonic, page 291

Salad Course:
Fruit and Mushroom Mix,* page 108

Main Dish:
Pumpkin Stew, page 90

Side Dishes:
Fried Wild Greens, page 107
Vegetable Risotto, page 128

Dessert:
Blupee Pudding, next page

Blupee Pudding

This fluffy and light Blupee pudding is mixed with blueberries, coconut whip cream, marshmallows, and topped with sprinkles!
No blupees are harmed in the making of this dish!

<8 servings	20 minutes	Vegan*	Gluten free

Ingredients:

1 prepared package of blue jello, see directions
Coconut Whip Cream, page 172
Blueberries
Mini marshmallows
Blue or white assorted sprinkles

Directions:

1. Prepare the blue jello according to its instructions, but before you refrigerate, thoroughly mix in a little less than 1/2 of your Coconut Whip Cream.

2. After the jello has firmed, whisk it to break it up and make it smooth.

3. In 8, or less if you prefer larger servings, small serving glasses, divide the ingredients in small layers. Alternate spoonfuls of jello and whip cream, and sprinkle in blueberries, marshmallows, and sprinkles as you go.

4. Top with the rest of the whip cream, and a few more sprinkles, serve immediately, and enjoy!

*Vegan- Make sure to use an agar agar based vegan jello or gelatin. If you can't find a blue variety where you live, don't worry! You can get a clear agar agar jello, then add blue food coloring to get the right color. You could also substitute a thick chia seed pudding, but it will have a very different texture.

Lon Lon Ranch Brunch

Made with fresh Lon Lon milk, eggs, and wildberries, this brunch spread includes hot savory omelets, sweet crepes, and a light platter of assorted fruits! Don't forget Epona's Breakfast on the next page!

4 Courses   Breakfast Menu

Beverages:
Lon Lon Milkshakes, page 279
or
Chateau Romani, page 283

Brunch:
Epona's Breakfast, next page

Honeyed Fruits, page 159

Vegetable Omelets, page 265

Wildberry Crepes, page 268

Epona's Breakfast

These garlic roasted carrots will have you jumping fences and racing across Hyrule field!
Not intended for equine consumption.

8 servings	10 minutes	Vegan	Gluten free

Ingredients:

1 pound baby carrots, with trimmed stems *(16 oz or 450 g)*
1/4 cup shredded fresh parsley *(15 g)*
1 tablespoon minced garlic, or more to taste *(9 g)*
1/4 cup water *(60 ml)*
Ground sea salt, to taste
Olive oil, optional

Game Guide

The Legend of Zelda:
Ocarina of Time
Majora's Mask
Four Swords Adventures
Breath of the Wild
Hyrule Warrior Legends

Carrots in The Legend of Zelda series can be used to spur horses, restore hearts, or increase speed or stamina!

Directions:

1. Preheat oven to 400 degrees Fahrenheit *(205 degrees Celsius)*.
2. Toss carrots, fresh parsley, garlic, and water together in a baking tray. Sprinkle sea salt and olive oil to taste on top.
3. Roast for about 30 minutes, stirring once halfway through. Carrots should be starting to brown in spots, if not, stir, and roast for an additional 5 to 10 minutes.
4. Let cool for a few minutes before serving, and enjoy!

Skull Kid Munch Menu

This snack spread is inspired by Skull Kid and Deku Scrubs! Plenty of finger foods makes this menu ideal for keeping a party fed, without going full out on dinner!

4 Courses	Snack Menu

Snacks:

Deku Dip, next page, served with pita chips and sliced raw vegetables.

Spicy Sautéed Peppers, page 124

Sautéed Nuts, page 125

Salt Grilled Greens,* page 101

*No need to actually grill them on a salt block if you are low on time; just prepare in a normal cast iron pan, with freshly ground rock salt! You can do this right after the Spicy Sautéed Peppers in the same pan, both dishes are very quick to prepare, and are great hot or cold.

Deku Dip

A regional recipe from Deku Forest, this garlic and pine nut hummus is perfect with crunchy carrots, sliced bell peppers, cucumbers, and pita chips!

| 8 servings | 10 minutes | Vegan | Gluten free |

Ingredients:

2 cans of chickpeas or garbanzo beans *(15 oz each)*
1 tablespoon minced garlic *(9 g)*
1/4 cup toasted pine nuts* *(35 g)*
2 tablespoons sesame seeds *(16 g)*
2 tablespoons fresh lemon juice *(30 ml)*
1/4 teaspoon cumin *(.5 g)*
1/4 teaspoon smoked paprika *(.5 g)*
A pinch of cayenne pepper
Salt to taste
Dipping snacks, like fresh sliced vegetables or chips

Game Guide

Freshly-Picked Tingle's Rosy Rupeeland.

6 Twisted Tusks
2 Gelatines
6 Explosive Claws

Directions:

1. In a blender, add 1 full can of beans, including liquid, and 1 drained can of beans, without liquid. Then add the rest of the ingredients in order.
2. Blend until smooth, then taste. You may want to add additional seasoning, cayenne pepper, lemon juice, or salt to taste, then blend again, until it suits you.
3. Transfer to a bowl, cover, and let sit in the refrigerator for an hour or so before serving. Eat within a week, and enjoy!

*You can toast them yourself by tossing them in a hot pan for a few minutes.

Termina Tea Time Menu

The following afternoon tea spread is inspired by The Legend of Zelda: Majora's Mask!
Enjoy caramelized Chateau Romani accompanied by an assortment of sweets!

4 Courses	Tea Menu

Beverages:
Chateau Romani Milk Tea, page 283

Appetizer:
Magic Beans, next page

Rock Sirloin Fudge, page 30

Egg Tarts, page 148

Miniature Carrot Cakes,* page 142
and
Coconut Whip Cream, page 172

*Prepare using a mini muffin tin.

Magic Beans

These themed cake balls are the perfect treat for a Termina Tea party!

32 servings*	10 minutes	Vegan	Gluten free

Ingredients:

1 finished and cooled cake, in a flavor of your choice**
1+ cup frosting, of a complementary flavor *(240+ ml)*
12 ounces of white candy melts or wafers *(340 g)*
Green, blue, yellow, and red food coloring
Toothpicks or cake pop sticks
Block of styrofoam, to dry cake pops
Edible shimmer or glitter, optional
A green pod tray, you can make one out of green paper

Game Guide

The Legend of Zelda: Ocarina of Time.

The Legend of Zelda: Majora's Mask.

The Legend of Zelda: Hyrule Warriors Legends.

Directions:

1. Use your hands to slowly break the cake apart into fine crumbs in a large bowl.
2. Add 1 cup of frosting, then mix until uniform. You want dough that will firmly keep its shape as a ball. If it is too dry, add a little bit more frosting at a time.
3. Roll the dough into bite sized balls, place on a platter, and chill for one hour.
4. Follow the candy melt directions for melting, and stir until smooth.
5. Divide the melted candy into 4 microwave safe bowls, then add a few drops of different food coloring to each. Mix, and add more food coloring, until you reach the color you desire. If it hardens, remelt in the microwave for a few seconds.
6. Spear a cake ball with a cake pop stick or toothpick, then gently roll it in the candy until covered. Stick them into the styrofoam block to dry. Repeat for all cake balls.
7. Once dry, lightly brush them with edible glitter, take them off their sticks, and serve on a green pod tray! Enjoy!

*About 32 small truffles, 8 of each color! Feel free to halve or quarter this recipe.
**A standard box mix size cake! Choose a cake that works for your diet, in whatever flavor you love; or get fancy and make 4 differently flavored cakes for each color Magic Bean!

This recipe was inspired by a backer of this cookbook. Erika R. Broadway, your enthusiasm and devotion spurred me on, thank you.

Tingly and Minish Dinner

This wholesome dinner is so satiating. Chunky meat, vegetable, and potato stew with wheat bread, complemented with Glazed Mushrooms, Super Sweetcorn, and Mashed Potatoes and Gravy. Follow with Fruit pie or Bum Peach Cobbler, or both!

5 Courses	Dinner Menu

Beverages:
Tingly Power Up Potion, page 300
Moka Chai's Mocha Chai, page 301

Soup Course:
Tasty Meat Stew, page 84
Wheat bread, page 95

Entrées:
Glazed Mushrooms,* page 110
Super Sweetcorn, next page
Mashed Potatoes and Gravy, page 104

Dessert:
Slice of Fruit Pie, page 154
Bum Peach Cobbler, next page

*Serve with toothpicks.

Super Sweetcorn

These two Tingly inspired recipes can be cooked at the same time, and by the time you are done eating dinner, the Bum Peach Cobbler will be cool enough to eat!

| 4 servings | 35 minutes | Vegan | Gluten free |

Ingredients:

4 ears of fresh sweet corn, husked
1 tablespoon brown sugar *(12.5 g)*
3 tablespoons water *(45 ml)*
Ground sea salt, to taste
Ground black pepper and red pepper flakes, to taste

Game Guide

Freshly-Picked Tingle's Rosy Rupeeland.

Super Sweetcorn

Directions:

1. Preheat the oven to 375 degrees Fahrenheit *(190 degrees Celsius)*.
2. In a shallow plate, mix brown sugar and water. Roll each ear of corn in the mixture to coat it, then sprinkle salt, black pepper, and red pepper flakes over the top to taste, and wrap individually in aluminum foil. Prepare Bum Peach Cobbler below.
3. Bake corn in a baking tray for 20 to 30 minutes, turning the corn over half way through. Carefully remove corn from foil, and serve immediately. Enjoy!

Bum Peach Cobbler

Ingredients:

2 cups ripe peaches, sliced *(500 g)*
1 cup rolled oats *(90 g)*
1/2 cup brown sugar *(90 g)*
1 teaspoon cinnamon, and pinch of nutmeg if you desire *(2.6 g)*
1/8 teaspoon salt *(.7 g)*
1/4 cup butter, or vegan butter *(55 g)*

Game Guide

Freshly-Picked Tingle's Rosy Rupeeland.

Bum Peaches

Directions:

4. In a bowl, mix together everything but the peaches. Pour half of this into a small glass baking dish, add the peaches, and stir. Pour the rest of the mixture on top.
5. Bake for 20 to 30 minutes, when the crumble on top is starting to brown, and it all smells delicious. Serve warm, top with ice cream, and enjoy!

Hearty Dinner Menu

Treat your loved ones to a romantically candle lit and Zelda inspired dinner. This hearty cuisine will fill heart containers on a special occasion.

4 Courses	Dinner Menu

Beverages:
Red Potion, page 277

or

The Hearty Elixir, page 297

Soup Course:
Creamy Heart Soup,* page 76

Entrées:
Hearty Salmon Meunière, page 216
Hearty Rice Balls,** page 175

Dessert:
Heart Containers, next page

*See page 76 to choose between a cool soup palette cleanser, or a traditional veggie cream soup. Either way, you'll add heart shaped dragon fruit slices for a romantic look!

**Choose what kind of rice balls you prefer, and shape as soft hearts instead of triangles.

Heart Containers

These heart shaped and raspberry filled shortbread cookies are so soft, delicious, and vegan!
Treat your loved ones to these beautifully baked heart containers!

~12 servings	1 hour	Vegan

Ingredients:
Heart shaped cookie cutters, 1 large, 1 small for windows

Rasberry Heart Filling:
1 cup raspberries *(150 g)*
1 1/2 tablespoons chia seeds *(15 g)*
2 teaspoons lemon juice, freshly squeezed *(10 ml)*
1/2 teaspoon vanilla extract *(2.5 ml)*
2 tablespoons honey *(30 ml)*

Shortbread Heart Container Cookies:
3/4 cup vegan butter, softened to room temperature *(80 g)*
1/2 cup sugar *(115 g)*
2 tablespoons sweetened almond milk *(30 ml)*
1/2 teaspoon almond extract *(2.5 ml)*
1 teaspoon vanilla extract *(5 ml)*
2 cups all purpose flour *(300 g)**
1/2 teaspoon salt *(2.5 g)*
1/2 teaspoon baking powder *(2.5 g)*
Powdered sugar, for garnish

*Gluten Free- Use a gluten free all purpose flour, or if you can find it, a gluten free all purpose pastry flour!

Heart Containers

Directions:

1. Heat raspberries in a small sauce pan over medium high heat, for 3 to 5 minutes, stirring continuously. It's done when the raspberries have broken apart into a sauce, but are still chunky. Turn heat to low, add chia seeds, lemon juice, vanilla extract, and honey, stir for 2 minutes, then remove from heat.

2. Preheat oven to 350 degrees Fahrenheit *(175 degrees Celsius)*, then prepare a large baking tray or two medium trays with parchment paper.

3. In a large bowl, beat the butter and sugar together with a wooden spoon until well mixed and fluffy, then mix in almond milk, almond extract and vanilla extract.

4. In a different bowl, sift your flour in through a sieve, then mix in the salt and baking powder until combined.

5. Slowly combine the dry flour mixture into the wet mixture, until it is a uniform dough. If necessary, add a little more flour if it is too sticky.

6. Flour a flat surface and roll out the dough very thinly, 1/8 inch thick *(.3 cm)*. Cut out 24 large hearts, then use the small heart cutter to cut out a window in 12 of the large hearts. With a spatula, place each heart carefully onto your baking tray, about 1 inch apart.

7. Bake for about 10 minutes, but monitor closely. It is far better to under cook these then to over cook them! The ideal cookie is a very light gold, so it crumbles easily.

8. Cool for 15 minutes, then assemble the cookies by spreading the heart filling over the full heart shape, then top with a window heart. Press gently together, then sprinkle a small puff of powdered sugar over each cookie. Serve immediately, or store in an airtight container at room temperature. Enjoy!

This recipe was inspired by a backer of this cookbook. Cody 'WhiteKnight' Baldree, your kindness and dedication is so cherished, thank you.

Skewers
Choose Your Skewer Adventure Game

Warning and Beware
This chapter is not like other chapters.
You and YOU ALONE are in charge of what happens in these recipes.

There are dangerous pointy objects, ingredients, adventures, and consequences. You must use all of your cooking talents and much of your common sense. Your decisions could end in deliciousness or disaster- or even death. But don't lose hope. YOU can go back and make a different choice to change the taste of your skewers!

The story begins...

You are reading from the best cookbook ever. You intend to use it to make Skewers, a type of delicious food made from various ingredients impaled and cooked on sticks. The first step looms ahead, you must prepare a sauce. Marinades and sauces are listed just below on the page, but you are immediately drawn to one. Ultimately, you decide:

>**Pineapple Barbecue**, turn to page 54.
>**Orange Teriyaki**, turn to page 53.
>**Garlic Rosemary Lemon**, turn to page 52.

>To skip the cutscene. Make simple mushroom skewers now, turn to page 66.
>You are confused. Turn to the Skewer Index on page 50.
>To find the Game Guides. Turn to the Skewer Game Guide on page 67.

Skewer Index

Skewers are particularly perfect for dinner parties or for children! Prepare and lay out all of the ingredients, then allow guests or kids to assemble their own skewers!
Cook them, and enjoy!

Delicious Combination Suggestions

Pineapple Barbecue Marinated Mushrooms and Tofu, with Broccoli, Onions, and Zucchini.

Orange Teriyaki Marinated Beef, with Mini Bell Peppers, Baby Tomatoes, and Red Onions.

Lemon Rosemary Garlic Marinated Salmon, with Brussels Sprouts, Lemon wedges, and Okra.

Skewer Tips and Tricks

Prepare yourself against the hidden dangers of skewers!

1. Prevent disease! No poultry is listed in the options here! First, the skewers in The Legend of Zelda: Breath of the Wild do not include any poultry. Second, the risk of contamination between the fresh ingredients, and by individuals making their own skewers, is very high when using raw poultry. Skip the sickness.

2. Raw meats should only be handled carefully by adults. Help children with their skewers, or limit them to vegetables.

3. Make sure everyone involved washes their hands before, AND after.

4. Metal skewers can burn fingers and tongues, be careful!

5. Wooden skewers can catch fire, especially over a fire or grill. You can prevent this by soaking them in water for at least 30 minutes before using them! If they do catch fire, you can blow them out easily.

6. If you have more supplies after eating, go ahead and assemble the rest of the ingredients onto skewers, but do not cook them. Instead, wrap them in plastic wrap and save them for up to 3 days. Cooked skewers don't keep as well as uncooked ones.

Garlic Rosemary Lemon

>You've chosen the Garlic Rosemary Lemon adventure from page 49!

| 1 cup *(240 ml)* | 5 minutes | Vegan | Gluten free |

Ingredients:

1/4 cup fresh lemon juice, about 2 large lemons *(60 ml)*
1 teaspoon lemon zest, finely grated *(2 g)*
1 tablespoon fresh rosemary, minced *(3.6 g)*
1 tablespoon garlic, minced *(9 g)*
1/2 tablespoon sugar *(7 g)*
1/2 teaspoon cracked black pepper *(1 g)*
1/2 teaspoon coarse sea salt *(3 g)*
1/2 cup extra virgin olive oil *(120 ml)*
1/4 teaspoon red pepper flakes or to taste, optional *(.5 g)*

Directions:

1. Add all ingredients except olive oil to a small mixing bowl. Whisk vigorously until salt and sugar have dissolved. Add olive oil, and whisk until combined.
2. Reserve half in a container you can easily drizzle from, the other half you will use as marinade in the next step! Make sure to vigorously stir before using, there may be some oil separation.

Next...

The zesty aroma from the marinade is wafting into your nostrils! Now more decisions await you! What main ingredients will you prepare and then marinate!? Will you pick one? All of them? It is up to you. Ultimately, you decide on:

>**Meat Skewers**, turn to page 55.
>**Fish Skewers**, turn to page 56.
>**Seafood Skewers**, turn to page 57.
>**Mushrooms Skewers**, turn to page 58.
>**Tofu Skewers**, turn to page 59.

Orange Teriyaki

>You've chosen the Orange Teriyaki adventure from page 49!

| 1 cup *(240 ml)* | 5 minutes | Vegan | Gluten free |

Ingredients:

1/4 cup water *(60 ml, 2 fl oz)*

1/4 cup fresh orange juice, about 1 orange *(60 ml, 2 fl oz)*

1/2 teaspoon orange zest, finely grated *(1 g)*

1/4 of a yellow onion, very finely diced

1/2 cup of soy sauce *(120 ml, 4 fl oz)*

1/2 cup brown sugar *(80 g)*

1/2 tablespoon garlic, minced *(9 g)*

1/2 tablespoon vegan Worcestershire sauce *(8 ml)*

1/4 teaspoon powdered ginger *(.5 g)*

Directions:

1. Add all ingredients to a small saucepan. Bring to a boil, then reduce heat to medium low, cover, and continue simmering for 15 minutes. Stir occasionally to prevent sticking.

2. Remove from heat, and reserve half in a container you can easily drizzle from.

Next...

The tangy aroma from the marinade is wafting into your nostrils! Now more decisions await you! What main ingredients will you prepare and then marinate!? Will you pick one? All of them? It is up to you. Ultimately, you decide on:

>**Meat Skewers**, turn to page 55.

>**Fish Skewers**, turn to page 56.

>**Seafood Skewers**, turn to page 57.

>**Mushrooms Skewers**, turn to page 58.

>**Tofu Skewers**, turn to page 59.

Pineapple Barbecue

>You've chosen the Pineapple Barbecue adventure from page 49!

| 1 cup *(240 ml)* | 5 minutes | Vegan | Gluten free |

Ingredients:

1/2 cup ketchup, or Lon Lon Ketchup, page 274 *(115 g)*
1/2 cup crushed pineapple and juice *(8 oz can)*
1 1/2 tablespoons brown sugar *(19 g)*
1 tablespoon soy sauce *(15 ml)*
1 tablespoon vegan Worcestershire sauce *(15 ml)*
1 tablespoon apple cider vinegar *(15 ml)*
1 teaspoon garlic, minced *(3 g)*
1/4 teaspoon red pepper flakes or to taste, optional *(.5 g)*

Directions:

1. Add all ingredients to a small saucepan. Bring to a boil, then reduce heat to medium low, cover, and continue simmering for 15 minutes. Stir occasionally to prevent sticking.
2. Remove from heat, and reserve half in a container you can easily drizzle from.

Next...

The sweet aroma from the marinade is wafting into your nostrils! Now more decisions await you! What main ingredients will you prepare and then marinate!? Will you pick one? All of them? It is up to you. Ultimately, you decide on:

>Meat Skewers, turn to page 55.
>Fish Skewers, turn to page 56.
>Seafood Skewers, turn to page 57.
>Mushrooms Skewers, turn to page 58.
>Tofu Skewers, turn to page 59.

Meat Skewers

>You've completed a marinade, and have now chosen the Meat Skewer!

>Vegan. You chose Meat Skewers, despite being a vegan. There is meat in Meat Skewers.
If you proceed, you will lose your vegan powers.
Go back in time to select a vegan alternative.

Ingredients:
1/2 cup of the marinade from the previous step *(120 ml)*
1 pound beef sirloin tips *(.5 kg or 450 g)*

Directions:
1. If necessary, cut beef sirloin tips into smaller bite sized cubes. Bigger will require longer cooking times, or result in medium rare meat.
2. Add raw beef sirloin tips to a resealable plastic bag, and then pour in a 1/2 cup *(120 ml)* of your marinade. Press out as much air as possible, and seal the bag.
3. Carefully squish everything around to make sure the meat is fully saturated, then refrigerate for at least one, ideally three or more hours.

Next...

The Meat is now marinating in the refrigerator, so all you can do now is wait… or can you? The second stage of skewer preparation is finished, and now you can prepare the bonus ingredients that will make your skewer into something grand! Or something terrible.

>Turn to the Bonus Ingredients, page 60.

Fish Skewers

>You've completed a marinade, and have now chosen the Fish Skewer!

>Vegan. You chose Fish Skewers, despite being a vegan. There is fish in Fish Skewers. If you proceed, you will lose your vegan powers. Go back in time to select a vegan alternative.

Ingredients:

1/2 cup of the marinade from the previous step *(120 ml)*

1 pound firm fleshed fish*, skinned and deboned *(.5 kg or 450 g)*

Directions:

1. Cut fish into bite sized cubes. Add fish to a resealable plastic bag, and then pour in a 1/2 cup *(120 ml)* of your marinade. Press out as much air as possible, and seal the bag.
2. Carefully squish everything around to make sure the fish is fully saturated, then refrigerate for at least one, ideally three or more hours.

*Tuna, Salmon, or Cod Lion all work well here. You want firm flesh so it will not slide off the skewer easily.

Next...

The Fish is now marinating in the refrigerator, so all you can do now is wait… or can you? The second stage of skewer preparation is finished, and now you can prepare the bonus ingredients that will make your skewer into something grand! Or something terrible.

>Turn to the Bonus Ingredients, page 60.

Seafood Skewers

> *You've completed a marinade, and have now chosen the Seafood Skewer!*

> *Vegan. You chose Seafood Skewers, despite being a vegan.*
> *There is seafood in Seafood Skewers.*
> *If you proceed, you will lose your vegan powers.*
> *Go back in time to select a vegan alternative.*

Ingredients:

1/2 cup of the marinade from the previous step *(120 ml)*
1 pound fresh seafood mix* *(.5 kg or 450 g)*

Directions:

1. Thaw any frozen ingredients first. Rinse and prepare your seafood. If preparing shrimp, peel and devein. Add seafood to a resealable plastic bag, and then pour in a 1/2 cup *(120 ml)* of your marinade. Press out as much air as possible, and seal the bag.
2. Carefully squish everything around to make sure the seafood is fully saturated, then refrigerate for at least one, ideally three or more hours.

*A frozen medley works well too, and has such diversity! Alternatively, feel free to choose just your favorite, an array of fresh shrimp, scallops, or octopus works well here!

Next...

The Seafood is now marinating in the refrigerator, so all you can do now is wait… or can you? The second stage of skewer preparation is finished, and now you can prepare the bonus ingredients that will make your skewer into something grand! Or something terrible.

>**Turn to the Bonus Ingredients**, page 60.

Mushroom Skewers

>*You've completed a marinade, and have now chosen the Mushroom Skewer!*

Ingredients:
1/2 cup of the marinade from the previous step *(120 ml)*
1 pound baby portobello or cremini mushrooms, or your favorite! *(.5 kg or 450 g)*

Directions:
1. Carefully wash and rinse your mushrooms. Leaving them whole, add them to a resealable plastic bag, and then pour in a 1/2 cup *(120 ml)* of your marinade. Press out as much air as possible, and seal the bag.
2. Carefully squish everything around to make sure the mushrooms are fully saturated, then refrigerate for at least one, ideally three or more hours.

Next...

The Mushrooms are now marinating in the refrigerator, so all you can do now is wait… or can you? The second stage of skewer preparation is finished, and now you can prepare the bonus ingredients that will make your skewer into something grand! Or something terrible.

>Turn to the Bonus Ingredients, page 60.

Tofu Skewers

>You've completed a marinade, and have now chosen the Tofu Skewer!

Ingredients:

1/2 cup of the marinade from the previous step *(120 ml)*

1 pound extra firm tofu, tempeh, or other alternative *(.5 kg or 450 g)*

Directions:

1. Pat your tofu dry, and then cut into bite sized cubes. Cubes should be large enough to not fall apart when they are skewered. Add them to a resealable plastic bag, and then pour in a 1/2 cup *(120 ml)* of your marinade. Press out as much air as possible, and seal the bag.

2. Carefully squish everything around to make sure the tofu is fully saturated, then refrigerate for at least one, ideally three or more hours.

Next...

The Tofu is now marinating in the refrigerator, so all you can do now is wait… or can you? The second stage of skewer preparation is finished, and now you can prepare the bonus ingredients that will make your skewer into something grand! Or something terrible.

>Turn to the Bonus Ingredients, page 60.

Bonus Ingredients

>You've prepared a marinade, used half of it, and now it's time to choose the extra ingredients! You can choose as few or as many as you like.
If preparing this for a dinner party or for children, separate ingredients into bowls by type.
If not, you can begin skewering right away!

Please wash all ingredients before proceeding to next step!
If anything proves too hard to skewer, boil it in water for a few minutes to soften.

Baby tomatoes - Leave whole, skewer through the middle.

Broccoli - Break into large bite sized florets. Recommended with the Orange Teriyaki marinade.

Brussels sprouts - Choose small sprouts, consistent in size, or cut them in half.

Corn on the cob - Husk, rinse, and then cut crosswise into 2 inch *(5 cm)* long chunks.

Baby Carrots - Raw carrots are difficult to skewer, cut into 2 inch *(5 cm)* lengths, boil for 5-10 minutes to soften. Skewer crosswise, not lengthwise.

Eggplant - Cut into bite sized cubes. Try Ratatouille by pairing with tomatoes, squash, zucchini, and the Garlic Rosemary Lemon marinade.

Lemon - Cut into thick wedges. While you might not want to eat the lemon by itself, it will flavor the whole skewer! Recommended with for fish skewers, particularly salmon.

Mini Bell Peppers - Leave whole. If not mini, cut into squares. Recommended for meat skewers.

Okra - Select small okra, and leave whole. Skewer crosswise, not lengthwise. Recommended with lemon, white fish, and Brussels sprouts.

Onions - Try red onions! Cut into quarters, and then toss the innermost layers. Or use whole or halved baby onions.

Orange - Cut into wedges.

Pineapple - Skin, cut, toss core, and then cut into cubes. Recommended for seafood skewers.

Potato - Baby red potatoes are ideal, sweet potato is good too! Leave whole for baby potatoes, or slice fully grown potatoes into large bite sized circles. Leave skin on to better keep them on the skewer, and skewer through the skin. If necessary, boil for 5 to 10 minutes to soften for skewering. Recommended for mushroom skewers.

Radish - Halve or quarter radishes into chunks, enjoy a kick of flavor in each bite!

Squash - Yellow summer squash is delicious. Cut into bite sized cubes, or if the squash is thin, bite sized circles.

Zucchini - Choose a thin zucchini, and chop into thick bite sized circles. Pair with baby carrots, potatoes, and onions and top with the Garlic Rosemary Lemon marinade for a deliciously savory vegan skewer.

Next...

Your Bonus Ingredients are now prepared, just waiting to be skewered!

You have finished the second stage of skewer preparation, and now you can prepare the bonus ingredients that will make your skewer into something grand! Or something terrible.

>Turn to the Skewering Directions, page 62

Skewering Directions

> *The time has come. You are nearing the point of no return. It is up to you now- sculpt your delicious masterpiece by alternating ingredients onto your skewer! Will you make a rainbow? Monotone? Try a never before tasted flavor combination? It is up to you!*

Supplies:
Wooden or Metal Skewers.*
Platter or baking sheet for completed skewers.

Directions:
1. Remove your marinated entrées from the refrigerator and empty into bowls.
2. One by one, skewer your chosen entrées and ingredients onto your skewer. Alternate between ingredients for better flavor. Leave at least 2 inches at the ends of each skewer.
3. Once your skewers are assembled, drizzle some leftover marinade over each.

Vegan- If one of your guests is vegan, please take care to keep vegan and meat ingredients separated through this process, and wash your hands after touching non-vegan ingredients.

*Wooden are a little less durable, but metal ones can result in burnt fingers or tongues. If using metal, choose 'flat skewers', which prevents the ingredients from spinning in place when you are trying to rotate them.

Next...

At last! Your skewers are complete, and await only the heat of your chosen cooking technique. Will you bake or grill your skewers? Roast them over an open fire?
Ultimately, you choose to:

>**Bake in an oven,** turn to page 63
>**Grill on a grill,** turn to page 64
>**Roast on an open fire,** turn to page 65
>**Eat your skewers raw,** turn to page 328

Baked Skewers

>You made the practical and succulent decision to bake your skewers! Preheat the oven!

Directions:

1. Preheat the oven to 450 degrees Fahrenheit *(230 degrees Celsius)*. Oil the surface of a large, clean baking sheet.
2. Carefully arrange skewers on the baking sheet. Leave space between each skewer to allow for proper cooking.
3. Cook skewers on the center rack for approximately 15 minutes, then flip the skewers once, and bake for an additional 15 minutes. Skewers should be browned, sizzling, but not burning. Next:
4. Vegan: As soon as your skewers look good, remove!
5. Meat: Remove one skewer and cut into the center of the meat. If it is too pink, bleeds reddish fluids, or is difficult to cut in the center, continue cooking for a few more minutes and check again on a different skewer.
6. When skewers are finished, remove them from the oven. Remember to not place cooked skewers onto any used dish that held raw meat. Drizzle any left over marinade over the freshly cooked skewers.

>Congratulations! You've made it through the chapter alive!
One final challenge awaits you… to try your creation! Enjoy!

The End

Grilled Skewers

>You made the fiery and flavorful decision to grill your skewers! Fire up the grill!

Directions:

1. Fully preheat the grill to medium high.
2. Once the grill is heated, and just before adding the skewers, oil the grilling surface using a grilling brush.
3. Carefully arrange skewers on the grilling surface. Leave space between each skewer to allow for proper cooking.
4. Cook skewers for approximately 15 minutes, rotating the skewers as you go, so each of four sides is grilled (approximately 3 to 5 minutes per side).
5. Vegan: As soon as your skewers look good, remove!
6. Meat: Remove one skewer and cut into the center of the meat. If it is too pink, bleeds reddish fluids, or is difficult to cut in the center, continue cooking for a few more minutes and check again on a different skewer.
7. When skewers are finished, remove from grill onto a new platter. Remember to not place cooked skewers onto any used dish that held raw meat. Drizzle any left over marinade over the freshly cooked skewers.

>Congratulations! You've made it through the chapter alive!
One final challenge awaits you… to try your creation! Enjoy!

The End

Roasted Skewers

>You made the adventurous and game accurate decision to roast your skewers over an open flame! Use your considerable survival instincts to start a fire!

>Please see the full Fire Cooking chapter guide and fire safety precautions on page 233.

Directions:

1. Start your cooking fire, please see the full guide and safety precautions on page 233. You will also need a fire grate to safely proceed with this choice, or very steady hands and a Fireproof Elixir, page 282. (That was a joke, please do not drink and play with fire.)
2. Once the fire is ready and the grate is both in place and heated, oil the grate surface using a grilling brush if possible.
3. Carefully arrange skewers on the grate surface. Leave space between each skewer to allow for proper cooking.
4. Cook skewers for approximately 10 to 15 minutes, turning as you go, so each of four sides is grilled, approximately 3 to 4 minutes per side. The time required really depends on the fire, add more wood if necessary. Use your best judgment, check any meat, and know that when cooking over an open fire, food often continues to cook for a few minutes after being taken off the fire.
5. Vegan: As soon as your skewers look good, remove!
6. Meat: Remove one skewer and cut into the center of the meat. If it is too pink, bleeds reddish fluids, or is difficult to cut in the center, continue cooking for a few more minutes and check again on a different skewer.
7. When skewers are finished, remove from fire onto a new platter. Remember to not place cooked skewers onto any used dish that held raw meat. Drizzle any left over marinade over the freshly cooked skewers. Be sure to let skewers cool before eating, especially if you have used metal skewers.

>Congratulations! You've made it through the chapter alive!
One final challenge awaits you… to try your creation! Enjoy!

The End

The Mushroom Skewer

Sure, there are a lot of mushroom skewer recipes out there, but this one is the one. You may want to double or triple this recipe.

6 Skewers	30 minutes	Vegan	Gluten Free

Ingredients:

1/4 cup avocado oil *(60 ml)*
1 teaspoon dill weed *(1 g)*
1 teaspoon garlic salt *(3 g)*
1 pound small mushrooms** *(.5 kg or 450 g)*
~6 wooden skewers

Directions:

1. Preheat oven to 400 degrees Fahrenheit *(200 degrees Celsius)*. Gently wash the mushrooms, and put them into a bowl.
2. Mix the avocado oil, dill, and garlic salt together, then drizzle about half of this mixture over the clean mushrooms. Mix together with your hands to coat the mushrooms.
3. Skewer 4 to 5 mushrooms per skewer, about 1 inch *(2.5 cm)* apart. Arrange them on a baking sheet.
4. With a basting brush or spoon, lightly brush the mushrooms with the oil mix again, on all sides.
5. Bake for 10 minutes. Take them out, brush on the oil again.
6. Bake for 5 minutes. Take them out, brush on the oil again.
7. Bake for 5 more minutes. When you take them out this time, they should be soft and brown. Smaller mushrooms might need less time, bigger mushrooms might need more.
8. Drizzle any excess oil mix atop if desired, allow to cool for a couple minutes before serving. If attending a party, bring more than twelve for the love of Hyrule. Enjoy!

*Baby portobellos are great, but an assortment is great too!

Skewers Game Guide

Use this chapter to make skewers in real life, but what about in game? Below you will find every skewer recipe from The Legend of Zelda: Breath of the Wild!

Fish Skewer

Any fish

Copious Fish Skewers

Any 4 different Seafood

Seafood Skewer

Any Crab or Snail

Mushroom Skewer

Any Mushroom

Copious Mushroom Skewers

Any 4 different Mushrooms

Fish and Mushroom Skewer

Any Fish
Any Mushroom

Gourmet Spiced Meat Skewer

Raw Gourmet Meat
Goron Spice

Prime Spiced Meat Skewer

Raw Prime Meat
&
Goron Spice

Spiced Meat Skewer

Goron Spice
&
Raw Meat

Meat Skewer

Any 3 or less Meat

Copious Meat Skewers

Any 4 different Meats

Meat and Mushroom Skewer

Any Meat
Any Mushroom

Soups and Stews

The following recipes range from the Elixir Soup, perfect for sick days, to Monster Soup, whose purple color will wow the potluck crowd. Comforting, warm, and wonderful; these recipes are crafted to quickly fill your health bar when you are feeling low.

Guide to Heartwarming Soups

"Only the pure of heart can make a good soup." - Ludwig van Beethoven

Soup making is less a science and more of an art. An ideal soup is different for each person who makes it, so taste test and adjust until your heart is content. Thicken with flour or cornstarch, add more or less of any ingredient, and remember when they say love is the secret ingredient; patience in preparing your ingredients and low heat for longer times make special soups.

The best soup is a surprise soup. After a tired day of adventuring, you return home hungry and cold, to find a mouth watering, wafting fragrance meeting you at the door. Served with a slice of bread and a smile, no words can convey this contentment. It is so easy to prepare a soup in twenty minutes at the beginning of the day, and leave it on low in a cooker until it is time for supper. Take this time to care for yourself or for your loved ones.

As you iterate on the soups and stews in this chapter, please take notes directly on the recipe pages, and write what you did differently. This is how mainstay family recipes are born. I hope these soups stay with you and bring you the sustenance you need to keep going.

Many of these recipes use bouillon as a base, but you are welcome to use soup stock instead. I love the Better Than Bouillon brand, and use their Seasoned Vegetable Base in the majority of the following recipes. I've also included the Wheat Bread recipe in this chapter, inspired by The Legend of Zelda: Breath of the Wild! Wheat bolillo buns go so well with soup!

Carrot Stew

Creamy orange, with hearty chunks of potatoes and Endura carrots, this stew will surely increase your stamina!

Serves 2	1 hour	Vegan	Gluten free

Ingredients:

1 tablespoon oil *(15 ml)*

2 teaspoons minced garlic *(6 g)*

1 yellow onion, chopped

1 pound baby carrots *(16 oz or 450 g)*

1 pound sliced cremini mushrooms, optional *(16 oz or 450 g)*

2 cups water *(480 ml)*

3 large gold potatoes

1 tablespoon vegetable bouillon** (15 ml)

1 bay leaf

1 tablespoon sugar *(12 g)*

1 teaspoon thyme *(1 g)*

1 teaspoon ground ginger *(2 g)*

2 teaspoons sweet paprika *(4.5 g)*

1/4 teaspoon turmeric, for color* *(1 g)*

2 reserved carrots with green tops per bowl, for accurate garnish

Dried parsley, for accurate garnish

Game Guide

The Legend of Zelda: Breath of the Wild.

Any Carrot

Fresh Milk

Goat Butter

Tabantha Wheat

*To achieve that beautiful orange color, accurate to The Legend of Zelda: Breath of the Wild, we just need a kick of turmeric yellow!

**Better Than Bouillon: Seasoned Vegetable Base, or similar.

Carrot Stew

Directions:

1. Heat oil and a splash of water in a large soup pot to medium high. Add garlic and onion, then cook covered, stirring occasionally for 5 minutes, until onions are beginning to brown.

2. Add another splash of water, baby carrots and mushrooms. Cook covered, stirring occasionally, for 7 minutes, until mushrooms are cooked.

3. Add water, potatoes, bouillon, bay leaf, sugar, thyme, ginger, sweet paprika, and turmeric. Cover and bring to a boil, then reduce heat to medium, and simmer for 45 minutes, stirring occasionally if necessary to prevent sticking. Or cook on low for several hours. The soup is done when the carrots and potatoes are soft all the way through.

4. Remove the bay leaf, serve in wooden bowls, garnish with reserved whole carrots on the side and a dash of dried parsley in the center. Enjoy!

Cream of Mushroom Soup

There's nothing like fresh, simple, and savory Cream of Mushroom Soup. Finally, a use for all of those mushrooms you obsessively collected!

Serves 2	30 minutes	Vegetarian	Gluten free

Ingredients:

2 tablespoons oil *(30 ml)*
1 pound cremini or mixed mushrooms, whole *(16 oz or 450 g)*
1/2 pound shiitake mushrooms, sliced *(8 oz or 225 g)*
1 tablespoon minced garlic *(9 g)*
1 yellow onion, very finely diced
1/2 tablespoon chicken bouillon, or vegetable bouillon* *(4 g)*
2 tablespoons all purpose flour or cornstarch *(20 g)*
1 teaspoon thyme *(1.5 g)*
1 cup water *(240 ml)*
1 cup milk *(240 ml)*
1/2 cup sour cream, optional *(120 ml)*
Dried parsley, for accurate garnish

Game Guide

The Legend of Zelda: Breath of the Wild.

Any Carrot
Fresh Milk
Goat Butter
Tabantha Wheat

Directions:

1. Heat oil in a soup pot to medium high. Add all of the mushrooms, then cover and cook for about 10 minutes, stirring occasionally. They are done when the mushrooms have released their juices and are starting to brown.
2. Add the garlic and onion, stir on medium heat for 1 minute.
3. Add bouillon, thyme, water and milk. Mix and simmer uncovered on medium high for 10 minutes, stir in flour a little at a time to thicken.
4. Add in the sour cream. Stir thoroughly and bring it to a light boil once more. Serve garnished with dried parsley, and enjoy!

*Better Than Bouillon: Roasted Chicken or Seasoned Vegetable Base, or similar.

Vegan- Unsweetened plain almond milk is better than actual milk in this recipe. Skip the sour cream, and use vegetable bouillon instead of chicken!

Elixir Soup

Prepared especially for Link by his grandmother, this is a simple broth soup served best on cold days to help replenish your hearts. Serve in heat proof jars for added authenticity.

Serves 2	45 minutes	Vegan	Gluten free

Ingredients:

1 tablespoon oil *(15 ml)*
1 medium onion, chopped
2 teaspoons minced garlic *(6 g)*
1/8 teaspoon ground ginger *(.25 g)*
1/4 teaspoon ground turmeric *(1 g)*
1 teaspoon ground cumin *(2 g)*
1/2 cup canned yellow lentils, rinsed and drained* *(190 g)*
3 cups of water *(720 ml)*
1 tablespoon chicken bouillon, or vegetable bouillon** *(8 g)*
1/8 teaspoon ground cayenne pepper, optional *(2 g)*
1 tablespoon lemon juice, optional *(15 ml)*
Fresh cilantro sprigs for garnish

Game Guide

The Legend of Zelda: The Wind Waker.

Given to Link by his Grandma on Outset Island.

Directions:

1. Heat oil, a splash of water, and onion together on medium high heat for about 5 minutes, until onion becomes translucent.

2. Add the garlic, ginger, turmeric and cumin. Stir briskly before adding the yellow lentils, water, and bouillon. Bring to a full rolling boil before reducing heat to medium to a soft boil until the lentils have are soft through, around 15 minutes.

3. Optional: For the smooth consistency accurate to The Legend of Zelda: The Wind Waker, transfer to a blender and puree!

4. Stir in lemon juice and cayenne pepper if desired, then ladle soup into jars. Garnish each with a couple cilantro sprigs. Enjoy!

*Canned is easier; or use dry but cook until soft before hand.
    **Better Than Bouillon: Roasted Chicken or Seasoned Vegetable Base, or similar.

Cream of Vegetable Soup

Pairs wonderfully with round crackers and sick days.

Serves 4	30 minutes	Vegan	Gluten free

Ingredients:

2 tablespoons oil *(30 ml)*

1 medium onion, finely chopped

1 large carrot, chopped

1 tablespoon minced garlic *(9 g)*

1 cup chopped green beans *(150 g)*

1 small head of baby bok choy, with leaves separated

1 teaspoon dried thyme *(1.5 g)*

1 teaspoon dried oregano *(1 g)*

1 teaspoon dried basil *(1 g)*

1 cup of cream style sweet corn, about half a 15 oz can *(8 oz or 225 g)*

3 cups milk, or water *(720 ml)*

1 tablespoon vegetable bouillon* *(8 g)*

~1/4 cup corn starch, to thicken** *(40 g)*

Dried parsley, for accurate garnish

Ground black pepper to taste

Game Guide

The Legend of Zelda: Breath of the Wild.

Any Vegetable, Herb or Flower (except carrots or pumpkin)

Fresh Milk

Rock Salt

Vegan- Use water instead of milk. Instead of cream style corn, use 1 cup *(240 ml)* of fresh or frozen corn. For more accurate texture, blend the corn with a splash of water before adding it to the soup. I also use way more garlic than I feel comfortable listing here.

*Better Than Bouillon: Seasoned Vegetable Base, or similar.

**You can also use all purpose flour, or instant mashed potatoes.

Cream of Vegetable Soup

Directions:

1. Heat a splash of water, olive oil, onion, and carrots in pan for a 5 minutes, until onions begin to brown.

2. Add another splash of water, garlic, green beans, and bok choy leaves, and continue to heat for 3 to 4 more minutes, stirring to prevent sticking.

3. Add thyme, oregano, basil, cream style corn, milk or water, and vegetable bouillon. Mix thoroughly, and then bring to a boil, stirring to prevent sticking.

4. Once boiling, turn heat to low, and thicken your soup with corn starch. Sprinkle a couple spoonfuls at a time and stir until your desired thickness is achieved. If the carrots are soft all the way through, it is done! If not, continue cooking on medium low for an additional 10 to 20 minutes.

5. Serve garnished with a sprinkling of dried parsley. Ground black pepper to taste, and enjoy!

Creamy Heart Soup

This chilled* Hydromelon and Radish soup is accurate to The Legend of Zelda: Breath of the Wild, and is garnished with a heart shaped slice of Voltfruit. According to Ashai from Gerudo Town, those who master the creation of Creamy Heart Soup are said to be able to master anything!

Serves 2	30 minutes	Vegan	Gluten free

Ingredients:

1 dragon fruit

1 ripe Honeydew Melon

2 small baby radishes, halved

1 tablespoon granulated sugar *(12 g)*

1 cup plain yogurt, or unsweetened almond yogurt *(245 g)*

1/4 cup coconut milk *(60 ml)*

2 tablespoons honey *(30 ml)*

2 ripe bananas, peeled

1 tablespoon fresh beets, finely diced, for color *(10 g)*

Game Guide

The Legend of Zelda: Breath of the Wild.

Hydromelon
Voltfruit
Any Hearty Radish
Fresh Milk

*If you would rather a traditional hot and creamy heart soup instead, use the Cream of Vegetable Soup recipe on page 74, and adorn it with dragon fruit hearts! Here, I couldn't resist trying to make this recipe accurate to the crazy The Legend of Zelda: Breath of the Wild ingredient list of hydromelon, voltfruit, radishes, and fresh milk!

Creamy Heart Soup

Directions:

1. Wash and cut your dragon fruit in half. Cut one half into 1/2 inch slices *(1.25 cm)*, then carefully cut these slices into 2 hearts. On the other half, use the melon baller to make balls, then put them into a mixing bowl. Set the hearts aside.

2. Use the melon baller on the honeydew melon next, you want 8 small melon balls. Put them into the mixing bowl, and add halved radishes, and sugar. Mix gently, then set aside.

3. Put 2 cups of the remaining ripe melon, yogurt, honey, bananas, and beets into the blender, and puree until very smooth. The blend should be a light pink; if not, add a bit more beets and blend again. Pour into two serving bowls. Chill in the refrigerator.

4. To serve, retrieve bowls, add an even portion of melon and dragon fruit balls to each, and garnish with the dragon fruit heart shape. Enjoy!

Creamy Meat Soup

Creamy Meat Soup, or Super Soup for the Tingle inclined, is the classic and chunky noodle soup you've been waiting for, ideal for when someone is feeling under the weather!

Serves 4	1 hour	Gluten free

Ingredients:

3 tablespoons oil *(45 ml)*
1 pound steak, cut into about 8 slices* *(16 oz or 450 g)*
1 medium onion, finely chopped
1 large carrot, chopped
1 tablespoon minced garlic *(9 g)*
1 cup chopped green beans *(150 g)*
1 small head of baby bok choy, with leaves separated
1 teaspoon dried thyme *(1.5 g)*
1 teaspoon dried oregano *(1 g)*
1 teaspoon dried basil *(1 g)*
1 cup of cream style sweet corn, about half a can *(200 g)*
3 cups milk, or water *(720 ml)*
1 tablespoon beef or vegetable bouillon ** *(8 g)*
~1/4 cup corn starch, to thicken*** *(30 g)*
Dried parsley, for accurate garnish
Ground black pepper to taste

Game Guide

The Legend of Zelda: Breath of the Wild.

Any Meat
Any Vegetable, Herb, or Flower
Fresh Milk
Rock Salt

Super Soup

Freshly-Picked Tingle's Rosy Rupeeland

5 Mini Apples
3 Rib Steak
3 Tough Meat

Vegan- In The Legend of Zelda: Breath of the Wild, this soup and the Cream of Vegetable Soup look exactly the same, barring a couple of slices of meat! Since that's the case, you can go try the vegan Cream of Vegetable Soup, on page 74!

*The meat appears to be 1/2 inch *(1.25 cm)* thick slices of steak, left whole. There are about two slices per soup!

**Better Than Bouillon: Roasted Beef or Seasoned Vegetable Base, or similar.

***You can also use all purpose flour, or instant mashed potatoes.

Creamy Meat Soup

Directions:

1. Add oil, then preheat your cast iron pan to medium high. Add steaks. Cover and sauté for 5 to 6 minutes on each side, until all steaks are done all the way through.
2. Transfer steaks and excess juices to a soup pot on medium high, then add a splash of water, onions, and carrots. Cook covered for 5 minutes, until onions begin to brown.
3. Add another splash of water, garlic, green beans, and bok choy leaves, then continue to cook for 3 to 4 more minutes, stirring to prevent sticking.
4. Add thyme, oregano, basil, cream style corn, milk or water, and vegetable bouillon. Mix thoroughly, and then bring to a boil, stirring to prevent sticking.
5. Once boiling, turn heat to low, and thicken your soup with corn starch. Sprinkle a couple spoonfuls at a time and stir until your desired thickness is achieved. If the carrots are soft all the way through, it is done! If not, continue cooking on medium low for an additional 10 to 20 minutes.
6. Serve soup in four bowls, and make sure there are two slices of steak in the center of each! Garnish with a sprinkling of dried parsley, add ground black pepper to taste, and enjoy!

Creamy Seafood Soup

Shrimp and scallops, delicious red bell pepper, paired with a silky cashew cream base, this soup is divine and reminiscent of long walks on the beach.

Serves 2	1 hour	Gluten free

Ingredients:

1/2 pound raw shrimp, peeled and deveined *(8 oz or 225 g)*
1/2 pound bay scallops *(8 oz or 225 g)*
1 tablespoon oil *(15 ml)*
1 yellow onion, finely chopped
1 large carrot, finely chopped
1 celery stalk, finely chopped
1/2 red bell pepper, finely chopped
2 yukon gold potatoes, finely chopped
1 cup corn, frozen is fine *(300 g)*
1 1/2 cup cashew cream *(360 ml)*
4 cups water *(960 ml)*
1 1/2 tablespoons vegetable bouillon* *(12 g)*
1 teaspoon Cajun seasoning** *(~1 g)*
1 teaspoon garlic, minced *(3 g)*
1/4 cup fresh chopped parsley *(15 g)*
1 tablespoon dried and finely shredded nori or seaweed *(5 g)*
Dried parsley, for accurate garnish

Game Guide

The Legend of Zelda: Breath of the Wild.

Any Seafood
Any Vegetable, Herb, or Flower
Fresh Milk
Rock Salt

Ocean Soup

Freshly-Picked Tingle's Rosy Rupeeland

3 Power Garlic
4 Sweet Potatoes
4 Tasty Squids
3 Salty Octopi

Vegan- 8 ounces *(225 g)* of oyster mushrooms instead of scallops, and chop up 8 ounces *(225 g)* or so of your favorite vegan protein to toss in. Tempeh works well here, so do meatless chicken products.

*Better Than Bouillon: Seasoned Vegetable Base, or similar.

**Cajun seasoning recipe: 1 part cayenne pepper, 1 part paprika, 1 part oregano, 1 part ground black pepper.

Creamy Seafood Soup

Directions:

1. Oil and preheat your large soup pot. Add a splash of water, shrimp, and scallops, cover, and cook for 8 to 10 minutes, until shrimp are pink, opaque and well cooked.

2. Gradually add all other ingredients in order, stirring between each addition. Cover, bring to a boil, then reduce heat to medium, and cook for 30 to 40 more minutes, stirring occasionally. Soup is done once potatoes are tender and well cooked.

3. Serve and garnish with a sprinkling of dried parsley. Enjoy!

Hearty Clam Chowder

A favorite of Ashai, who teaches cooking in Gerudo Town, this is a creamy coastal clam chowder, perfect with crackers. No snails in this dish, but you are welcome to add some!

Serves 2	30 minutes

Ingredients:

1 tablespoon butter *(14 g)*
1 yellow onion, finely chopped
2 tablespoons all purpose flour *(20 g)*
1 cup water *(240 ml)*
1 tablespoon vegetable bouillon* *(8 g)*
3 large yukon gold potatoes, cut into bite sized cubes
2 cans chopped clams, with juice *(20 oz or 550 g)*
2 cups cream *(480 ml)*
1 bay leaf
1/2 teaspoon ground thyme *(.75 g)*
2 teaspoons dried parsley *(3 g)*
A few sprigs of fresh parsley

Game Guide

The Legend of Zelda: Breath of the Wild.

Fresh Milk
Tabantha Wheat
Goat Butter
Hearty Blueshell Snail

Seafood Soup

Freshly-Picked Tingle's Rosy Rupeeland

3 Power Garlic
3 Sweet Potatoes
3 Tasty Squids

Vegan- Use 1/4 cup vegan butter *(55 g)*, and 1/4 cup *(40 g)* all purpose flour instead. Replace clams with 12 ounces *(350 g)* of chopped white button mushrooms, and 8 ounces *(225 g)* of oyster mushrooms, and add them when you add the potatoes. For cream, use unsweetened soy milk (almond will do if you can't do soy), and add 1 tablespoon *(15 ml)* red wine vinegar to this. You'll notice that this chowder is close, but is missing a sort of 'ocean' taste. Add about 1 teaspoon *(1 g)* of ground dried seaweed to help!

Gluten free- Instead of the flour, use 2 tablespoons of corn starch *(16 g)*, mixed in 3 tablespoons of water until all clumps are gone.

*Better Than Bouillon: Seasoned Vegetable Base, or similar.

Hearty Clam Chowder

Directions:

1. Heat butter in a large soup pot to medium high. Add onion, cover and cook, stirring occasionally, until translucent, about 5 minutes.

2. Slowly stir in flour to avoid clumping, and mix until dissolved. Then add water, bouillon, potatoes, juice from cans of clam, cream, bay leaf, thyme, and dried parsley. Stir constantly until it is brought to a light simmer.

3. Reduce heat to medium low, cover, and simmer for 15 minutes.

4. Add the clams, and let cook for an additional 5 to 7 minutes, until clams are firm. Make sure to not bring it to a boil!

5. Remove the pot from heat, and remove the bay leaf. Serve garnished with a sprig of fresh parsley. Enjoy!

Meat Stew or Tasty Stew

A wholesome and chunky stew of veggies and beef will satisfy any construction worker after a hard day of work! Perhaps this is why it is Hudson's favorite dish! Try the spicy variant from Rito Stable, or call it 'Tasty Stew' if you love Tingle!

Serves 4	2 hours	Gluten free

Ingredients:

2 tablespoons olive oil *(30 ml)*
1 pound stew or steak beef, cut into strips *(16 oz or 450 g)*
2 tablespoons minced garlic *(18 g)*
1 yellow onion, chopped
~2 tablespoons beef bouillon* *(16 g)*
5 cups water *(1200 ml)*
1 can tomato paste *(6 oz or 170 g)*
1 tablespoon sugar *(12.5 g)*
2 tablespoons dried parsley *(10 g)*
1 teaspoon ground thyme *(1.5 g)*
2 bay leaves
1 pound baby carrots, keep whole or chop *(16 oz or 450 g)*
3 large yukon gold potatoes, cut into 1 inch cubes
1 cup corn, fresh or frozen *(320 g)*
1 cup peas, fresh or frozen *(320 g)*
Instant mashed potatoes or corn starch, optional to thicken
1 green onion, chopped, for garnish
~1 tablespoon cayenne pepper, for Spicy Meat Stew *(5 g)*

Game Guides

The Legend of Zelda: Breath of the Wild.

Any Meat
Tabantha Wheat
Goat Butter
Fresh Milk

Spicy Meat Stew

Add one of the following to the original recipe:
Spicy Pepper
Sunshroom
Warm Safflina
Sizzlefin Trout

Tasty Stew

Freshly-Picked Tingle's Rosy Rupeeland.

4 Thick Meat
4 Baby Sharks
4 Bitter Newts

Vegan- No beef and use vegetable bouillon instead to enjoy this as a chunky Vegetable Stew, ideal for cool weather!

*Better Than Bouillon: Roasted Beef Base, or similar.

Meat Stew or Tasty Stew

Directions:

1. Heat a splash of water and oil in a large soup pot to medium high. Add beef, garlic, and onion. Sauté and stir for 10 minutes, until beef is browned.

2. Add bouillon and water, tomato paste, sugar, parsley, thyme, bay leaves, baby carrots, potatoes, corn, peas, and cayenne pepper if desired. Cover, and simmer for 60 to 80 minutes stirring occasionally. Taste, and add more bouillon if desired.

3. The stew is done when the potatoes and carrots slide easily off of an inserted fork.

4. If necessary, thicken your stew by adding a spoonful of instant mashed potatoes or corn starch at a time, stir, and repeat until you have your desired stew consistency.

5. Serve topped with chopped green onion. Enjoy!

Monster Soup

Even if you choose not to add Monster Extract, you will be surprised at the purple of this soup! Serve to the amazement of your dinner guests, and to the delight of their stomachs!

Serves 6	1 hour	Vegan	Gluten free

Ingredients:

1 tablespoon oil *(15 ml)*
1 tablespoon garlic, minced *(9 g)*
1 large yellow onion, finely diced
8 baby purple potatoes, chopped, about 1 pound *(.5 kg)*
4 large purple carrots, chopped, about 1 pound *(.5 kg)*
5 cups hot water *(1200 ml)*
~2 tablespoons vegetable bouillon* *(20 g)*
2 teaspoons ground thyme *(3 g)*
1/2 cup fresh chopped parsley *(30 g)*
1 bay leaf
1 large beet, very finely diced**
Shelled pumpkin seeds,*** optional
Fresh parsley, for garnish
Monster Extract, page 173, or purple food coloring, to reach desired color
Instant mashed potatoes or corn starch, to thicken if desired
Optional: 1/2 cup whole wheat rotini noodles, peas, and corn. Delicious, but can take away from the purple color. Add noodles with the water, add peas and corn with the beet!

> ## Game Guide
> *The Legend of Zelda: Breath of the Wild.*
>
> Monster Extract
> Tabantha Wheat
> Fresh Milk
> Goat Butter

*Better Than Bouillon: Seasoned Vegetable Base, or similar.

**Generally this is more than enough to achieve a violent purple color! If you want the purple to be really over the top, add some Monster Extract or purple food coloring!

***The Legend of Zelda: Breath of the Wild picture makes it look like teeth are floating on top of the soup- pumpkin seed 'teeth' do the trick!

Monster Soup

Directions:

1.   In a large soup pot, mix oil, a splash of water, garlic, and onions on medium high. Cover and let cook for 5 minutes, until onions are translucent.

2.   Add potatoes and carrots to the pot. Cover and let cook for an additional 3 to 4 minutes.

3.   Add the hot water, making sure it covers everything by half an inch *(1.25 cm)* or so, then add the vegetable bouillon, thyme, parsley, and bay leaf. Bring to a boil, reduce heat to medium, and cook covered for 30 minutes, stirring occasionally. Taste and add more bouillon if desired.

4.   Add the very finely diced beet, mix thoroughly, and cook covered for an additional 15 minutes, stirring occasionally. Thicken if desired by stirring in instant mashed potatoes or corn starch, a little at a time.

5.   When carrots and potatoes are soft all the way through, if desired, stir in a few drops of Monster Extract to achieve a more violent purple. Serve garnished with pumpkin seeds and a sprinkling of parsley. Enjoy!

Monster or Super Stew

Delicious chunks of unidentifiable monster parts swimming in a spicy purple broth!*
Or, if you prefer the Tingle inspired Super Stew variant, leave out the purple!

Serves 4	1 hour	Gluten free

Ingredients:

1 tablespoon oil *(15 ml)*
1/2 teaspoon sesame oil *(7 ml)*
2 teaspoons garlic, minced *(6 g)*
2 tablespoons soy sauce *(30 ml)*, use gluten free if necessary
1/4 lb beef sirloin, chopped strangely *(4 oz or 115 g)*
1 tablespoon beef or vegetable bouillon** *(8 g)*
3 cups water *(720 ml)*
1 tablespoon chili flakes *(7 grams)*
4 dried anchovies
8 ounces mixed frozen seafood, thawed *(225 g)*
1/2 small yellow onion, diced
8 ounces Shiitake mushrooms, chopped strangely *(225 g)*
1/2 zucchini diced
8 ounces hard tofu, chopped strangely *(225 g)*
1 fresh chili, sliced
2 teaspoons anchovy sauce *(6 g)*
Monster Extract, page 173, for a slight purple gray, or:
Purple 'Gel' Food Dye, for a very vibrant purple

Game Guide

The Legend of Zelda: Breath of the Wild.

Any Meat
Any Seafood
Monster Extract

Super Stew

Freshly-Picked Tingle's Rosy Rupeeland

4 Thick Meat
4 Baby Sharks
4 Bitter Newts
4 Spicy Prawns

Vegan- Replace beef with either more tofu or tempeh, and replace the seafood and anchovies with the chopped stems of large mushrooms and a sprinkling of shredded dried nori.

*It's easy to look at the ingredients here, and turn the page immediately. But trust me. This recipe was adapted from Korean style seafood stews, and is actually delicious- especially if you enjoy spicy foods. Add more chili flakes or fresh chilies if you are feeling adventurous!

**Better Than Bouillon: Roasted Beef or Seasoned Vegetable Base, or similar.

Monster or Super Stew

Directions:

1. Heat oil in a large soup pot to medium high. Add sesame oil, garlic, soy sauce, and beef. Cook covered for 6 to 7 minutes, until beef is lightly browned, and cooked through.

2. Add bouillon, water, chili flakes, anchovies, frozen seafood, yellow onion, and Shiitake mushrooms. Bring to a boil, and boil for 5 minutes.

3. Add the zucchini, tofu, fresh chili, and anchovy sauce, boil for another 5 minutes.

4. Turn heat down to medium low, then add the Monster Extract or purple gel food coloring. Add a little at a time, mixing as you go, until you arrive at the shade of purple you desire!

5. Serve, and tell no one what you put in it. Enjoy!

Pumpkin Stew

The main ingredient is one of the famous Kakariko Village Fortified Pumpkins!
Serve this stew straight from your freshly baked pumpkin!

Serves 4	3 hours	Vegan	Gluten free

Ingredients:

1 tablespoon oil, plus extra for baking *(15 ml)*
1 medium yellow onion, chopped
2 tablespoons garlic, minced *(18 g)*
4 cups water *(960 ml)*
1/2 pound baby carrots, chopped *(8 oz or 225 g)*
2 medium sized golden Yukon potatoes, chopped
1 large sweet potato, chopped
1 can black beans, drained *(15 oz or 425 g)*
1 cup yellow corn *(320 g)*
2 teaspoons salt, or to taste *(11 g)*
1 teaspoon ground thyme *(1.5 g)*
2 tablespoons dried parsley *(10 g)*
2 tablespoons vegetable bouillon* *(16 g)*
1 pumpkin, around 10 pounds** *(4.5 kg)*
Dried parsley, for garnish
Ground black pepper, to taste

Game Guide

The Legend of Zelda:
Breath of the Wild.

Fortified Pumpkin
Tabantha Wheat
Goat Butter
Fresh Milk

*Better Than Bouillon: Seasoned Vegetable Base, or similar.

**A large, squat pumpkin works best, about the size of a basket ball! You want it steady so it does not tip over in the oven, and you want to be able to cut out a top large enough so that you can serve from it later! Also, it's best to select a pumpkin that was grown specifically to be eaten, not just a Halloween pumpkin! Choose a 'baking' pumpkin if you can.

Pumpkin Stew

Directions:

1. Preheat oven to 325 degrees Fahrenheit *(160 degrees Celsius)*. Put oil, onion, and garlic into a large pan, along with a splash of water. Heat covered on medium high for about 6 minutes, until onions are starting to caramelize.

2. Add in water, carrots, potatoes, black beans, yellow corn, salt, thyme, dried parsley, and vegetable bouillon. Cover and bring to a boil. Let simmer for 30 minutes, stirring around every 10 minutes. You want the potatoes and carrots to be easy to cut through.

3. Wash the pumpkin, and cut out the top. Remember to use an angle when cutting so the top doesn't fall in later, and cut out a large enough top that it will be easy later to serve from. Scoop out all of the seeds, and pull out most of the strings. Do not scrape the flesh out, it will become part of the stew.

4. Pour or ladle the stew into the pumpkin, and cover with the top. Try not to over fill the pumpkin! Take a spoonful or two of oil, and lightly brush all of the outside of the pumpkin. Place on a sturdy baking dish or tray, the pumpkin may sweat or leak while baking.

5. Bake the pumpkin for around 2 hours. It is ready when the flesh is tender, a knife will slip in from the outside easily. Better to under bake then over bake this, take it out as soon as you think it is done.

6. Stir thoroughly, and taste. Depending on the size of your pumpkin, you may want to add a teaspoon *(5 ml)* or so of additional vegetable bouillon, and stir again.

7. Serve directly from the pumpkin! With each scoop, scrape some of the tender pumpkin meat from the inside, then garnish with a sprinkle of dried parsley, and ground black pepper. Enjoy!

Veggie Cream Soup

A delicious and chunky array of vegetables complement one another in this tomato based soup, one of the specialties of Kakariko's budding chef, Koko!

Serves 4	25 minutes	Vegan	Gluten free

Ingredients:

1 tablespoon oil *(15 ml)*
1 yellow onion, chopped
1 tablespoon garlic, minced *(9 g)*
2 pounds tomatoes, mixed baby and large, chopped *(900 g)*
1 cup baby carrots, very thinly diced *(300 g)*
2 golden yukon potatoes, finely chopped
3 cups water *(720 ml)*
1 cup milk or 1 cup additional water *(240 ml)*
2 tablespoons vegetable or chicken bouillon* *(16 g)*
1/2 cup peas, fresh or frozen *(160 g)*
1/2 cup corn, fresh or frozen *(160 g)*
1/3 cup fresh parsley, or 1 tablespoon dried *(20 g or 5 g)*
1/3 cup fresh basil, or 1 tablespoon dried *(10 g or 2 g)*
1/4 teaspoon freshly ground black pepper, or to taste *(.5 g)*
1 whole small carrot with green top per bowl, for garnish

Game Guide

The Legend of Zelda: Breath of the Wild.

Any Carrot or Pumpkin
Fresh Milk
Rock Salt

*Better Than Bouillon: Seasoned Vegetable Base or Roasted Chicken, or similar.

Vegan- It might be necessary to thicken the soup by stirring in some instant mashed potatoes, cornstarch or all purpose flour.

Veggie Cream Soup

Directions:

1. Put oil, onion, garlic, and tomatoes into a soup pan, along with a splash of water. Heat covered on medium high for about 6 minutes, until onions are starting to brown. The tomatoes should be disintegrating, mix until they are broken apart.
2. Add 1 cup of water *(240 ml)*, carrots, and potatoes. Cover, bring to a boil, then cook, stirring occasionally, for an additional 7 minutes, or until potatoes and carrots are soft and cooked all the way through. Add more water if necessary, the smaller you chop, the faster this will be.
3. Add last 2 cups water *(480 ml)*, milk, vegetable bouillon, peas, corn, parsley, basil, and black pepper if desired. Heat on medium for 10 minutes, stirring occasionally, until it is hot all the way through.
4. If desired, lightly blend for a creamier texture.
5. Ladle into bowls, and serve with a whole carrot with top stuck in to the side. Enjoy!

Lava Soup

This molten lava soup is bright red, with black pebbles and golden gems!

Serves 4	30 minutes	Vegan	Gluten free

Ingredients:

1 tablespoon minced garlic *(9 g)*
1 medium yellow onion, finely diced
1 tablespoon vegetable bouillon* *(8 g)*
3 cups water *(720 ml)*
2 jars roasted red peppers, rinsed, drained, chopped *(24 oz or 680 g)*
1 medium carrot, very thinly sliced into rounds
1 tablespoon red curry paste *(16 g)*
1/2 teaspoon sugar *(2 g)*
1/4 teaspoon salt *(1.5 g)*
1 can black beans, drained and rinsed thoroughly *(8 oz or 225 g)*
1/2 cup corn *(160 g)*
1 cup coconut milk *(240 ml)*

> ### Game Guide
> *The Legend of Zelda: Oracle of Seasons.*

Directions:

1. Heat a splash of water and oil in a large soup pot to medium high. Add garlic, and onion. Sauté and stir for 5 minutes, until onions are soft.
2. Add bouillon and water, roasted red peppers, carrots, red curry paste, sugar, and salt. Bring to a boil, then cover and simmer on medium heat for 20 minutes, until vegetables are soft. Taste, and add more bouillon if desired.
3. Blend soup until mostly smooth.
4. Stir in beans, corn, and coconut milk, and while stirring frequently, heat until hot all the way through, but not boiling.
5. Serve topped with chopped green onion. Enjoy!

*Better Than Bouillon: Seasoned Vegetable Base, or similar.

This recipe was inspired by a backer of this cookbook. Kara Roncin, your attention to detail has made this book bigger and better! Thank you.

Wheat Bread

These wheat bread bolillos are so soft and springy on the inside, with a crunchy exterior. They are perfect for mopping up leftover soup and stew!

6 bolillos	2 hours	Vegan

Ingredients:

1/4 cup warm water *(60 ml)*

1/4 cup agave nectar or honey *(60 ml)*

1 tablespoon vegan butter, room temperature *(14 g)*

1 tablespoon active dry yeast *(8.25 g)*

3/4 teaspoon salt *(4 g)*

1 cup whole wheat flour *(150 g)*

1 3/4 cup unbleached flour *(265 g)*

~3/4 cup warm water *(180 ml)*

1/2 cup cold water *(120 ml)*

1 teaspoon cornstarch *(2.5 g)*

Square pads of butter or vegan butter, for side garnish

Game Guide

The Legend of Zelda: Breath of the Wild.

Tabantha Wheat
&
Rock Salt

Wheat Bread

Directions:

1. In a large bowl, mix warm water, agave, butter, and yeast together. Let sit for 5 minutes, mixing occasionally, until everything has dissolved.

2. Add salt, wheat flour, and unbleached flour, mix until it is uniform. Slowly add a bit of warm water at a time, mixing and folding between, until it just forms a large dry ball. Let it stand for a few minutes.

3. Add a little more warm water at a time, folding and kneading between, until the dough ball is smooth without cracking, but not sticky.

4. Grease a smooth surface with butter, and place the dough there. Cover with a small bowl or plastic wrap, then let it rise for 30 minutes. Prepare a greased baking sheet, large enough for 6 or fewer bolillos. The smaller these are made, the crunchier they will be!

5. Knead the dough by hand for a minute, and then separate it into 6 balls.

6. With your hands, flatten a ball, then roll it up into a bolillo shape. Pinch the ends of each bolillo into a taper, then set them on the baking sheet. Let them rise until they have doubled, about 45 minutes.

7. Preheat oven to 375 degree Fahrenheit *(190 degrees Celsius)*.

8. In a small sauce pan, dissolve cornstarch in cold water, then bring to a boil. Brush the cornstarch mixture over each fully risen bolillo.

9. With a sharp knife, slash each bolillo 3 times like < | | | > so they look like The Legend of Zelda: Breath of the Wild Wheat Bread.

10. Bake for about 30 minutes, until they are golden brown. Cool them for at least 10 minutes, then enjoy!

Salt Grilling

In this chapter, ingredients are seared atop a block of sizzling Himalayan rock salt! Explore an array of different salt-seared dishes inspired by The Legend of Zelda: Breath of the Wild. From meats and mushrooms to greens and vegetables, the end result is a deliciously singed and salt encrusted meal; not too salty, and sure to wow a dinner party.

If you'd rather a simpler experience without a salt block, all of these recipes can be prepared similarly in a skillet or on a grill. Add a pinch of ground rock salt to the bottom of the skillet or rub some into the sides of each ingredient.

Tools

First, a salt block, at least 2 inches *(2.5 cm)* thick to prevent cracking when you heat your block. Second, a steel holder that will fit your block. Salt blocks are heavy, fragile, and will be horrendously hot, a steel holder is for your own safety. Please use gloves too.

Technique

Heat slowly or, in rare cases, it may shatter. To sear food, the surface needs to be about 450 degrees Fahrenheit *(230 degrees Celsius)*. You can use a grill, or you can heat it in the oven, then move it to the stove top on a high setting for the actual grilling. Heat it slowly over the course of an hour, 20 minutes on 250 degrees Fahrenheit *(120 degrees Celsius)*, then 20 on 375 *(190 degrees Celsius)*, then 450 *(230 degrees Celsius)* for the last 20.

Maintenance

Salt blocks do not last forever, but, you can still get a few good years of weekly use out of a 2 inch thick block! Take care in handling it, any fractures caused by dropping it can cause it to shatter upon the next re-heating. To clean it after use, let it cool slowly to room temperature, then scrub off any food with plain water and wipe it down; soap is unnecessary because of the salt-content and should not be used. Fully dry it, and keep it in a dry space. Remember, this is salt, if left to soak or run through a dishwasher, it will dissolve.

Final Notes

After use, your salt block may discolor, become stained by the food you've cooked on it, or it might even look like its been cracked. These things happen, and are normal. As long as you are heating it up slowly each time, it is fine to continue using it. In the event of a break, do not continue grilling with your salt block, instead, grind it up and use it as salt!

Salt Grilled Crab

These salt encrusted crab cakes are mouth-watering, and can be made into large patties for a main course, or tiny patties for a party platter! This recipe pairs nicely with the Veggie Cream Soup, page 92, or Glazed Veggies, page 111.

Serves 2	25 minutes

Ingredients:

12 to 16 ounces of crab meat *(350 to 450 g)*
1 cup bread crumbs, or crushed saltine crackers *(100 g)*
1/4 cup plain hummus *(60 g)*
2 lemons, 1 juiced, 1 wedged for garnish
1/2 teaspoon garlic powder *(1.5 g)*
1 egg
1/4 cup finely chopped sweet red pepper *(40 g)*
2 green onions, finely chopped
Gooey Tartare, page 232, optional tartar sauce garnish

Game Guide

The Legend of Zelda: Breath of the Wild.

Rock Salt
&
Any Crab

Vegan- Substitute crab with 8 ounces *(225 g)* of garbanzo beans, and 8 ounces *(225 g)* of hearts of palm. Or, you can try a vegan crab meat alternative, like Match Meat's crab. For the egg, use 1 tablespoon *(15 ml)* each of oil, hot water, and ground flax seed, and let sit for 5 minutes before using.

Note- This recipe is for crab cakes, when the actual in game recipe looks more like a whole roasted crab served on a leaf. Please feel free to serve that at your next party instead.

If you'd rather a simpler experience without a salt block, this recipe can be prepared in a normal skillet or on a grill. Just add ground rock salt to the bottom of the skillet or rub some into the sides of each crab cake.

Salt Grilled Crab

Directions:

1. Oil and slowly preheat your salt block to 450 degrees Fahrenheit *(230 degrees Celsius)* in the oven.

2. While the salt block is heating, add crab, crumbs, hummus or mayo, one lemon's juice, garlic powder, egg, red pepper, and green onion together in a bowl. Mix gently but thoroughly.

3. Shape the mixture into cakes of any size. However, know that the larger and flatter they are, the more salt encrusted they will be, and the thicker they are, the more time they will take to cook. About 1 inch *(2.5 cm)* thick patties take around 5 minutes to cook on each side. Add more crumbs if the cakes are soggy!

4. Place your cakes on the salt block in the oven. Cook for 5 minutes, flip, then cook for another 5 minutes. Remove a cake to carefully test the center, and remove if the center is fully opaque. If the meat is still translucent, continue cooking.

5. Garnish with lemon wedges, and a drizzle of Gooey Tartare if desired, and serve! Enjoy!

Salt Grilled Fish

Freshly chopped salsa served over seared and salted fish is on the menu.
If you want it to have a bit more kick, add more cayenne pepper!

Serves 2	20 minutes	Gluten free

Ingredients:

2 fillets of halibut or your favorite fish
1/4 teaspoon freshly ground black pepper *(.5 g)*
1 lime, 1/2 juiced, 1/2 wedged for garnish
1/8 teaspoon cayenne pepper *(.2 g)*
1/4 red onion, finely diced
1/4 cup chopped cilantro *(12.5 g)*
1 tomato, diced
1 medium bell pepper, yellow or orange
1 can black beans, rinsed and drained *(15 oz or 425 g)*

Game Guide

The Legend of Zelda: Breath of the Wild.

Rock Salt
&
Any Fish or Snail

Directions:

1. Oil and slowly preheat your salt block to 450 degrees Fahrenheit *(230 degrees Celsius)* in the oven.
2. While the salt block is heating, pat the fillets dry with a towel on both sides. Lightly season with ground black pepper on both sides.
3. In a bowl, combine half the lime's juice, cayenne pepper, red onion, cilantro, tomato, bell pepper, and beans. Mix thoroughly.
4. Place the fillets onto the salt block, cook either in the oven or on the stove top. Grill for 5 minutes on both sides, the fish is done when browned, and flesh can be flaked with a fork. The center should change from translucent to opaque.
5. Serve each fillet piping hot, with salsa on top, and garnish with a lime wedge. Enjoy!

If you'd rather a simpler experience without a salt block, this recipe can be prepared in a normal skillet or on a grill. Just add a ground rock salt to the bottom of the skillet or rub some into the sides of each fillet.

Salt Grilled Greens

Salty, crispy, delicious, and satisfying! A good pair to any of the Rice Ball chapter recipes!

Serves 2	15 minutes	Vegan	Gluten free

Ingredients:
12 Brussels sprouts
1 bunch asparagus, trimmed
2 full carrots
1 small zucchini
3 cups of spinach, for bedding *(100 g)*

Game Guide
The Legend of Zelda: Breath of the Wild.
Rock Salt
&
Any Vegetable, Herb, or Flower

Directions:
1. Oil and slowly preheat your salt block to 450 degrees Fahrenheit *(230 degrees Celsius)* in the oven.
2. While the salt block is heating, be sure to thoroughly wash all of the vegetables and pat them dry. Cut the Brussels sprouts in half, and cut the carrots and zucchini into quarters lengthwise.
3. Once your salt block is preheated, use tongs to carefully place all vegetables onto the salt block, except for the spinach. Keep in mind, the more surface area of the vegetable that touches the block, the stronger the flavor will be.
4. Cook in the oven for about 7 minutes, no need to flip. Greens should be browned on one side and relaxed but not too limp. Serve over spinach, and enjoy!

If you'd rather a simpler experience without a salt block, this recipe can be prepared in a normal skillet or on a grill. Just add ground rock salt to the bottom of the skillet or toss some with the ingredients before cooking.

Salt Grilled Meat

Salt-grilled beef fillets paired with a tangy rosemary sauce, this recipe seeks to satisfy your taste buds.

Serves 2	25 minutes	Gluten free

Ingredients:

1 to 2 pounds beef tenderloin *(450 to 900 g)*
1/4 cup butter *(55 g)*
1 yellow onion, finely chopped
1 teaspoon minced garlic *(3 g)*
1/3 cup balsamic vinegar *(80 ml)*
2 teaspoons dried rosemary *(2.4 g)*
1/4 cup fresh chopped parsley *(15 g)*

Game Guide

The Legend of Zelda: Breath of the Wild.

Rock Salt
&
Raw Meat or Raw Bird Drumstick

Directions:

1. Oil and slowly preheat your salt block to 450 degrees Fahrenheit *(230 degrees Celsius)* in the oven.
2. While the salt block is heating, cut the beef tenderloin into approximately 1 inch *(2.5 cm)* thick circular fillets. Pat dry on both sides, and let sit.
3. In a sauce pan, melt butter on medium heat, then add onion. Cook covered for 5 to 6 minutes, until onions are just beginning to brown, then add vinegar, and rosemary. Sauté for an additional 5 minutes, until sauce is syrupy, then remove from heat.
4. Place the fillets onto the salt block, cook in the oven for 5 minutes on both sides. Use a knife to test the center to make sure it is cooked to your taste.
5. Serve with sauce drizzled over each fillet. Enjoy!

Vegan- Substitute the tenderloin with large mushroom tops. You can also use your favorite meat substitute! Tempeh is great with this recipe. Proceed normally with vegan butter, but lightly oil both sides of your substitute to prevent sticking.

If you'd rather a simpler experience without a salt block, this recipe can be prepared in a normal skillet or on a grill. Just add ground rock salt to the bottom of the skillet or rub some into the sides of each tenderloin fillet.

Salt Grilled Mushrooms

Mushrooms paired with mashed potatoes and a brown mushroom sauce is a warm and comforting meal that goes well with a side of glazed vegetables.

Serves 2	45 minutes	Vegan	Gluten free

Ingredients:

1 pound large mushrooms* *(16 oz or 450 g)*
Mashed potatoes and mushroom gravy, page 104, optional

Game Guide

The Legend of Zelda: Breath of the Wild.

Any Mushroom
&
Rock Salt

Directions:

1. Oil and slowly preheat your salt block to 450 degrees Fahrenheit *(230 degrees Celsius)* in the oven.
2. Cut the stalks off of the mushrooms, clean, and dry. Oil each side lightly, then add to the salt block in the oven. Cook for five minutes on each side. They are done when they are browned and slightly shriveled. Serve with mashed potatoes, with mushroom gravy drizzled over everything. Enjoy!

*Large portobellos are easy to find, but use your favorite mushrooms!

If you'd rather a simpler experience without a salt block, this recipe can be prepared in a normal skillet or on a grill. Just add ground rock salt to the bottom of the skillet or rub some into the sides of each mushroom.

Mashed Potatoes and Mushroom Gravy

While not mentioned specifically, many recipes are beautifully paired with one or both of these delectable dishes! Serve with salt-grilled meals, cast iron sautés, or skewers!

Serves 4	30 minutes	Vegan	Gluten free

Mashed Potatoes Ingredients:
4 medium yukon gold potatoes, chopped
1/4 cup butter, room temperature *(55 g)*
1/4 cup fresh chopped parsley *(15 g)*
1 tablespoon minced garlic *(9 g)*
2 chives, chopped
1 teaspoon sea salt, or to taste *(5 g)*
1/4 teaspoon ground black pepper *(1 g)*

Mushroom Gravy Ingredients:
1 tablespoon butter *(14 g)*
1 teaspoon minced garlic *(3 g)*
1 pound mushrooms, very finely chopped *(450 g)*
1 yellow onion, finely chopped
3/4 cup vegetable stock *(160 ml)*
2 to 3 tablespoons cornstarch *(16 to 24 g)*

Directions:

1. Mashed Potatoes: Toss potatoes into a large pot filled with water. Bring to a boil, then boil for around 20 minutes. Potatoes are done when they fall easily off of an inserted fork. Transfer them to a bowl, and add butter, parsley, garlic, chives, sea salt and ground black pepper. Mix and mash until potatoes are to your desired texture. Taste test and adjust.

2. Mushroom Gravy: In a sauce pan on medium heat, add butter, garlic, small mushrooms and onion. Let cook covered, stirring occasionally, for 7 minutes, until onions are translucent and mushrooms are browned, then add vegetable stock. Stir in a bit of flour at a time, mixing to avoid clumps. Reduce heat to low, and allow to simmer while you cook everything else. If after everything is finished the gravy still needs thickening, add a spoonful or two of the mashed potatoes, and mix them to dissolve.

Cast Iron Cooking

Link often cooks on double handled cast iron skillets found inexplicably in the wilderness! Here is a guide for the acquisition, use, and maintenance of such skillets. The following recipes can also be prepared over a fire, see the Fire Cooking chapter guide on page 233.

Cast Iron

Cast iron is heavy, can develop a 'non-stick' surface, withstands heat like a Goron, is nearly indestructible, and heats evenly; ideal for one pot meals with no need for constant stirring. You can use metal spatulas, and transfer from the stove, to the oven, to directly over a fire!

Equipment

There are many great brands, and you can buy new or used. I use the Lodge brand, which is easily and cheaply found online. The 10.25 inches *(26 cm)* Cast Iron Skillet is a good starter, and is generally affordable. If you crave game accuracy and need Link's wilderness pan, go for the more expensive 17 inch *(43 cm)* Cast Iron Frying Pan with Loop Handles. For utensils, avoid plastics which might melt, use either wooden or metal spatulas. A well-fitting lid is crucial for many recipes as well, so make sure to get one that fits the skillet you buy.

Seasoning

Most new skillets are seasoned a little bit. Seasoning is just the act of rubbing a little oil all over your skillet, heating it up until it just starts to smoke, then letting it cool. Over time, this process creates a smooth, 'non-stick' surface. This happens naturally when you cook, but doing it at least once before using a new pan is good. As oil is reheated in your skillet over and over, it fills in the natural pores and cracks with a very hard polymer.

Maintenance

Maintain your cookware by using it! Oil it, heat it, prepare your food. Afterward, rinse out any remaining food, scrub the full pan, a steel scrubber works well, then dry it thoroughly with a towel. Oil it again and wipe off the excess oil before storing it. Is it safe to use soap? Yes, you will not dislodge the polymer with normal kitchen soap. Just make sure you lightly oil your skillet after washing. Rust might happen if you leave it wet, but just scrub it out, dry it, and oil it. Again, these are indestructible, so don't worry so much!

Energizing Glazed Meat

This honeyed and succulent steak, is delicious and simple to prepare! 10/10 with rice!

Serves 2	15 minutes	Gluten free

Ingredients:

1 tablespoon oil *(15 ml)*

2 lb tri-tip beef, cut into 4 large chunks *(1 kg)*

1/4 teaspoon black pepper *(.5 g)*

1/4 teaspoon salt *(1.5 g)*

2 tablespoons honey *(30 ml)*

1/4 cup soy sauce *(60 ml)*

1/4 cup brown sugar *(40 g)*

2 teaspoons finely chopped fresh ginger *(4 g)*

1 tablespoon minced garlic *(9 g)*

3 tablespoons roasted sesame seeds *(25 g)*

Game Guide

The Legend of Zelda: Breath of the Wild.

Courser Bee Honey
&
Any Meat

Directions:

1. Oil and preheat your cast iron skillet to medium high. Add black pepper, salt, honey, soy sauce, brown sugar, ginger, and garlic, stir to combine.

2. Add meat to skillet, flip and coat each side with sauce. Cook covered at med-heat for 7 minutes. If the sauce starts to stick, reduce heat, add a splash of water, and lengthen the cook time. Add the sesame seeds, flip meat, then cook for an additional 7 minutes. Cut into the center of the meat to verify it is cooked all the way through.

3. Serve two large chunks per plate, drizzle the excess sauce on top, garnish with green onion, and enjoy!

Vegan- For tempeh, tofu, or similar, preheat skillet to high, and add it after the oil, before the sauce. Sear each side, use a metal spatula to flip, decrease heat to medium, then add the sauce as normal. It's ready when the dish is simmering! Replace honey with agave, maple syrup, or your favorite similar glaze.

Fried Wild Greens

Wild and green? This recipe must be one of Tingle's favorites!

Serves 2	10 minutes	Vegan	Gluten free

Ingredients:

1 tablespoon sesame oil *(15 ml)*
1 tablespoon minced garlic *(9 g)*
1 handful long stemmed broccoli*
6 to 8 fresh Brussels sprouts, halved
1 baby bok choy, vertically chopped
1 can baby corn, drained *(15 oz or 425 g)*
1 tablespoon fresh ginger, finely minced *(12 g)*, or 1 teaspoon ground ginger *(1.8 g)*
2 tablespoons soy sauce *(30 ml)*
1 tablespoon brown sugar *(12 g)*
1 tablespoon water *(15 ml)*
Cayenne pepper to taste

Game Guide

The Legend of Zelda: Breath of the Wild.

Any Vegetable, Herb, or Flower

Directions:

1. Oil and preheat your cast iron skillet to medium high. Once it is hot, add all the ingredients, stir to combine, cover, and cook for 5 to 7 minutes, stirring occasionally. Do not cook for too long! As soon as the Brussels sprouts are cooked through and the broccoli has changed color but before everything wilts, remove from heat.
2. Serve immediately, and enjoy!

*If you can, purchase broccolini, tender stem broccoli, or similar! If not, just take normal broccoli, but chop vertically to try to preserve most of the stems!

Fruit and Mushroom Mix

This warm salad includes a base of fresh spinach, topped with Hylian rice, sautéed mushrooms, dried fruits, chopped walnuts and a balsamic ginger vinaigrette! This recipe is for one large salad, double it for two!

Serves 1	15 minutes	Vegan	Gluten free

Ingredients:
3/4 cup cooked wild grain rice *(200 g)*
2 tablespoons water *(30 ml)*
1/4 pound baby portobello mushrooms* *(4 oz or 115 g)*
2 cups baby spinach *(60 g)*
1/4 cup walnuts, chopped *(30 g)*
1/4 cup mixed dried fruits, chopped *(50 g)*
2 tablespoons Parmesan cheese, grated, optional *(10 g)*

Game Guide

The Legend of Zelda: Breath of the Wild.

Any Fruit
&
Any Mushroom

Balsamic Ginger Vinaigrette:**
1/2 cup olive oil *(120 ml)*
1 teaspoon sesame oil *(15 ml)*
1/4 cup balsamic vinegar *(60 ml)*
2 tablespoons soy sauce *(30 ml)*
2 tablespoons brown sugar *(25 g)*
2 teaspoons minced garlic *(6 g)*
2 tablespoons minced ginger *(18 g)*

*Feel free to use a mix of mushrooms!

** This makes enough for several uses, store sealed in the refrigerator, and always shake before using!

Fruit and Mushroom Mix

Directions:

1. Prepare wild grain rice.
2. Prepare vinaigrette in a bottle or jar. Add all vinaigrette ingredients, then shake vigorously until well combined. Shake again before using!
3. Oil and preheat your cast iron skillet to medium high, add 2 tablespoons of water *(30 ml)*, a tablespoon of vinaigrette, portobello mushrooms, and chopped walnuts. Cover and cook for 6 to 7 minutes, stirring occasionally, until mushrooms are tender and brown. Remove from heat.
4. Prepare a large bowl for your salad. Add baby spinach, then hot rice, mushrooms, walnuts, dried fruits, and cheese if desired. Top with drizzled vinaigrette to taste. Enjoy!

Glazed Mushrooms

A simple recipe for honey caramelized mushrooms,
with a dash of balsamic vinegar to make it tangy!

Serves 2	10 minutes	Vegan	Gluten free

Ingredients:

2 tablespoons oil *(30 ml)*
1 tablespoon honey *(15 ml)*
1 pound baby portobello mushrooms, quartered *(16 oz or 450 g)*
2 tablespoons balsamic vinegar* *(30 ml)*
1 tablespoon dried parsley *(5 g)*
1/2 teaspoon ground thyme *(2 g)*
1/2 teaspoon dried rosemary *(.5 g)*
Salt and Pepper to taste

Game Guide

The Legend of Zelda:
Breath of the Wild.

Courser Bee Honey
&
Any Mushroom

Directions:

1. Add all ingredients to a bowl with a lid. Gently mix until everything is coated.

2. Oil and preheat your cast iron skillet to medium high. Once hot, pour the ingredients from the bowl in, be sure to scrape in all of the sauce. Add a splash of water, then cook covered for 6 to 7 minutes, stirring occasionally.

3. Once the mushrooms are tender and brown, remove from heat. Serve immediately and enjoy!

*Vinegar can be overpowering to some! If you don't like it, leave it out. If you're unsure, use only 1 tablespoon *(15 ml)*, you can always add more if you like it!

Glazed Veggies

Forage for a few Endura carrots for this recipe, and good luck procuring the honey!
Courser Bees can be smoked out of their hives with a lit torch.

Serves 2	1 hour	Vegan	Gluten free

Ingredients:

3 tablespoons oil *(45 ml)*

2 to 3 tablespoons water *(30 to 45 ml)*

1/2 teaspoon ground thyme *(.7 g)*

1/2 teaspoon salt *(3 g)*

1/2 teaspoon ground black pepper *(1 g)*

3 large parsnips, thickly sliced

3 large carrots, thickly sliced

3 large golden beets, coarsely chopped

1 large turnip, coarsely chopped

1/2 cup honey *(120 ml)*

Game Guide

The Legend of Zelda: Breath of the Wild.

Courser Bee Honey
&
Any Vegetable, Herb, or Flower

Directions:

1. Preheat oven to 450 degrees Fahrenheit *(230 degrees Celsius)*. Oil and preheat your cast iron skillet to medium high, and mix all ingredients, except for the honey, together. Cover and cook for 5 minutes. Stir, and then drizzle the honey over everything. Mix until all vegetables are coated.

2. Cover and cook in the oven for 30 to 45 minutes, until vegetables are tender and easy to poke through with a fork.

3. Serve directly from the cast iron skillet, and enjoy!

*Don't peel! Wash thoroughly, and experience stronger flavors and textures by leaving the peel on.

Herb Saute

Sauté and then roast in the oven for an incredible and aromatic taste!
Don't forget the Goron Spice!

Serves 2	35 minutes	Vegan	Gluten free

Ingredients:

2 tablespoons oil *(30 ml)*
2 teaspoons garlic *(6 g)*
1 tablespoon dried parsley *(5 g)*
2 teaspoons dried oregano *(2 g)*
1 teaspoon dried rosemary *(1 g)*
1/2 teaspoon salt *(3 g)*
1 red onion, cut into wedges
4 small red potatoes, coarsely chopped
1 medium zucchini, cut into half circles
1 red pepper, coarsely chopped
1 cup baby portobello mushrooms, optional *(8 oz or 225 g)*
1/2 teaspoon Goron Spice, page 188, or mild curry powder *(1 g)*

Game Guide

The Legend of Zelda:
Breath of the Wild.

Goron Spice
&
Any Vegetable, Herb, or
Flower

Directions:

1. Preheat oven to 450 degrees Fahrenheit *(230 degrees Celsius)*. Oil and preheat cast iron skillet to medium high.

2. Add oil, garlic, parsley, oregano, rosemary, and salt to pan, then stir thoroughly to combine. Add all other ingredients, and continue stirring so all vegetables are coated with herbs. Cook for 6 minutes uncovered to brown some edges. Sprinkle the Goron Spice over everything.

3. Cover, then transfer cast iron skillet to the oven, and cook uncovered for 25 minutes.

4. Serve straight out of the cast iron skillet, and enjoy!

Meat and Seafood Fry

This is a surf and turf style dish that combines succulent beef with ahi tuna, seared and served with a tangy sauce. This recipe is for medium rare, but cook to your desired taste.

Serves 2	20 minutes	Gluten free

Ingredients:

1/2 pound beef tenderloin* *(.25 kg)*
1/2 pound sushi grade ahi tuna *(.25 kg)*
Sea Salt and ground black pepper, to taste
3 tablespoons oil *(45 ml)*
1 cup shredded cilantro *(50 g)*
1 tablespoon toasted sesame seeds *(8 g)*
1 teaspoon minced ginger *(3 g)*
1 teaspoon minced garlic *(3 g)*
3 tablespoons soy sauce *(45 ml)*
1 lime worth of freshly squeezed lime juice
1 teaspoon brown sugar (4 g)

Game Guide

The Legend of Zelda: Breath of the Wild.

Any Gourmet Meat
&
Any Seafood

Directions:

1. Prepare beef tenderloin and ahi tuna by slicing into 1.5 inch *(3.8 cm)* thick fillets. Pat dry, then season all sides with salt and ground black pepper. Set aside.
2. In a bowl, combine sesame seeds, cilantro, lime juice, garlic, ginger, soy sauce, sugar, and 1 tablespoon oil *(15 ml)*.
3. Oil your skillet with 2 tablespoons oil *(30 ml)*, preheat to medium high.
4. Once the skillet is hot, sear the fillets for one to two minutes on each side. Decrease the heat to medium and add the sauce. Mix and check meat with a knife to make sure it is cooked to your taste. If it needs more time, increase heat, cover, and flip meat every few minutes until you are satisfied. Once the sauce is simmering, it is ready to serve. Cut the fillets into chunks if you choose, serve it with left over sauce from the skillet drizzled over the top, and enjoy!

Vegan- This is a mainly meat dish, but the sauce goes well with firm tofu and mushroom fillets.

Meat Pie or Veggie Pie

These are small hand held pies, delightfully crunchy on the outside, while steamy and scrumptious on the inside. This recipe makes 4 hand sized pies.

Serves 2	1 hour	Vegan if desired

Ingredients:
Crust:*

2 cups plain flour *(300 g)*

2 tablespoons sugar *(25 g)*

1 teaspoon salt *(6 g)*

1/4 cup butter, or coconut oil *(55 g)*

1/4 cup almond yogurt *(245 g)*

1/3 cup milk, unsweetened almond milk works *(80 ml)*

1 tablespoon fresh yeast *(9 g)* or 4 teaspoons active dry yeast *(11 g)*

1 tablespoon milk *(15 ml)*

2 tablespoons milk, for glaze *(30 ml)*

2 tablespoon honey or sugar, for glaze *(30 ml)*

Game Guide

The Legend of Zelda: Breath of the Wild.

Tabantha Wheat
Goat Butter
Rock Salt
Any Meat

Filling:

1/2 pound chuck steak, finely chopped or 2 medium zucchini, chopped *(.25 kg)*

1/4 cup water, or more as necessary *(60 ml)*

1 teaspoon minced garlic, or more to taste *(3 g)*

1 small yellow onion, finely chopped

2 large golden yukon potatoes, very finely chopped

2 large carrots, finely chopped

1/2 cup peas *(160 g)*, and an additional 1/2 cup corn *(160 g)* if desired

2 teaspoons vegetable bouillon*** *(10 ml)*

1/2 teaspoon thyme *(1.5 g)*

Vegan- Add zucchini at the same time as the other vegetables, and add black beans!

*Or use bought pie crust dough! You can also make full size pies instead of hand sized.

**If the dough won't stick, paint on a little bit of water as glue to help!

***Better Than Bouillon: Seasoned Vegetable Base, or similar.

Meat Pie or Veggie Pie

Directions:

1. Crust: Add flour, sugar, salt, butter, yogurt, and milk to mixing bowl. Beat 100 times, until thick and mostly consistent. Dilute your yeast with 1 tablespoon milk *(15 ml)*, and mix. Add to the mixing bowl, folding it in a few times, and then knead with your clean hands until mixture is uniform. Cover mixing bowl, and set aside for 2 hours.

2. Filling: Oil and preheat your cast iron skillet to medium high. Add the chuck steak, and cook for 5 to 8 minutes, stirring occasionally. Once no pink is visible when it is cut, add water, garlic, yellow onion, potatoes, carrots, peas, vegetable bouillon, and thyme. Cover and cook for 10 minutes, stirring occasionally to prevent sticking; you may need to add more water. Once carrots and potato are tender, thicken with cornstarch if necessary, then remove from heat and make the pies.

3. Once the crust dough has rested for 2 hours, preheat your oven to 400 degrees Fahrenheit *(200 degrees Celsius)*. Then sprinkle flour on your clean work surface, and plop the dough in the center. Sprinkle more flour on top of everything. Using your rolling pin, roll the dough until it is even and flat, large enough for about three 7 inch *(18 cm)* diameter circles. Cut these circles free hand, or buy laying a small plate down, and tracing the edges with a knife. Put the circles to the side, and knead the excess dough back together. Roll it into your fourth circle.

4. Add a scoop of your filling to the center of a circle. Carefully fold one side of the dough to the other, lining up the edges to create a half circle. With a fork, press along the edges of the seam to secure the dough together,** then with a knife, poke a small slit in the top to vent. Repeat steps for the remaining circles.

5. Prepare a baking sheet with aluminum foil, then place the pies on the sheet, leaving at least 2 inches *(5 cm)* between each pie for even cooking. In a small glass, mix together 2 tablespoons *(30 ml)* milk with 2 tablespoons *(30 ml)* honey, then glaze the tops of each pie with a brush or spoon.

6. Cook at 400 degrees Fahrenheit *(200 degrees Celsius)* for 10 minutes, then check on them. Bake for a few more minutes at a time; until they are both golden brown and have firm cooked bottoms.

7. Allow to cool for 10 minutes before serving, and enjoy!

Meat and Rice Bowl

Juicy tenderloin piled high with brown sesame sauce and green onions, and an optional kick of chili; East Akkala and Serenne Stable's favorite dish just might be yours too.

| Serves 2 | 25 minutes | Gluten free |

Ingredients:

~2 cups cooked rice *(300 g)*
2 pounds beef tenderloin, sliced into thick slabs* *(1 kg)*
1 tablespoon minced garlic *(9 g)*
1 large yellow onion, sliced into long thin pieces
1 tablespoon brown sugar *(12.5 g)*
1 tablespoon sake** *(15 ml)*
1 tablespoon mirin *(15 ml)*
1 tablespoon soy sauce *(15 ml)*
1 tablespoon toasted sesame seeds *(8 g)*
Cayenne pepper, to taste, optional
2 green onion, chopped into 2 inch pieces

Game Guide

The Legend of Zelda: Breath of the Wild.

Hylian Rice
Any Meat
Rock Salt

Vegan- Tempeh and mushrooms work well here, but my favorite is big slabs of zucchini!

*If it is hard to slice, try partially freezing it and then slicing it. Teriyaki beef tenderloin is amazing here.

**Sake and mirin may not be on hand, and may be difficult to find. If you have neither, add 2 tablespoons *(30 ml)* of white wine, and an additional teaspoon *(4 g)* of sugar. If you don't have white wine, just add another tablespoon *(15 ml)* of soy sauce and call it good.

Meat and Rice Bowl

Directions:
1. Prepare rice.
2. Oil and preheat your cast iron skillet to medium high. Add garlic, onion, sake, soy sauce, sesame seeds, mirin and sugar. Cook covered for 5 to 7 minutes, stirring occasionally, until onions are browned.
3. Add beef to skillet, and coat both sides with sauce. Cook covered for 5 to 7 minutes, then flip and cook for an additional 5 to 7 minutes, until meat is cooked all of the way through.
4. Serve beef on top of bowls of fresh rice, top with chopped green onion, and drizzle with left over sauce from the skillet. Enjoy!

Mushroom Risotto

The appeal of a well made risotto is a hot, well textured comfort meal, and the chilly Mushroom Risotto is much loved by Gerudo Town, but the conventional recipe can be found in Ivee's diary in Hateno Village. Choose your own seasoning to make this risotto your own.

Serves 4	35 minutes	Vegan	Gluten free

Ingredients:

1 pound small whole mushrooms, like enoki *(16 oz or 450 g)*
4 large whole portobello mushrooms, for accurate garnish
2 teaspoons minced garlic *(6 g)*
1 small yellow onion, finely chopped
1 cup Carnaroli or Arborio dry rice *(200 g)*
3 cups vegetable broth *(720 ml)*
1/2 cup fresh or frozen corn *(160 g)*
3/4 cup shelled edamame *(115 g)*
2 teaspoons of your favorite spice blend* *(4 g)*
Sprigs of basil, for garnish

Game Guide

The Legend of Zelda: Breath of the Wild.

Hylian Rice
Goat Butter
Rock Salt
Any Mushroom

Directions:

1. Oil and preheat your cast iron skillet to medium. Add all mushrooms, garlic, onion, and a splash of water, then cover, cook, and stir occasionally until the mushrooms are juicy, approximately 7 minutes. Set aside the large mushrooms.

2. Increase heat to high, then add dry rice to the skillet. Cook while stirring constantly for 2 minutes to lightly brown the rice before adding all of the broth. Reduce heat to medium, cover and let simmer for about 15 minutes, stirring occasionally. Once the rice is tender and but there's still a bit of broth left, proceed.

3. Add the corn, edamame, and spice blend. Mix thoroughly, then cover and let simmer for about 7 more minutes. The dish is ready when the rice is fully cooked, and the broth is gone! Enjoy!

*The intended spice was Goron Spice, page 188 , but Italian spice blends make this risotto divine, so choose your favorite!

Mushroom Saute

Sometimes, you only have mushrooms in your inventory. This is the flavorful result!

Serves 2	10 minutes	Vegan	Gluten free

Ingredients:

1 tablespoon oil *(15 ml)*
1 pound mixed whole mushrooms* *(16 oz or 450 g)*
1 tablespoon garlic, minced *(9 g)*
1 tablespoon dried parsley** *(5 g)*
2 teaspoons ground sage *(1.5 g)*
1 tablespoon dried rosemary *(3.6 g)*
2 teaspoons ground thyme *(3 g)*
1 tablespoon truffle oil, optional *(15 ml)*

Game Guide

The Legend of Zelda: Breath of the Wild.

Goron Spice
&
Any Mushroom

Directions:

1. Oil and preheat your cast iron skillet to medium high. Add all ingredients except the truffle oil. Cover and cook for 6 to 7 minutes, stirring occasionally, until mushrooms are tender and brown. If desired, drizzle truffle oil on top, and stir once more.
2. Serve on its own, or on top of meat, salad, or pasta! Enjoy!

*The Legend of Zelda: Breath of the Wild platter holds a mix of various mushrooms, so choose your favorites, or explore what is available! Never eat a mushroom you do not know personally.

**You are welcome to use the game accurate Goron Spice, page 188, for this recipe instead of the spices listed here!

Poultry Pilaf

A tasty omelet style chicken fried rice, inspired by Japanese 'Omurice' dishes!

Serves 2	30 minutes	Gluten free

Ingredients:

3 cups cooked rice *(450 g)*
2 chicken breasts, cooked, shredded
1 tablespoon oil *(15 ml)*
1 teaspoon minced garlic *(3 g)*
1 yellow onion, diced
1/2 cup diced carrot, fresh or frozen *(160 g)*
1/3 cup peas, fresh or frozen *(100 g)*
1/3 cup corn, fresh or frozen *(100 g)*
1/4 cup water *(60 ml)*
2 tablespoons ketchup* or Lon Lon Ketchup, page 274 *(30 ml)*
3 eggs
1 green onion, chopped for garnish

Game Guide

The Legend of Zelda: Breath of the Wild.

Any Raw Bird
Hylian Rice
Goat Butter
Bird Egg

Vegan- This recipe still tastes great without eggs or poultry, so you can go without and add soft tofu, cooked lentils, mushrooms, eggplant, or broccoli instead!

*This recipe is inspired by Japanese 'Omu-Rice' dishes, which are usually flavored with normal ketchup! 2 to 3 tablespoons *(30 to 45 ml)* is ideal for most people, but please taste test to find the best amount for you!

Poultry Pilaf

Directions:

1. Prepare chicken and rice. About 1 cup dry rice *(175 grams)* yields enough for this recipe. Chicken can be cooked covered in your skillet with 1 teaspoon oil *(5 ml)* and a splash of water, then removed once fully cooked.

2. Combine oil, garlic, onion, and carrots in the skillet, cook covered on medium high heat for 5 to 7 minutes, until carrots are tender and onion is translucent.

3. Add peas, corn, chicken, water and ketchup to skillet, mix thoroughly, cook covered on medium heat for 5 minutes, until ingredients are hot all the way through.

4. Increase heat to medium high, add rice and mix thoroughly. In the center of the skillet, clear out a space to the bottom. Crack all three eggs directly into the space, and beat them. Once they reach a smooth runny consistency, mix all of the ingredients and stir. The eggs will scramble while you stir, once the eggs are cooked, decrease heat to low.

5. Serve with a sprinkling of chopped onions on top. Enjoy!

Stuffed Pumpkins

Koko is a master at this succulent pumpkin recipe, but you can always substitute stuffed orange bell peppers if you don't want to travel all the way to Kakariko Village for one of their famous fortified pumpkins!

Serves 4	1 hour	Gluten free

Ingredients:

2 cups cooked brown rice *(300 g)*
1 tablespoon oil *(15 ml)*
1/2 pound lean ground beef *(.25 kg)*
2 individual sized pumpkins or 4 orange bell peppers*
2 to 3 tablespoons oil *(30 to 45 ml)*
1 medium onion, chopped
1 large carrot, chopped into coins
1 tablespoon garlic, minced *(9 g)*
1/4 cup soy sauce *(60 ml)*
3 tablespoons brown sugar *(40 g)*
1/8 teaspoon cayenne pepper, optional to taste *(.25 g)*
1/2 cup corn, fresh or frozen *(160 g)*
1/2 cup peas, fresh or frozen *(160 g)*
Fresh basil leaves for garnish

Game Guide

The Legend of Zelda: Breath of the Wild.

Fortified Pumpkin

&

Any Meat

Vegan- Leave out the meat and add in summer squash or zucchini to make Veggie stuffed pumpkins, or if you'd like an alternative, roughly cut Tempeh works well!

*Try to purchase ones that are squat, that sit well without tipping over, baking or sweet, 3 to 4 pound *(1.3 to 1.8 kg)* pumpkins are best. For bell peppers, always choose the ones that have 4 prongs on the bottom, not 3. They might be sweeter and sit more firmly.

Stuffed Pumpkins

Directions:

1. Prepare brown rice, and preheat oven to 400 degrees Fahrenheit *(200 degrees Celsius)*.

2. Heat oil and ground beef on medium high, stirring occasionally, until no traces of pink remain, about 7 to 8 minutes. During this, wash the pumpkins or orange peppers, and then carefully cut off their tops. Don't throw away the tops, you'll use them later! Remove the inner seeds and strings from each pumpkin or pepper, but make sure to not scrape away the pumpkin flesh. Rub them inside and out with 2 to 3 tablespoons of oil *(30 to 45 ml)*, then arrange them on a baking tray.

3. Add garlic, onion, carrots, soy sauce, brown sugar, and cayenne pepper to the skillet with the cooked beef. Combine, then cover and cook for 4 to 5 minutes, until onions are translucent.

4. Add corn, peas, and rice to the pan, mix thoroughly. Turn the heat off, and scoop the mixture into each pumpkin or pepper, pouring any extra sauce on top of each. Replace the tops.

5. Cook the pumpkins in the oven for 45 minutes, or 25 minutes for bell peppers, checking occasionally. They are done when they are relaxed and sweating. You should be able to easily slide a knife into the pumpkins.

6. Serve each individually, with top removed on the plate, garnished with a couple fresh basil leaves. Enjoy!

Spicy Sautéed Peppers

Link picked a peck of Spicy Peppers! This recipe piles them high on a platter like they appear in The Legend of Zelda: Breath of the Wild, perfect for serving at a party! These will certainly keep guests warm in cold regions.

Serves 6	10 minutes	Vegan	Gluten free

Ingredients:

12 whole baby red peppers, stems and all

1/4 cup water *(60 ml)*

2 teaspoons lime juice *(10 ml)*

1/2 teaspoon salt *(3 g)*

1/2 teaspoon ground cumin *(1 g)*

1/2 teaspoon dried oregano *(.5 g)*

1/4 teaspoon ground cayenne pepper, to taste *(.5 g)*

Game Guide

The Legend of Zelda: Breath of the Wild.

Spicy Pepper

Directions:

1. Oil and preheat your cast iron pan to medium high. Add all the ingredients, and mix thoroughly. Cook uncovered for 7 minutes, gently stirring to prevent sticking. Peppers are done when soft but still brightly colored! The final result should still have a bit of crunch!

2. Serve your Spicy Sautéed Peppers stacked high on a plate, and enjoy!

Deku Nuts or Sauteed Nuts

These are wonderfully sugared and sautéed pecans, best eaten warm, if you're careful not to burn your tongue! Pack them for an ideal snack while you are exploring!

Serves 2	15 minutes	Vegan	Gluten free

Ingredients:

2 cups pecans* *(8 oz or 225 g)*
1 teaspoon oil *(15 ml)*
1/4 cup sugar *(60 g)*
2 tablespoons maple syrup *(30 ml)*
1 teaspoon ground cinnamon *(2.6 g)*
1/4 teaspoon cloves *(.5 g)*
1/2 teaspoon salt *(3 g)*

Game Guide

The Legend of Zelda: Breath of the Wild.

Acorn
or
Chickaloo Tree Nut

Deku Nuts

The Legend of Zelda: Ocarina of Time Majora's Mask Twilight Princess Super Smash Bros. Hyrule Warriors Legends

Directions:

1. Oil and preheat your cast iron skillet to medium. Add all ingredients except the nuts, mixing for about 5 minutes until it has melted into a smooth sauce.
2. Add the pecans, and stir until they are all coated. Decrease heat to low, and cook uncovered for 5 minutes while keeping an eye on the pan. Stir occasionally, if it smells like it's about to start burning, remove from heat and proceed to next step!
3. Pour nuts and sauce into a single layer on a large plate. Chill in the refrigerator for a minimum of one hour, or eat them while they are hot! Enjoy!

* Unsalted pecan halves are wonderful here, but use your favorite! In his infinite wisdom, Link's appear to be whole walnuts with an acorn on top.

Spicy Pepper Steak

This mouth watering recipe smells divine and is served with peppers and broccoli drizzled with a sweet and spicy sauce.

Serves 2	20 minutes

Ingredients:

2 steaks, 1/2 pound each *(8 oz or 225 g each)*

3 tablespoons whole wheat flour *(25 g)*

2 tablespoons oil *(30 ml)*

2 teaspoons minced garlic *(6 g)*

1 yellow onion, sliced into long strips

1/3 cup brown sugar *(65 g)*

1/3 cup soy sauce (80 ml)

2/3 cup water *(160 ml)*

1 jalapeño finely chopped, optional to taste

Your favorite hot or chili sauce, optional to taste

1 green bell pepper, finely diced

2 cups broccoli florets, about 3 heads worth

2 sprigs basil, for accurate garnish

4 red sweet snacking peppers, for accurate garnish

Game Guide

The Legend of Zelda: Breath of the Wild.

Spicy Pepper
&
Any Meat

Vegan- Spicy Pepper Broccoli! The delicious, spicy brown sauce of this recipe goes so well with broccoli, just add as much broccoli as you can fit into your skillet while still being able to cover it.

Gluten free- Use cornstarch instead of wheat flour.

Spicy Pepper Steak

Directions:

1. Sprinkle flour on top of your steaks, then massage until steaks are coated with flour.

2. Oil and preheat your cast iron skillet to medium high, then add garlic, onion, and steaks. Stir, cover, and cook for 3 to 4 minutes on each side. Steaks should be medium to medium rare.

3. Add brown sugar, soy sauce, water, jalapeño, and your choice of hot sauce to the steaks. Mix until sugar is dissolved.

4. Add green pepper and broccoli. Cook covered on medium high for 7 more minutes, stirring occasionally. It is done when the broccoli is tender but still bright green. Cut into steaks to make sure they are done to your taste.

5. Serve each steak with a sprig of basil on top, and with broccoli on one side and two sweet snacking peppers on the other. Drizzle left over sauce from the skillet over everything, and enjoy!

Vegetable Risotto

*Hylian rice cooked in flavored vegetable broth to soft perfection,
with an assortment of fresh vegetables, and a sprinkling of cheese if desired.
Perfect for quiet nights after the quests are turned in.*

Serves 4	30 minutes	Vegan	Gluten free

Ingredients:

2 teaspoons minced garlic *(6 g)*
1 small yellow onion, finely chopped
1 cup Carnaroli or Arborio dry rice *(200 g)*
3 cups vegetable broth *(720 ml)*
2 small zucchini, finely chopped
1 cup baby spinach, shredded*
1/2 cup fresh or frozen peas *(160 g)*
1/2 cup baby tomatoes, halved or whole *(75 g)*
1/4 cup fresh chopped parsley *(4 g)*
2 tablespoons Parmesan cheese, finely grated, optional *(10 g)*

Game Guide

*The Legend of Zelda:
Breath of the Wild.*

Any Carrot or Pumpkin
Hylian Rice
Goat Butter
Rock Salt

Directions:

1. Oil and preheat skillet to medium. Add the garlic and onion, then let cook, stirring occasionally for five minutes. Onions should be soft and translucent, not yet browning.

2. Add dry rice to skillet, sauté while stirring continuously for 2 minutes to lightly brown the rice, then add all of the broth. Cover and let simmer for about 15 minutes, stirring occasionally. The rice should be soft but not quite done, with a little broth left.

3. Add the zucchini, spinach, peas, tomatoes, parsley and cheese. Mix thoroughly, then cover and let simmer for about 7 more minutes. The dish is ready when the rice is fully cooked! You can serve over a bed of spinach, with a further sprinkling of Parmesan on top if you desire. Enjoy!

Vegan- Skip the cheese! Thicken if necessary with corn starch or instant mashed potatoes, and add garlic salt to taste.

Chu Jelly Preserves

Inspired by the rainbow of Chus and Chuchus found in The Legend of Zelda series, this chapter transforms these enemies into actual, delicious jelly!

From the lemon zest Yellow Chu Jelly, to the spicy strawberry Red Chu Jelly, to the rare chocolate raspberry Black Chu Jelly, these delightful jellies serve perfectly atop scones, toast, ice cream and more! They make wonderful gifts too!

Guide to Jelly Preserves

New to the world of fruit preserves? Don't worry! It is simpler than you think, and you will never again have to buy expensive jars of fruit jelly from the store!

1. In the next two pages, I have laid out two processes: Preparation and Conclusion, that will be referred to in each recipe.

2. Additionally, you will need pectin! Any brand should do fine, but I prefer the ones that don't come in packets, that way you can more easily measure out an exact amount. I use Ball's Real Fruit Flex Batch Pectin.

3. Do not cut or reduce the sugar in these recipes. It is chemically necessary for the jelling process!

4. Finally, please wash all of your ingredients, and your hands, thoroughly before starting, and throughout the process if necessary. Good hygiene means a longer shelf life!

Preparation

Use these instructions to prepare for each recipe in this chapter!

Preparation Supplies:

-4 or 5 half pint, 8 oz, canning jars per recipe. Each recipe results in about 4 jars, but you can prepare a 5th just in case.

-1 jar lifter. A real jar lifter would be safest and best, but sturdy tongs wrapped with clean rubber bands or similar can work. Just be careful, the jars and water will be very hot.

-1 large soup pot, big enough to submerge your jars comfortably

-1 trivet. This will sit inside the soup pan, underneath your jars. I like silicon trivets, but you can also use a carefully placed hand towel.

-1/4 cup distilled white vinegar. *(60 ml)* This is especially important for homes with hard water.

Preparation Directions:

1. Wash your jars, lids, and bands thoroughly in hot, soapy water. Fully rinse and let air dry.
2. Check each jar for any cracks or chips. Do not use if there are any.
3. Make sure your trivet and soup pot are clean, place the trivet inside, and add the vinegar.
4. Arrange your jars, no lids, just the jars, in the pot, and try to make sure they are not touching if possible. Fill the pot and jars with hot water, until the jars are fully submerged.
5. Place the pot on the stove top, cover, and bring to a boil. Once it reaches a boil, turn the heat slightly down, but enough to maintain a light boil, and continue boiling covered for at least 10 minutes.
6. Proceed with chosen recipe!

Conclusion

Use these instructions to conclude each recipe in this chapter!

Conclusion Directions:

1. Remove the canning jar pot from heat, and carefully remove the jars with a jar lifter. Pour all of the water back into the pot.

2. Ladle, spoon, or pour the preserves into the jars. A funnel would be helpful. Leave exactly 1/4 inch *(.5 cm)* of head space at the top of each jar. Then, with a clean, damp paper towel, clean the rim of each jar.

3. Center the lids on each jar, and tighten each with a ring. Jars differ, follow your jar's instructions. Do not tighten it too much, you want to use just your finger tips, and tighten it until there is good resistance. The air in the top of the jar needs to escape during the next step, tightening it too much prevents that from happening.

4. Carefully submerge each jar back into the soup pot. Make sure there is at least an inch or two of water above the jars. You do not want the jars to become exposed at any point.

5. Cover the canning soup pot, then bring it to a boil. Depending on your altitude, keep it boiling hard for 5 minutes for less than 1,000 feet *(<300 meters)*, 10 minutes for less than 6,000 feet *(<1800 meters)*, or 15 minutes for more than 6,000 feet *(>1800 meters)*.

6. Remove the pot from heat, and set out a thick towel over the counter. Carefully remove the jars, and lay them out on the towel. If any of your jars are oozing, put them back into the pot, off heat, and let them cool slowly for ten minutes. Leave the jars on the towel alone. You may hear them pop, chirp, and make other happy noises, this is natural. If they don't make any noises that is normal too, and they are still happy, don't worry.

7. After a few hours, once the jars are completely cool, you can check the seals. Remove just the rings and pick up the jar straight up, 1 or 2 inches from the counter, by the lid, with just your finger tips. If it holds, you've done it! The jars are sealed! Replace the ring, screw tightly, make sure the jar is perfectly clean, mark the jar with the date, and store in a cool dark place. If everything was done right, it has a shelf life of around 2 years. If the lid doesn't hold, that's okay! Once opened, the preserves will be good for up to 3 months as long as it is refrigerated. Either way, enjoy!

Red Chu Jelly

This spicy jam is made with strawberries and a chili! Ideal over ice creams, or atop meat dishes. It shouldn't explode on impact, but avoid testing that anyway.

4 jars	1 hour	Vegan	Gluten Free

Ingredients:

3 cups strawberries, washed with tops removed *(500 g)*
1 fresh jalapeño pepper*
1/2 tablespoon apple cider vinegar *(7 ml)*
1 tablespoon lemon juice *(15 ml)*
1/4 teaspoon cinnamon *(.6 g)*
1/8 teaspoon ground ginger *(.25 g)*
3 1/2 cups of sugar *(700 g)*
3 tablespoons pectin *(25 g)*

Game Guide

The Legend of Zelda Series.

Drops from Red Chus or Chuchus, and Fire Chuchus. Can also be made in The Legend of Zelda: Breath of the Wild by exposing Chuchu Jelly to fire.

Directions:

1. Prepare using the Preparation instructions in the intro for this chapter on page 130.
2. With your hands or a masher, crush the strawberries in a bowl. Leave chunks for the texture you desire.
3. Add crushed strawberries and pectin to a pan on high heat. Stir constantly, and bring to a full boil that does not dissipate with stirring.
4. Add sugar, apple cider vinegar, lemon juice, cinnamon, ground ginger, and chili pepper. Bring to a full boil again, and boil while stirring for 1 full minute.
5. Remove from heat, carefully remove the jalapeño pepper shell, then skim off any foam.
6. Follow the Conclusion instructions in the intro for this chapter on page 131, and enjoy!

*For a nice spicy punch that will help you brave the cold regions, split it down the middle, scoop out the seeds and toss them in, and then toss the shell in too. For more mild, leave it whole.

Yellow Chu Jelly

Sweet lemonade style jelly, this sour and sweet preserve will surely shock your senses!
Serve with tea and scones for a delightful afternoon snack.

| 4 jars | 1 hour | Vegan | Gluten Free |

Ingredients:

1 lemon, washed and sliced into thin circles
2 cups juiced lemons with pulp* *(480 ml)*
Lemon zest to taste
3/4 cup water *(180 ml)*
4 tablespoons pectin *(33 g)*
1 cup honey *(240 ml)* or 2 cups sugar *(400 g)*

Game Guide

The Legend of Zelda Series.

Drops from Yellow Chus or Electric Chuchus. Can also be made in The Legend of Zelda: Breath of the Wild by exposing Chuchu Jelly to electricity. In The Legend of Zelda: Twilight Princess, it can be used as Lantern Oil.

Directions:

1.   Prepare using the Preparation instructions in the intro for this chapter on page 130. Also put three spoons into the freezer.

2.   On high heat in a large pan, combine water, lemon slices, juice, pulp, and zest. Stir until mixed, cover, and bring to a boil.

3.   Add the pectin, stir to dissolve, and bring to a full boil that does not dissipate with stirring. Add honey, then return to full rolling boil. Continue boiling while stirring for 1 full minute. Lemon preserves are tricky to thicken, retrieve one spoon from the freezer, and scoop a small amount of the preserves out. Allow it to cool for a few seconds, and test the thickness. If it is still too syrupy, continue boiling while stirring for a few more minutes, until it thickens a bit more. Test again as necessary until it achieves desired thickness. Lemon jelly is notoriously difficult to set properly.

4.   Remove from heat and skim any foam off the top.

5.   Follow the Conclusion instructions in the intro for this chapter on page 131, and enjoy!

*About 8 large lemons
   Vegan- This recipe does use honey, but that 1 cup of honey can be replaced with 2 cups of sugar! Proceed as directed!

Green Chu Jelly

This space intentionally left blank.

4 jars	1 hour	Vegan	Gluten Free

Ingredients:

3 cups kiwi flesh, about 7 kiwis *(500 g)*
3 tablespoons pectin *(25 g)*
4 cups sugar *(900 g)*
1 tablespoon lemon juice *(15 ml)*
1 cup unsweetened pineapple juice *(240 ml)*

Game Guide

The Legend of Zelda: The Wind Waker, and Twilight Princess.

Drops from Green Chus or Chuchus, but in Twilight Princess these can only be found in the Wii and HD version after a Blue and Yellow Chu merge, and the resultant Green Chu Jelly has no effect.

Directions:

1. Prepare using the Preparation instructions in the intro for this chapter on page 130.
2. Add the kiwi flesh and pectin to a pan on high heat. Mash them while stirring, and bring to a full boil that does not dissipate with stirring.
3. Add sugar, lemon juice, and pineapple juice. Bring to a full boil again, and boil while stirring for 1 full minute.
4. Remove from heat, and skim off any foam.
5. Follow the Conclusion instructions in the intro for this chapter on page 131, and enjoy!

Blue Chu Jelly

Fresh blueberries paired with just a taste of mint results in a jelly that is just as invigorating as a blue potion! For an extra blue look, use a blue glass jar!

4 jars	1 hour	Vegan	Gluten Free

Ingredients:
4 cups blueberries, crushed *(500 g)*
3 tablespoons pectin *(25 g)*
4 cups sugar *(900 g)*
1 tablespoon lemon juice *(15 ml)*
8 fresh peppermint leaves, minced

Game Guide

The Legend of Zelda Series.

Drops from Blue Chus or Chuchus. In The Legend of Zelda: Breath of the Wild, Chuchu Jelly is neutral, and can be changed into any other Chuchu Jelly with elemental exposure.

Directions:

1. Prepare using the Preparation instructions in the intro for this chapter on page 130.
2. In a large pan, add washed and crushed blueberries and pectin on high heat.
3. Bring to a full boil that does not dissipate with stirring. Add sugar, lemon juice, and minced peppermint leaves, then return to full rolling boil. Continue boiling while stirring for 1 full minute.
4. Remove from heat, and skim any foam off the top.
5. Follow the Conclusion instructions in the intro for this chapter on page 131, and enjoy!

Purple Chu Jelly

Purple Chu Jelly has a random effect when used, so good luck!
Use a new mix of berries for a new flavor each time you try this recipe!

| 4 jars | 1 hour | Vegan | Gluten Free |

Ingredients:

3 to 4 cups of random berries, crushed *(500 g)*
3 tablespoons pectin *(25 g)*
3 cups sugar *(675 g)*
1/2 teaspoon chili powder, optional *(1 g)*

Game Guide

The Legend of Zelda:
Twilight Princess.

Drops from Purple Chus.

Directions:

1. Prepare using the Preparation instructions in the intro for this chapter on page 130.
2. In a large pan, combine washed and crushed berries, and pectin on high heat.
3. Bring to a full boil that does not dissipate with stirring. Add sugar, and chipotle chili powder if desired, then return to full rolling boil. Continue boiling while stirring for 1 full minute.
4. Remove from heat, and skim any foam off the top.
5. Follow the Conclusion instructions in the intro for this chapter on page 131, and enjoy!

Rare and White Chu Jelly

This is a home style apple pie style jam whose smell will bring you a sense of nostalgia. Especially delicious over French vanilla ice cream.

| 4 jars | 1 hour | Vegan | Gluten Free |

Ingredients:

4 cups peeled, cored, chopped, apples *(500 g)*
2/3 cup water *(160 ml)*
1/2 tablespoon lemon juice *(7 ml)*
3 tablespoons pectin *(25 g)*
2 1/2 cups sugar *(550 g)*
1/2 teaspoon ground cinnamon *(1 g)*
1/2 teaspoon ground cloves *(1 g)*
1/2 teaspoon ground nutmeg *(1 g)*

Game Guide

The Legend of Zelda: Twilight Princess.

Rare Chu Jelly is dropped by Rare Chus, and is identical to Great Fairy's Tears.

The Legend of Zelda: Breath of the Wild.

White Chu Jelly is dropped by Ice Chuchu, or can be made by exposing Chuchu Jelly to ice.

Directions:

1. Prepare using the Preparation instructions in the intro for this chapter on page 130.

2. In a large pan, combine apples, water, and lemon juice on high heat. Cover, and simmer for 10 minutes.

3. Add the pectin, stir to dissolve, then bring to a full boil that does not dissipate with stirring. Add sugar, then return to full rolling boil. Continue boiling while stirring for 1 full minute.

4. Remove from heat, skim any foam off the top, and then add cinnamon, cloves, and nutmeg. Stir until thoroughly mixed.

5. Follow the Conclusion instructions in the intro for this chapter on page 131, and enjoy!

Black Chu Jelly

This forbidden food cannot be found through normal game play, we only know of its existence through the game data of The Legend of Zelda: Twilight Princess. Enjoy this forsaken treat made of raspberries and chocolate!

| 4 jars | 1 hour | Vegan | Gluten Free |

Ingredients:

3 heaping cups raspberries *(400 g)*

3 tablespoons pectin *(25 g)*

3 cups sugar *(675 g)*

1 to 2 tablespoons black cocoa powder* *(7 to 15 g)*

> ### Game Guide
> *The Legend of Zelda: Twilight Princess.*
>
> Consuming forbidden Black Chu Jelly results in the loss of one heart. That's thankfully not the case in real life.

Directions:

1. Prepare using the Preparation instructions in the intro for this chapter on page 130. Also put 3 spoons into the freezer.

2. Add raspberries and pectin to a pan on high heat. Mash them while stirring, and bring to a full boil that does not dissipate with stirring.

3. Add the sugar, then add black cocoa powder to taste, it's very strong. I recommend adding and mixing in a little at a time and taste testing. Bring to a full boil again, and boil while stirring for 1 full minute. Check thickness by taking a small amount out with a frozen spoon and allow it to cool. Continue boiling for a few additional minutes if necessary, until desired cooled thickness is reached.

4. Remove from heat, and skim off any foam.

5. Follow the Conclusion instructions in the intro for this chapter on page 131, and enjoy!

*Try to find actual black cocoa powder! It will result in a very dark jelly!

Desserts

Welcome to the largest chapter in this book! From the highly thematic Rock Hard Food and Monster Cake to classics like Apple Pie and Carrot Cake, this chapter covers it all!

Vegan and Vegan Curious Folks

The majority of these desserts are vegan by default. I find that vegan desserts are less heavy, more delicious, and less likely to upset stomachs! In taste testing, no one suspected that these recipes were vegan (even the Bean Monster Cake), so you can serve with confidence!

Gluten Free Folks

In this chapter, as with this book, I try to avoid adding gluten unnecessarily. Where practical, the following recipes avoid gluten all together, or restrict it to just the crust, that way a gluten free alternative can be easily substituted.

However, I do not always succeed, I am sorry. In those cases, I try to provide an alternate recipe or substitution instructions! I wish you all a happy stomach!

Apple Pie

This delectable Apple Pie is a favorite of Rito Village, though Lakeside Stables loves the hasty variation! Serves 6, or just 1 if you're ambitious.

6 servings	1.5 hours + cooling	Vegan

Ingredients:
Crust:
2 cups all purpose flour *(300 g)*
1 teaspoon salt *(5.6 g)*
2 tablespoons granulated sugar *(25 g)*
1/2 cup cold butter or cold coconut oil *(110 g)*
3 to 4 tablespoons ice water *(45 to 60 ml)*
9 inch pie pan *(~23 cm)*
1 tablespoon real maple syrup *(15 ml)*

Filling:
6 cups sliced Honeycrisp apples* *(750 g)*
2 tablespoons lemon juice *(30 ml)*
1/4 cup all purpose flour *(40 g)*
2 teaspoons ground cinnamon *(5 g)*
1/2 teaspoon ground nutmeg *(1 g)*
1/4 teaspoon ground cloves *(.5 g)*
1 teaspoon vanilla extract *(5 ml)*
2 tablespoons real maple syrup *(30 ml)*
1/4 cup brown sugar *(50 g)*

Glaze:
1 tablespoon maple syrup *(15 ml)*
1 tablespoon hot water *(15 ml)*
Mint leaves, for garnish
Apple slices, for garnish

> ## Game Guide
> *The Legend of Zelda: Breath of the Wild.*
>
> Tabantha Wheat
> Cane Sugar
> Goat Butter
> Apple

Vegan- Be sure to use Coconut oil instead of butter!
Gluten Free - Use 2 cups of all purpose gluten free flour when making the pie crust, or purchase a gluten free pie crust to substitute!

*This is roughly over 3 pounds, around 8 to 10 apples total. You can use your favorite kind of apple, I just love Honeycrisp apples, and I think it makes a noticeable difference! Leave the peels on for better flavor.

Apple Pie

Directions:

1. Crust: Combine flour, salt, and sugar in a bowl. Use your clean hands to thoroughly mix. Add the cold butter or coconut oil, and knead with hands until consistent and crumbly. You could use a mixer here, but Link doesn't have a mixer be realistic.

2. Add ice water until you can just roll the dough into a ball without crumbling and cracking. Add one spoonful of ice water at a time, kneading thoroughly before adding another. You will likely need 3 to 4 tablespoons *(<60 ml)* of ice water, but it will depend on your flour. Err on the side of crumbly instead of soupy. Once it reaches a dough consistency, separate it into two halves, and roll them both into balls. Cover and place in the refrigerator. Link did have access to a refrigerator.

3. Filling: Wash your apples thoroughly, core them, and slice them thinly. You are welcome to peel them, but keeping the peel adds a punch of flavor. Add the apple slices and all other filling ingredients to a bowl, and mix thoroughly. Set aside without covering.

4. Preheat the oven to 400 degrees Fahrenheit *(205 degrees Celsius)*.

5. Remove one ball of dough from the refrigerator. Lightly flour a clean surface, and use a rolling pin to roll out the dough into a large circle. Make sure to rotate the dough after every few rolls to prevent sticking. Carefully lift the circle, lay it centered over your pie dish, and gently press in the sides and bottom so there are no gaps. Cut any excess trim.

6. Mix your apple filling once more, then dump it into the pie or ceremoniously place each apple slice to make perfect layers of concentric circles. If there is too much filling, don't worry, that's not true, just make a happy mound.

7. Remove the second ball from the refrigerator. Now you will make the top of the pie, and you can spend as much or as little time on this as you wish. The Legend of Zelda: Breath of the Wild crust is a woven top with what appears to be a rolled and fluted edge. To make a woven top, first roll out the dough, and cut it into long and thin strips. Place half of the strips carefully over the top of the pie, all facing one direction. Then, fold every other strip half back, place a strip, unfold the folded strips over the top, and fold back the other strips, to place another strip, repeat. Once done with the weave, you can trim any excess, and use it to roll a long edge piece with your hands. Wind this around the edge of the pie, and use your fingers to secure it to the bottom pie crust. Then you can make it pretty with indents from your fingers, or a fork. Any excess dough can be used to make decorations like koroks and leaves, fairies, rupees, or blupees!

8. Mix 1 tablespoon maple syrup with 1 tablespoon hot water *(15 ml each)*, then brush this glaze onto the crust of your pie. Take a picture with your Sheikah Slate before you put it in the oven.

9. Bake on a baking sheet for 20 minutes, then reduce heat to 375 degrees Fahrenheit *(190 degrees Celsius)*. Add a pie crust shield or metal foil to the edges if desired, to prevent browned edges. Bake for an additional 30 minutes. Remove from the oven, and don't worry, it will thicken as it cools. Cool to room temperature, about 2 hours, before slicing and serving. Garnish with mint leaves and extra apple slices for accuracy, and enjoy!

Carrot Cake

On February 21st, 1986, Link was born with the release of the first The Legend of Zelda game. This nostalgic and scrumptious cake is the perfect way to celebrate. Happy Birthday Link! You can use Swift or Endura carrots for this made from scratch recipe.

6 servings	1 hour	Vegan

Ingredients:

9 inch round cake pan, or cupcake tray with inserts *(~23 cm)*
Coconut oil for pan
2 cups all purpose flour *(300 g)*
1 teaspoon baking soda *(4.6 g)*
1 teaspoon baking powder *(5 g)*
2 teaspoons cinnamon *(5 g)*
1 teaspoon nutmeg *(2 g)*
1/2 teaspoon cloves *(1 g)*
1/2 teaspoon salt *(3 g)*
3 cups grated carrots *(330 g)*
1 1/2 cups brown sugar *(270 g)*
2 tablespoons ground flaxseed *(14 g)*
6 tablespoons hot water *(90 ml)*
1/2 cup olive oil *(120 ml)*
1 teaspoon vanilla extract *(5 ml)*
1 tablespoon apple cider vinegar *(15 ml)*
Almond milk, if necessary*

Garnish:**

~1/4 cup granulated sugar *(60 g)*
6 realistic candy carrots, or baby carrots with stems
Coconut Whip Cream, page 172, or similar

> ### Game Guide
>
> *The Legend of Zelda: Breath of the Wild.*
>
> Tabantha Wheat
> Cane Sugar
> Goat Butter
> Any Carrot

*Sometimes the batter just isn't as moist as it should be. If this is the case and the batter seems dry, then add a little bit of sweetened vanilla almond milk, or water, a spoonful at a time, and mix until it is nice and whippy!

**The Legend of Zelda: Breath of the Wild version does not have frosting, which you might normally associate with Carrot Cake! Instead the in game model, and this recipe, has a light sprinkling of sugar on top, with a small dollop of coconut whip cream and a baby carrot with stem on each slice.

Carrot Cake

Directions:

1. Preheat the oven to 350 degrees Fahrenheit *(175 degrees Celsius)*. Use coconut oil to coat the bottom and sides of the pan thoroughly.

2. In a glass measuring cup, mix 2 tablespoons ground flaxseed *(30 ml)* with 6 tablespoons freshly boiled water *(90 ml)*. Once mixed, let sit for 5 minutes.

3. Sift the flour, baking soda, baking powder, cinnamon, nutmeg, cloves, and salt together in a large mixing bowl, and then add the grated carrot, brown sugar, oil, vanilla, and apple cider vinegar. Beat thoroughly until well mixed, and then add your flax egg mixture from the measuring cup. Beat again until the texture is smooth.

4. Once well mixed and fluffy, pour your batter into the cake pan. Bake in the oven for 30 minutes, and then test with a toothpick in the center. If the toothpick comes out without batter, it is ready! If not, let it cook for an additional 3 to 4 minutes before testing again.

5. Take the cake out of the oven, then carefully run a knife along the edges of the pan to prevent sticking. Flip the cake onto a plate or cooling rack, and lift the pan from the cake.

6. Hand sprinkle sugar onto the top of the cake, about 1/4 cup total, then allow to cool for at least 30 minutes.

7. Serve the cake immediately, or keep it sealed and covered in the refrigerator. Garnish each slice of carrot cake with a dollop of coconut whip cream, and a carrot! Enjoy!

Dubious Food

A mass of green goo, with pixelated chunks of purple, and bones sticking out. Yuck! The raspberry and lemon marrow filled white chocolate bones really shine in this sweet green tea pudding!

| ~3 servings | 1 hour | Vegan | Gluten free |

Ingredients:
2 cups sweetened vanilla almond milk *(480 ml)*
1/2+ cup chia seeds *(110 g)*
2 tablespoons matcha green tea powder* *(12 g)*
1/2 tsp almond extract *(2.5 ml)*
1/2 tsp vanilla extract *(2.5 ml)*
1 cup raspberries and black berries *(150 g)*
Optional, large green tapioca pearls
Optional, green food coloring**

Marrow-filled Bones:***
A long bone shape baking or chocolate mold
1 pound of white chocolate or baking chips *(16 oz or 450 g)*
1/2 cup granulated sugar *(110 g)*
1/2 cup raspberries *(75 g)*
1 teaspoon lemon juice *(5 ml)*
3 teaspoons powdered pectin, *(.5 oz or 15 g)*

Game Guide

The Legend of Zelda: Breath of the Wild.

Food with monster parts or critters

or

Seasoning without food

or

Monster parts without critters

or

Critters without monster parts

*Or more, for a greener color look and flavor.
**For an otherworldly green, feel free to add green food dye!
　　**Alternatively, you could make bone shaped cookies, or replace with purchased bone candy! Please do not use real bones.

Dubious Food

Directions:

1. Goo: Combine milk, chia seeds, matcha powder, almond and vanilla extract in a bowl. Stir until matcha is fully dissolved, then top with berries, stir roughly, then cover, and refrigerate for at least 4 hours.

2. Bones: Carefully melt the white chips. Fill your bone mold 1/3 of the way with melted chips, then knock the mold carefully against a hard surface to set it and get rid of air bubbles. Tilt the mold sideways in each direction to coat some of the sides of the bones with melted chips. Freeze the molds while you make the filling.

3. Bone Filling: Mix sugar, raspberries, and lemon juice in a saucepan over medium heat. Bring to a boil, then add the pectin in a little at a time, stirring constantly. Bring down to a light boil, and continue stirring for 5 minutes. Then remove from heat, and place in the freezer to cool. When both the filling and bone mold are cool to the touch, proceed to the next step.

4. Remelt the remaining white chips, and take the bone mold and filling from the freezer. Carefully, a piping bag or similar is helpful here, add a thick line of filling to each bone.

5. Fill the remaining mold with the rest of the melted white chips, taking care to coat the edges and then the filling. Knock the mold carefully against a hard surface, and then chill until icy cold to the touch. When it is icy cold, carefully remove the bones from the mold, but if any break, don't worry, it's accurate!

6. When the Goo has set, remove it from the refrigerator, and chop it roughly. Serve the Goo in a mound on each plate, and artfully stick a bone or two in each. Enjoy!

Egg Pudding

You can't beat the lightly sweet deliciousness of Japanese style purin!
If you want to avoid the Cuccos, I've included a vegan version too!

| 4 servings | 45 minutes | Vegan | Gluten free |

Sauce:
1/3 cup granulated sugar *(75 g)*
1/4 cup water *(60 ml)*
~4 Egg pudding molds*

Egg Pudding Ingredients:
1 1/4 cup milk *(300 ml)*
1/4 cup granulated sugar *(55 g)*
1/2 teaspoon vanilla extract *(2.5 ml)*
3 large eggs

Vegan Pudding Ingredients:
2 cups sweetened almond milk, or similar *(480 ml)*
1 tablespoon agar agar flakes *(4 g)*
2 tablespoons sugar *(25 g)*
1 teaspoon vanilla extract *(5 ml)*
1/2 cup extra firm silken tofu *(8 oz or 225 g)*

Garnish:
4 small sprigs of mint leaves

Game Guide
The Legend of Zelda:
Breath of the Wild.

Fresh Milk
Bird Egg
Cane Sugar

*These are very simple and cheap aluminum tins! Search for 'egg pudding cups' or 'mini pie pans', and choose one you like. Go for a reusable, not disposable- you can use these for the Egg Tart recipe also! This recipe makes about 4 puddings, depending on the shape and size you get.

Egg Pudding

Directions:

1. For the sauce, add 1/3 cup sugar *(75 g)* and 1/4 cup water (60 ml) to a saucepan. Simmer on medium while stirring occasionally until sugar has completely dissolved. Then without stirring, increase heat slightly to medium high until the mixture is golden brown, then remove from heat immediately, and let it cool for a few minutes. Rinse your pudding molds so they are slightly wet, and then pour the sauce evenly into each pudding mold.

2. For the pudding, add the milk, sugar, vanilla extract, (and agar agar flakes if vegan) to the saucepan, heat at medium for 4 to 6 minutes, stirring until sugar (and agar agar flakes) are fully dissolved and mixture is hot to the touch, but not boiling.

3. In a bowl, add the eggs or silken tofu. Beat until smooth, then gradually pour the hot milk mixture from the saucepan into the bowl. Mix until consistent, then pour it all back into the saucepan. Heat on medium high for an additional 2 to 3 minutes, stirring constantly.

4. Pour this mixture through a strainer into the bowl, to help create a smooth texture. Then pour evenly into your pudding molds, on top of the sauce.

5. Cover each mold with foil. Select a pan with a lid that can fit all the molds while covered. Add a trivet or towel and about a half inch of hot water to the bottom of the pan, then add each of your molds. Cover with a lid, and heat on low for about 20 minutes to steam the puddings. Check occasionally to make sure there's still a good amount of water at the bottom. Turn off the heat and let stand, covered, for an additional 10 minutes.

6. To serve cold, refrigerate until cool. To serve warm, slide a toothpick around the edge of each mold, and overturn onto a small serving dish. Garnish with mint leaves, and enjoy!

Egg Tart

This is a sweet and firm South Akkala Stable style tart!
Enjoy these soft vanilla and cinnamon egg tarts.

12 tarts	1 hour	Vegetarian

Ingredients:
Crust:

12 tart tins
1 cup powdered sugar *(125 g)*
3 cups all purpose flour *(450 g)*
1 cup butter, room temperature *(220 g)*
1 egg, beaten
1/2 teaspoon vanilla extract *(2.5 ml)*

Filling:

2/3 cup granulated sugar *(150 g)*
1 1/2 cups water *(360 ml)*
8 large eggs, beaten
1 cup milk, sweetened almond works well *(240 ml)*
1/2 teaspoon vanilla extract *(2.5 ml)*
1/2 teaspoon ground cinnamon *(1.3 g)*
Mint sprigs for garnish

Game Guide

The Legend of Zelda:
Breath of the Wild.

Tabantha Wheat
Bird Egg
Cane Sugar
Goat Butter

Egg Tart

Directions:

1. Crust: In a medium bowl, sift powdered sugar, and flour together. Mix in butter with a wooden spoon until the mixture is crumbly. Stir in one egg and vanilla extract. Dough should be moist but thick. Add more butter if it is too dry, or more flour it if is too greasy. Shape dough into 1 1/2 inch balls *(3.8 cm)*, then gently press them into the tart tins. Firmly cover the bottom, and press it into the sides so that it goes slightly over the edge. Flatten the edge with your fingers to look like The Legend of Zelda: Breath of the Wild model.

2. Filling: Preheat the oven to 450 degrees Fahrenheit *(230 degrees Celsius)*. In a medium saucepan, combine the granulated sugar and water, and bring to a boil over medium high heat. Cook until sugar is dissolved and mixture is consistent, just a couple minutes.

3. Remove from heat and cool to room temperature. Strain the beaten eggs, and mix them into the hot sugar mix. Then mix the milk, vanilla, and cinnamon in. Beat until you have a smooth consistency.

4. Strain the mixture for a smooth texture, then pour carefully into the tarts.

5. Bake for 15 to 20 minutes, until the edges are golden brown, the filling has puffed, and an inserted toothpick comes out dry.

6. Cool for at least 20 minutes, then garnish with a mint sprig on the side, and enjoy!

Fried Bananas

Crispy, sweet, perfectly served atop pancakes, ice cream, or anything!
Also great for distracting certain enemies! You can find this mighty recipe inside Misa's
recipe book in the Slippery Falcon General store in Rito Village!

| 2 servings | 15 minutes | Yigan | Gluten free |

Ingredients:

2 barely ripe bananas,* peeled and sliced in half lengthwise
1/2 cup all purpose flour *(75 g)*
1 tablespoon rice flour *(10 g)*
2 tablespoons brown sugar *(25 g)*
1/4 teaspoon cinnamon *(.7 g)*
1/8 teaspoon cloves *(.25 g)*
1/8 teaspoon vanilla extract *(.5 ml)*
3/4 cup water *(180 ml)*
3 tablespoons oil *(45 ml)*

Game Guide

The Legend of Zelda:
Breath of the Wild.

Mighty Bananas
Tabantha Wheat
Cane Sugar

Garnish:**

Coconut Whip Cream, page 172, or similar
2 banana leaves, 1 for each plate
2 pink Japanese anemone flowers, or similar, 1 for each plate

*Don't use overripe bananas, the ideal is to use bananas with a small amount of green tinge.

**The Legend of Zelda: Breath of the Wild recipe is two halves of a fried banana on top of a banana leaf, with a side of whipped cream and what appears to be, after careful research, a pink Japanese anemone flower; also known as the Windflower. Of course, any similar pink flower with yellow center will work! For more information regarding finding banana leaves, there is a guide on page 199!

Fried Bananas

Directions:

1. In a mixing bowl, combine flour, rice flour, sugar, cinnamon, cloves, vanilla, and water. You are looking for a pancake batter type consistency; if it is too dry, add a spoonful of water at a time until the texture improves.
2. Oil and preheat a frying pan, adding an additional 3 tablespoons of oil *(45 ml)*. Once the oil is hot, not smoking just hot, proceed to next step.
3. Dip the sliced bananas into the batter, thickly coating both sides. Tongs are very helpful here. Arrange onto the pan, and fry for 2 to 3 minutes, until golden brown on bottoms. Flip, and fry for an additional 2 to 3 minutes.
4. Plate your fried bananas atop a banana leaf, garnish with coconut whip cream and pink flower on the side, and enjoy!

Fruitcake

Excuse me, Princess... Here's your birthday cake! This Tres Leches inspired cake is light, juicy, spongy, with strawberries inside and fruit on top.
This fruitcake is Zelda's favorite, and the recipe can be found in the Hyrule Castle Library! You'll also find slices of this delicious cake at Wheaton and Pita's Bakery.

6 servings	2 hours	Vegetarian

Ingredients:

1 teaspoon oil *(15 ml)*
1/4 teaspoon salt *(1.5 g)*
1 and 1/2 teaspoon baking powder *(7.5 g)*
1 cup all-purpose flour *(150 g)*
5 whole large eggs, separated
3/4 cup sugar *(165 g)*
1/3 cup whole milk *(80 ml)*
1 teaspoon vanilla extract *(5 ml)*
1/4 cup sugar *(60 g)*
1/4 cup heavy whipping cream *(60 ml)*
1 cup evaporated milk *(8 oz or 240 ml)*
1 cup sweetened condensed milk *(8 oz or 240 ml)*

Frosting and Toppings:

2 1/2 cups heavy whipping cream *(600 ml)*
3 tablespoons granulated sugar *(40 g)*
1 lb fresh strawberries *(.5 kg)*
2 kiwis, peeled and sliced
1 cup blueberries *(8 oz or 225 g)*
1 mandarin orange, peeled and separated into wedges

Game Guide

The Legend of Zelda: Breath of the Wild.

Apple or Wildberry
Any Fruit
Tabantha Wheat
Cane Sugar

The Legend of Zelda: The Minish Cap

Slice of Cake

Fruitcake

Directions:

1. Preheat the oven to 350 degrees Fahrenheit *(175 degrees Celsius)*. Oil two 9 inch round cake pans *(~23 cm)*, then lightly flour the sides and bottom with a few pinches of all purpose flour.
2. Prepare 3 mixing bowls, 2 large and 1 medium. For the medium bowl, add the salt, baking powder, and flour. Whisk them together and then set aside.
3. Separate 5 eggs into the two other bowls, egg whites into one, egg yolks into the other.
4. For the egg yolk bowl: Add 3/4 cup sugar *(165 g)* to the yolks, and then beat by hand for 100 strokes. Add 1/3 cup milk *(80 ml)* and 1 teaspoon vanilla extract *(5 ml)*, then pour the flour mixture from the medium bowl into the yolk mixture. Beat for 50 strokes, until combined.
5. For the egg white bowl: beat egg whites with a whisk through the foamy stage until soft peaks form. When you lift the whisk, a cute little mountain should form underneath. Add the remaining 1/4 cup sugar, and then continue whisking until it begins to stiffen, then stop. Carefully add the egg white mixture to the yolk bowl, folding again and again until they are combined. Try not to over mix at this stage.
6. Divide the batter evenly into the two cake pans, and bake at 350 degrees Fahrenheit (*175 degrees Celsius)* for 30 minutes. Check with a toothpick at the 25 minute mark, and again at 30 minutes. When the toothpick comes out cleanly from the center, it is done! Flip the cakes onto a wire rack or plate, and allow to cool for 20 minutes. Trim any uneven edges.
7. While the cakes are cooking and cooling, freeze a large mixing bowl and whisk. Also prepare the milk syrup by combining the heavy whipping cream, evaporated milk, and sweetened condensed milk in a large measuring cup. Set aside.
8. When the cakes have cooled, place one cake flat side down on a cake platter or serving dish. Use a fork to poke holes straight down all over the cake. Go all the way to the edges, and go all the way through to the plate with each poke. Carefully pour half of the milk syrup over the top, spreading it to the edges with a spoon, and then set aside to absorb.
9. In the mean time make the frosting! Retrieve your frozen bowl and whisk from the freezer. Add 2 and 1/2 cups heavy whipping cream *(600 ml)* and 3 tablespoons sugar *(40 g)* to the bowl. Beat vigorously with the frozen whisk until it is thick but still spreadable.
10. Frost the top of the poked and saturated cake, leaving enough frosting in the bowl to coat the rest of the cake later. Lay out sliced strawberries all over the top.
11. Take the second cake and lay it with the flat side up. Repeat the fork poking on this cake, and then put it on top of the layer of strawberries atop the other cake.
12. Carefully pour the remaining milk syrup over your top layer, smoothing with a spoon to make sure the cake is saturated. Wait for 20 minutes, allowing the syrup to absorb.
13. Frost the rest of the cake, smoothing out the frosting on the top and sides with a spoon. Adorn the top of the cake with the sliced kiwi, blueberries, mandarin orange, and more strawberries. Slice the cake thickly, and enjoy!

Fruit Pie

Kara Kara Bazaar's favorite chilly fruit pie, topped with a variety of fresh fruit and cream! You can also enjoy slices of fruit pie in The Legend of Zelda: The Minish Cap!

| 2 small pies | 1 hour | Vegan | Gluten free |

Ingredients:
Crust:
1 cup all purpose flour *(150 g)*

1/2 teaspoon salt *(2.8 g)*

1 tablespoons granulated sugar *(12.5 g)*

1/4 cup cold coconut oil or butter *(55 g)*

2 to 3 tablespoons ice water *(30 ml to 45 ml)*

Two 5 inch pie pans *(~13 cm)*

Filling and Garnish:
1/3 cup sugar *(80 g)*

1 teaspoon cornstarch *(2.5 g)*

1/4 cup water *(60 ml)*

1 large egg or 1 flax egg*

1 tablespoon lemon juice *(15 ml)*

1/4 teaspoon vanilla extract *(1.25 ml)*

1 heaping cup of your favorite fruit** *(8 oz or 225 g)*

Coconut Whip Cream, page 172, or similar

2 orange slices per pie

2 large green grapes per pie

2 small strawberries or large raspberries per pie

3 blueberries per pie

1 sprig of mint per pie

Game Guide
The Legend of Zelda: Breath of the Wild.

Any Fruit (except Apple)
Tabantha Wheat
Cane Sugar
Goat Butter

The Legend of Zelda: The Minish Cap

Slice of Pie

*Mix 1 tablespoon ground flaxseed with 3 tablespoons boiling water *(15 ml per tablespoon)*. Let sit for five minutes.

**Choose your favorite, or make several kinds! Blueberries are my favorite here.

Fruit Pie

Directions:

1. Crust: Combine flour, salt, and sugar in a bowl. Use your clean hands to thoroughly mix. Add the cold coconut oil or butter, and knead with hands until consistent and crumbly.

2. Now you will add ice water until it is just doughy enough to roll into a ball without crumbling and cracking. Add one spoonful of ice water at a time, kneading thoroughly before adding another. You will likely need 3 to 4 spoonfuls of ice water, but it will depend on your flour. Err on the side of crumbly instead of soupy. Once it reaches a dough consistency, separate it into two halves, and roll them into balls. Cover and place in the refrigerator.

3. Preheat oven to 400 degrees Fahrenheit *(205 degrees Celsius)*. In a medium saucepan, add all filling ingredients except for the fruit. Heat over medium about 5 to 7 minutes, stirring constantly until it is smooth, thick, and starting to bubble.

4. Add your desired filling fruit, and stir gently while heating for another minute or two. Try not to mash the fruit, and remove from heat.

5. Remove pie dough from the refrigerator. Clear a clean surface, lightly flour it, and roll out two circles. Make sure to rotate it after every few rolls to prevent from sticking. Carefully lift and center over your pie pans, and gently press in the sides and bottom so there are no gaps. Roll any overhanging trim into a pretty edge.

6. Pour filling into crusts, then bake on a baking sheet for 12 minutes. Turn down the oven to 375 degrees Fahrenheit *(190 degrees Celsius)*, optionally add aluminum foil or a pie crust shield around the edge of the pie to prevent the edges from browning too much. Bake for an additional 15 minutes, or until the middle of the pie crust is done. Let it cool at room temperature for around 2 hours, until it is firm.

7. Just before serving, garnish with coconut whip cream and fruit toppings for accuracy. Enjoy!

Honeyed Apple

This is one of Koko's many specialties from Kakariko village!
To turn these into Monster Apples, add purple food gel or Monster Extract, page 173!

| 6 servings | 20 minutes | Vegetarian | Gluten free |

Ingredients:

6 Honeycrisp apples*
6 thick wooden sticks
A candy thermometer
2 cups sugar *(450 g)*
1/2 cup buckwheat honey, raw *(120 ml)*
1 tablespoon lemon juice *(15 ml)*

Game Guide

The Legend of Zelda: Breath of the Wild.

Apple
&
Courser Bee Honey

*Honeycrisps are wonderful here! Try to select apples with firm bottoms that will sit without rolling.

Honeyed Apple

Directions:

1. Prepare a glass of ice cold water. Remove the apple stems, clean your apples, and then firmly stick wooden sticks through tops. Prepare a baking tray with a sheet of baker's parchment, to place the apples on once they are done.

2. Oil and preheat a sauce pan to medium high, then add sugar, honey, and lemon juice. Carefully bring to a boil, stirring constantly, and check the temperature frequently. When foam builds, remove from the heat, continue stirring until it recedes, then replace it on the heat. Repeat until the candy reaches 300 degrees Fahrenheit *(150 degrees Celsius)*. With a spoon, drop a small amount of candy into the glass of ice cold water. If the result is a hard ball, you can proceed! If it is still soft, put it back on for another minute and try again.**

3. With caution, spin an apple into the candy, coating all sides, and then place it upright on the parchment. Repeat for each apple, then allow to cool to room temperature. Candy coating should be hard.

4. You can cut the apples into wedges for easy eating, or eat them fresh on the stick! Enjoy!

**Some people prefer softened candy instead of hard on their apples. It's a bit messier, but a bit easier to eat. If you would prefer soft, continue to test the candy in the ice water as you go, then remove the candy from heat when you reach the consistency you prefer!

Honey Candy

Do you think while sailing the lonely seas for adventure, Link ever gets seasick?
Not while armed with this tangy, energizing, and stomach calming candy!

| ~6 candy | 20 minutes | Vegetarian | Gluten free |

Ingredients:

A candy mold, Link uses a sphere mold
A candy thermometer
1/2 cup buckwheat honey, raw *(120 ml)*
2 tablespoons lemon juice *(30 ml)*
1 teaspoon ginger, minced *(3 g)*
1/4 cup powdered sugar *(30 g)*

Game Guide

The Legend of Zelda:
Breath of the Wild.

Courser Bee Honey

Directions:

1. Prepare a glass of cold water with ice.

2. Oil and preheat a sauce pan to medium high, then add honey, lemon juice, and ginger. Carefully bring to a boil, stirring constantly, and check the temperature frequently. When foam builds, remove from heat, continue stirring until it recedes, then replace it on the heat. Repeat until the candy reaches 300 degrees Fahrenheit *(150 degrees Celsius)*. With a spoon, drop a small amount of candy into the glass of ice cold water. If the result is a hard ball, you can proceed! If it is still soft, put it back on for another minute and try again.

3. With extreme caution, spoon or pour candy into the mold. Once the mold is filled, let it cool to room temperature, until the candy is hard.

4. Prepare a small dish with the powdered sugar.

5. Pop each candy out of the mold, then roll it in powdered sugar to lightly cover the sides. This will hopefully prevent the candy from sticking to itself, other candy, and you.

6. Store in an airtight container, this is especially important if you live in a humid environment. You want to keep them very dry, or they will get sticky. Storing in a refrigerator is a good idea! Storing them in the car is not a good idea, though using them for car sickness is effective! Enjoy!

Honeyed Fruits

This is an easy and delectable platter of delicious sliced fruits, topped with a drizzled spiced honey sauce! This recipe includes The Legend of Zelda: Breath of the Wild ingredients, but feel free to include whatever fruits are your favorite or in season!

2 servings	10 minutes	Vegetarian	Gluten free

Ingredients:

1/4 cup apple juice *(60 ml)*
1/4 teaspoon cinnamon or apple pie spice *(.65 g)*
1/4 cup honey *(60 ml)*
Fresh mint leaves
1 orange, sliced
1 cup grapes *(150 g)*
4 strawberries
1/4 of a pineapple, thickly chopped
1/4 of a melon, balled

Game Guide

The Legend of Zelda: Breath of the Wild.

Courser Bee Honey
&
Any Fruit (besides Apple)

Directions:

1. In a small saucepan, bring apple juice to a soft boil.
2. While waiting for the apple juice to boil, prepare your fruits and arrange them on the platter.
3. Once boiling, take the apple juice off the heat, and add cinnamon and honey.
For a few minutes, stir alternating clockwise and counter-clockwise, until honey has fully disintegrated.
4. Drizzle your spiced honey sauce over the fruit, and enjoy!

Vegan- Try agave instead of honey, or an additional 1/4 cup sugar.

Hyoi Pears

Use these pears to attract and control seagulls!
These cinnamon and sugared baked pears smell and taste divine.

4 servings	1.5 hours	Vegan	Gluten free

Ingredients:

4 small ripe pears, about 1.5 pounds, peeled *(~.7 kg)*
1 tablespoon lemon juice *(15 ml)*
1/2 teaspoon ground cinnamon *(1.3 g)*
1/8 teaspoon ground cloves *(.25 g)*
1/4 cup brown sugar *(45 g)*
1/2 cup water *(120 ml)*
Coconut whip cream, page 172, optional

Game Guide

The Legend of Zelda: The Wind Waker.

These pears can be purchased for your bait bag from Beedle's Shop Ship.

Directions:

1. Preheat oven to 350 degrees Fahrenheit *(175 degrees Celsius)*.
2. Core each peeled pear from the bottom, to leave the rest and stem whole. To make it look like the Hyoi Pears found in The Legend of Zelda: The Wind Waker, carve out three holes to appear like a face. Two small holes for the eyes, and one larger one for the mouth. Rub lemon juice over each pear, then place them in a small, greased baking dish.
3. Mix cinnamon, cloves, brown sugar, and water together, then pour over the pears into the baking dish.
4. Bake for 45 minutes to an hour, and spoon juices over the pears every 10 to 15 minutes. They are ready when easy to cut with a spoon all the way through.
5. Keep warm in the oven at 200 degrees Fahrenheit *(95 degrees Celsius)* until ready to serve. Garnish with coconut whip cream if desired, and enjoy!

Monster Rice Balls

There are two options for this recipe! A dessert version is below, made out of purple puffed rice and peanut butter. The savory version can be found on page 182. This recipe makes about 4 large treats, but multiplies easily.

4 servings	25 minutes	Vegan	Gluten free

Ingredients:

2 cups crispy rice cereal *(60 g)*
1/2 cup peanut butter, or alternative *(130 g)*
1/2 cup brown rice syrup* *(120 ml)*
Monster Extract, page 173, or purple food coloring
4 cut sheets of dark fruit leather 'nori'**

Game Guide

The Legend of Zelda: Breath of the Wild.

Hylian Rice
Rock Salt
Monster Extract

Directions:

1. Pour crispy rice into a large bowl, and lay a platter with baking paper.
2. Add peanut butter, syrup, and Monster Extract to a saucepan over medium heat. Stir until it has melted and color is even, add more for a more vibrant purple!
3. Once mixture has liquefied and is hot, pour it immediately and carefully into the large bowl of crispy rice. Mix it well, scraping the sides, until it is well combined.
4. Make sure it is cool enough to touch, then scoop approximately 1/2 cup *(120 ml)* prepared and rice into your hand. Using both hands, firmly shape and smooth the rice ball into a softened triangle, like an onigiri. After completing a rice ball, lay it flat on the baking paper. Repeat approximately 3 more times to make 4 total rice balls.
5. Cut your fruit leather into strips, so you can add them to one side of your rice ball. Fold one fruit strip around each rice ball.
6. Refrigerate for 30 minutes, arrange the Monster Rice Balls on a plate, and enjoy!

*You can alternatively use maple syrup or honey and it will still turn out great! You may need to add a bit more to help with sticking at the end. That said, I still recommend the brown rice syrup as the best for this particular recipe.

**You want something similar to a fruit roll up here.

Monster Cake

Suspiciously, this recipe is found in the Hyrule Castle, labeled as the Chancellor's favorite! Below are two recipes for different diets, a chunky chocolate traditional cake, or a delectable black bean brownie cake!

Bean Monster Cake

6 servings*	30 minutes	Vegan	Gluten free

Bean Monster Cake Ingredients:**

1 can of black beans, drained and well rinsed *(15 oz or 425 g)*
1/2 cup chocolate chips *(3 oz or 85 g)*
1/2 cup chopped walnuts *(60 g)*, just leave out for allergies
1/2 cup quick oats *(45 g)*
1/3 cup delicious honey or maple syrup* *(80 ml)*
1/4 cup coconut oil *(60 ml)*
2 tablespoons cocoa powder *(15 g)*
2 tablespoons granulated sugar *(25 g)*
2 teaspoons vanilla extract *(30 ml)*
1/2 teaspoon baking powder *(2.5 g)*
1/4 teaspoon salt *(1.5 g)*

Game Guide

The Legend of Zelda: Breath of the Wild.

Tabantha Wheat
Cane Sugar
Goat Butter
Monster Extract

Bean Monster Cake Directions:

1. Preheat oven to 350 degrees Fahrenheit *(174 degrees Celsius)*. Add all ingredients together, and mix thoroughly with a knife. For a finer cake texture, use a food processor or blender, but a knife adds realism, and chunky Monster Cake is great!
2. When you are satisfied with the texture, add to a greased round cake tin, mini cakes tin, cupcake tin, or, my favorite, a mini cupcake tin.
3. Bake for 15 to 18 minutes, depending on your tin. Cool in the refrigerator for an hour, then remove from the tin.
4. Continue with Frosting Directions, page 164.

*For life size, triple, and use two 7" diameter *(18 cm)*, 4" tall *(10 cm)* cake tins.
**This recipe is vegan and gluten free, use chocolate that works for your diet.

~ 162 ~

Monster Cake

Here you will find a chunky chocolate traditional cake!

Traditional Monster Cake

6 servings*	1 hour	Vegetarian

Traditional Monster Cake Ingredients:

2/3 cup butter, room temperature *(150 g)*

1 2/3 cups sugar *(375 g)*

3 large eggs

1 1/3 cups milk *(320 ml)*

1 teaspoon vanilla extract *(5 ml)*

2 cups all purpose flour *(300 g)*

1/3 cup cocoa powder *(40 g)*

1 1/4 teaspoons baking soda *(5.75 g)*

1 teaspoon salt *(5.6 g)*

Game Guide

The Legend of Zelda: Breath of the Wild.

Tabantha Wheat

Cane Sugar

Goat Butter

Monster Extract

Traditional Monster Cake Directions:

1. Preheat oven to 350 degrees Fahrenheit *(175 degrees Celsius)*. Add butter and sugar to a large bowl, mix until smooth. Add eggs, milk, and vanilla extract, then beat until smooth. In a new dry bowl, combine flour, cocoa, baking soda, and salt; mix thoroughly. Slowly add the dry mix to the large bowl, mixing until everything is added and smooth.

2. Pour batter into a greased round cake tin, mini cakes tin, cupcake tin, or, my favorite, a mini cupcake tin.

3. Bake for 35 to 45 minutes, depending on your tin. An inserted toothpick should come out clean or with a few crumbs, no wet batter. Cool for 30 minutes.

4. Continue with Frosting Directions, page 164.

*For life size, triple, and use two 7" diameter *(18 cm)*, 4" tall *(10 cm)* cake tins.

Frosting and Horns

8 servings   45 minutes   Vegan   Gluten free

Frosting Ingredients:

3 and 3/4 cups powdered sugar *(470 g)*

3 tablespoons coconut oil or butter *(45 ml)*

1/4 cup vanilla almond milk *(60 ml)*

2 teaspoons vanilla extract *(10 ml)*

Monster Extract, page 173, or purple food coloring

~1 tablespoon cocoa powder *(8 g)* for coloring

Horns:

16 ounces of white chocolate *(450 g)*

1/3 to 1/2 cup corn syrup *(80 to 120 ml)*

Monster Extract or purple food dye

Frosting Directions:

1. Horns: melt the white chocolate, either in a double boiler, microwave, or carefully over a fire. Cool for 5 to 10 minutes, so you can touch it comfortably.

2. Add 1/3 cup corn syrup to the bowl of chocolate, stir until absorbed. Pour onto a cool clean surface, like a counter or shield. Knead the chocolate and add small amounts of corn syrup until it reaches a good consistency, like play dough.

3. Add the monster extract a little at a time, kneading it through until it is purple!

4. Prepare a tray for the finished horns. For one large cake, make 2 large balls. For many smaller cakes, separate the chocolate into similarly sized balls, enough for 2 horns per cake. Roll each ball into a little pointed cone, then gently curve the cone. Once each horn is done, place the tray in the refrigerator to harden.

5. Frosting: You can buy or make your frosting! You'll need half chocolate, and half purple. To make, add all frosting ingredients to a new bowl except Monster Extract and cocoa powder. Beat with a wooden spoon until smooth. You want it very thick, but spreadable.

6. In a new bowl, dye one half purple for the center frosting. Dye the other half brown with cocoa powder for the top frosting. Alter the consistency and color if necessary; if the frosting is too thin, add more powdered sugar, too thick, more milk.

7. Cut each cake or cupcake carefully in half, unless they are small enough to use two per cake. Spread the purple frosting in their centers, then reassemble them.

8. Add the chocolate frosting to a pipette bag or a zip lock bag with a tiny hole in the corner. Add a chocolate swirl to the top of each cake.

9. Add two horns to each cake, pointed upwards. Enjoy!

Hot Buttered Apple

Koko in Kakariko Village is more than happy to share this recipe with you!
A spiced sautéed apple recipe, served with coconut whip cream!

2 servings	15 minutes	Vegan	Gluten free

Ingredients:

2 tablespoons butter or vegan butter *(30 g)*
2 large Honeycrisp apples, cored and thinly sliced
1 teaspoon cornstarch *(2.5 g)*
1/4 cup cold water *(60 ml)*
1/4 cup brown sugar *(50 g)*
1/2 teaspoon cinnamon or apple pie spice *(1.5 g)*
Fresh mint leaf garnish, for accurate garnish
Coconut whip cream, page 172, or similar
1 small Honeycrisp apple, left whole and uncooked, for garnish

Game Guide

The Legend of Zelda:
Breath of the Wild.

Apple
&
Goat Butter

Directions:

1. Oil and preheat your cast iron skillet to medium heat. Melt the butter, add the apple slices. Cook on medium heat for 6 to 8 minutes, stirring constantly. It's ready when the apples are easy to slice through.

2. Mix the cornstarch and water together, then add to the skillet. Add in brown sugar and cinnamon. Bring to a boil, and cook for an additional 2 minutes, stirring occasionally.

3. Remove from heat. You can keep this warm at 200 degrees Fahrenheit *(95 degrees Celsius)* in the oven until it is time for dessert, or you can serve immediately. Garnish with the untouched apple, coconut whip cream and mint leaves on the side, and drizzle the excess sauce on top! Enjoy!

Nutcake

In The Legend of Zelda: Breath of the Wild, the Nutcake looks suspiciously like a loaf of banana nut bread! Below you will find a fluffy and delectable Nutcake, with or without nuts! Inspired by Misa's recipe book in Rito Village!

| 8 servings | 30 minutes | Vegan |

Ingredients:

4 very ripe bananas *(about 1.5 cups, 12 oz, or 350 g)*
2 tablespoons ground flaxseed *(14 g)*
1/3 cup vanilla almond milk *(80 ml)*
1/3 cup butter or vegan butter *(70 g)*
2 tablespoons maple syrup *(30 ml)*
2 teaspoons vanilla extract *(10 ml)*
1 teaspoon cinnamon *(2.6 g)*
1/4 cup chopped walnuts *(30 g)*
3 tablespoons pumpkin seeds *(24 g)*
1/3 cup brown sugar *(60 g)*
1/2 cup rolled oats *(45 g)*
1 teaspoon baking soda *(4.6 g)*
1/2 teaspoon baking powder *(2.5 g)*
1/2 teaspoon sea salt *(2.8 g)*
1 1/2 cups whole grain flour *(225 g)*
Additional walnuts and pumpkin seeds for topping

Game Guide

The Legend of Zelda: Breath of the Wild.

Any Nut
Tabantha Wheat
Cane Sugar
Goat Butter

Nutcake

Directions:

1. Preheat the oven to 350 degrees Fahrenheit *(175 degrees Celsius)*. Butter a standard loaf pan.

2. In a large mixing bowl, mash bananas, then add ground flax, milk, vegan butter, maple syrup, vanilla extract, cinnamon, walnuts, and pumpkin seeds. Beat thoroughly until chunky but creamy.

3. Add the following into the mixing bowl one by one, stirring between each. Brown sugar, rolled oats, baking soda, baking powder, salt, and flour. Beat until consistent, until all flour has been incorporated.

4. Pour dough into your buttered loaf pan, and smooth the top with a spoon before adding a handful of additional walnuts and pumpkin seeds in an even, thin layer. Press them slightly into the top so they stick.

5. Bake in the center of the oven, uncovered, for 45 to 60 minutes. At 45 minutes, stick a butter knife through the center; if it's still raw, continue for another 5 to 15 minutes. When it is done, the top will be dry, golden, and stiff, and an inserted knife will come out clean.

6. Remove from the oven, and slide a knife around the sides to release the loaf. Carefully remove it from the pan, and allow to rest on a plate or cooling rack. Let cool for 30 minutes to an hour.

7. Serve cut into thick slices, and serve with a garnish of butter! Enjoy!

Pumpkin Pie

A seasonal treat, fresh from Olkin's pumpkin patch in Kakariko Village!
Using fresh pumpkin makes a world of difference in a pumpkin pie!
Select a 'sugar' or 'pie' pumpkin that feels heavy for its size, and enjoy the fortifying results!

| 6 servings | 1.5 hours | Vegan | Gluten free |

Filling Ingredients:

2 cups pureed pumpkin* *(~16 oz to 480 ml)*
3/4 cup vanilla almond milk *(180 ml)*
3/4 cup brown sugar *(135 g)*
1/4 cup cornstarch *(30 g)*
1/4 cup real maple syrup *(60 ml)*
1 teaspoon cinnamon, or more to taste *(~2.5 g)*
1 teaspoon vanilla extract *(5 ml)*
1/4 teaspoon ground cloves *(.5 g)*
1/8 teaspoon ground ginger *(.25 g)*
1/8 teaspoon ground nutmeg *(.25 g)*
1/4 teaspoon salt *(1.5 g)*

Game Guide

The Legend of Zelda:
Breath of the Wild.

Fortified Pumpkin
Tabantha Wheat
Cane Sugar
Goat Butter

Crust:

1 standard size graham cracker pie crust or 12 mini graham cracker pie crusts
Coconut whip cream, page 172, or similar, for garnish

*I urge you, fresh pumpkin is best! Use a pie pumpkin, just remove seeds and strings, scrape pumpkin flesh into a blender, blend, and use immediately! Or, a 15 ounce can *(425 g)* of pureed pumpkin, not pumpkin filling, will taste great too!

Gluten free- Use a gluten free pie crust, King Arthur Flour makes a good one.

Pumpkin Pie

Directions:

1. Preheat oven to 350 degrees Fahrenheit *(175 degrees Celsius)*. Add all filling ingredients to a mixing bowl, and beat until thoroughly mixed, about 100 times.
2. Pour the pie filling into pie crust(s). If using mini pie crusts, place them on a baking tray to make it easier to get them in and out of the oven.
3. Bake in the oven for 60 minutes.
4. Carefully remove from the oven, the pies will still be very hot, and they will not have fully set yet. Be careful not to spill them.
5. You can leave them out to cool, or place them in the refrigerator for a few hours to firm up.
6. Serve with a swirl of coconut whip cream on top! Enjoy!

Rock Hard Food

Have fun getting your hands dirty making edible 'rocks', and then eat them like a Goron! This recipe makes about 24 small rocks, and is easily doubled.

| 6 servings | 20 minutes | Vegan | Gluten free |

Ingredients:

1 and 1/4 cup graham cracker crumbs* *(120 g)*
1/4 cup sugar *(60 g)*
1/2 teaspoon ground cinnamon *(1.3 g)*
1/4 teaspoon ground nutmeg** *(.5 g)*
1/2 cup peanut butter or alternative *(125 g)*
1/3 cup honey or maple syrup *(80 ml)*
1/2 cup hot chocolate powder, for normal rocks *(60 g)*
1/2 cup powdered sugar, for frosted rocks *(60 g)*

Game Guide

The Legend of Zelda: Breath of the Wild.

Wood
or
Ore

Directions:

1. Mix crumbs, sugar, and spices in a large bowl. Add peanut butter and honey or maple syrup to the bowl. Stir the mixture with a fork until well-mixed. If the mixture is too dry to form balls, add a small amount of water and mix again!

2. Prepare two small bowls, place the cocoa powder in one, and the powdered sugar in the other. Set out a plate for the finished rocks!

3. Then, using your hands, make small bite sized balls from the dough. Err on the small side, these are very rich! But you can make larger Talus rocks if you wish!

4. Place each ball into either; the hot chocolate powder, for rocks; or powdered sugar, for frosted rocks. Then roll the ball over and over until it is covered with cocoa or sugar. Place each finished rock onto the plate.

5. Once all of the rocks are finished, cover, and refrigerate for an hour or more. Serve chilled and enjoy!

Gluten Free- Use gluten free graham style crackers!
*Cinnamon and honey flavored cookies, if you can't find them, other cookies work too! Toss them into a bag and crush to make crumbs!
**If you know you love nutmeg, use 1/2 teaspoon here. *(1 g)*

Simmered Fruits

A variety of fruits, simmered in a sweet sauce, and served hot!
This dessert soup is ideal to keep warm in the winter.
This recipe serves 2, but can be multiplied if you want Copious Simmered Fruits.

2 servings	15 minutes	Vegan	Gluten free

Ingredients:

1/2 cup mango juice, or similar *(120 ml)*
1/2 cup orange juice *(120 ml)*
1/4 cup granulated sugar *(60 g)*
1 1/2 tablespoons tapioca flour* *(12 g)*
1 orange, peeled and wedged
1 peach, sliced
1/2 cup blueberries *(75 g)*
1 cup small strawberries, whole but with stems removed *(150 g)*

Game Guide

The Legend of Zelda:
Breath of the Wild.

Any Fruit

Directions:

1. In a medium pan, mix mango juice, orange juice, sugar, and tapioca. Bring to a boil, reduce heat to medium low, cover, and stir occasionally for 6 minutes.
2. Add all of the fruit. Cover and continue to simmer for an additional 6 minutes, stirring occasionally.
3. Remove from heat, and serve into small bowls. Cool for a few minutes before serving with a spoon. Enjoy!

*If you want a thicker sauce, add more! The Legend of Zelda: Breath of the Wild recipe has a thin sauce the fruits are swimming in, but Link isn't exactly a chef so do what you want! You could also add small or large pearl tapioca to this recipe for fun!

Coconut Whip Cream

Several recipes throughout this book include a garnish of whip! Below you will find a delicious vanilla coconut whip, the perfect topping for a variety of desserts!

| 2 cups* | 10 minutes | Vegan | Gluten free |

Ingredients:

1 can chilled coconut cream, not milk** *(~14 oz or 400 g)*
1 metal mixing bowl and spoon, frozen in the freezer over night
1 teaspoon vanilla extract *(5 ml)*
2 to 4 tablespoons granulated sugar *(25 g to 50 g)*

Directions:

1. Remove the coconut cream from the refrigerator, being careful not to shake it. Open it gently, and scoop the coconut cream solids into the frozen bowl.
2. Whip the coconut cream with the frozen spoon until it thickens and peaks begin to form, then add vanilla extract and 2 tablespoons of sugar *(25 g)*. Continue to whip for a few minutes, adding more sugar if necessary to achieve a luscious whipped texture.
3. Use immediately, or store covered in the refrigerator for up to a week, or sealed in the freezer for a few months. Enjoy!

*About 2 cups or 240 ml, enough for about 6 servings.
**Be sure to buy the cream and not the milk! Chill the coconut cream over night in the refrigerator so that the solids can be scooped out without much liquid.

Monster Extract

A devious natural food dye that creates monstrously purple dishes! For a smoothie version, please turn to page 298. Two versions are below; blueberries result in a light purple, beets result in a more vibrant red purple. Or, you can use purple food coloring!

8 servings	10 minutes	Vegan	Gluten free

Blueberry Ingredients:
1/2 cup blueberries, fresh or thawed frozen *(75 g)*
1/3 cup water *(80 ml)*

Game Guide

The Legend of Zelda: Breath of the Wild.

Monster Extract

Blueberry Directions:
1. Add blueberries and water to a blender, then blend until very smooth.
2. Strain the mixture to remove any remaining lumps. You should be left with a fine purple liquid.
3. Pour into an airtight container, like a potion bottle, and store for up to a month in the refrigerator.
4. To use, add a teaspoon at a time to a dish, stirring in between, until your desired color is reached. Enjoy!

Beet Ingredients:
1 ripe medium beet, diced
2 cups water *(480 ml)*

Beet Directions:
1. Bring beets and water to a light boil in a medium sauce pan.
2. Boil lightly for 30 minutes or more, until at least half the water has evaporated.
3. Strain into an airtight container, like a potion bottle, and store for up to a month in the refrigerator.
4. To use, add a teaspoon at a time to a dish, stirring in between, until your desired color is reached. Enjoy!

Rice Balls

The following recipes are based off a delectable and versatile Japanese dish, onigiri! These shaped balls of rice are easy meals to pack for lunch, often have ingredients stuffed inside them or wrapped around them, and are so diverse in flavor!

Each of these recipes produce 4 medium rice balls. You can multiply or divide the recipe if you want to prepare more or less! You can also make them smaller if you desire.

On page 186, I have included a Rice for Rice Balls recipe; specialized instructions for making onigiri rice. These instructions will be referred to in the coming recipes!

Tips and Tricks

The type of rice is crucial, be sure to use Japanese short grain rice, and check out the Rice Ball Rice recipe on page 186. Other varieties may not stick properly.

It is important to prepare fresh rice every time! Old rice will not mold well into rice balls.

Want to add some crunch to your rice balls? Turn your onigiri into yaki onigiri, by oiling up a pan, preheating to medium high, and frying your rice balls for a couple minutes on each side.

You can make a whole bunch of different rice balls at once, just prepare enough rice for all of them, then stuff and wrap them each differently!

Keep rice balls fresh by wrapping them in plastic wrap and storing them in the refrigerator. If stored in this way, rice balls should last for a few days. If left at room temperature, they should last about a day.

Veggie Rice Balls

The recipe in The Legend of Zelda: Breath of the Wild is rice plus any vegetable, so let your imagination run wild! Below includes green onions and peas, but throw in your favorite!

4 rice balls	30 minutes	Vegan	Gluten free

Ingredients:

Prepared Japanese short grain rice, see page 186
2 green onions, chopped
1/2 cup peas *(160 ml)*
1/2 teaspoon grated fresh ginger *(1 g)*
1 teaspoon garlic, minced *(3 g)*
1 tablespoon soy sauce *(15 ml)*
1/2 tablespoon brown sugar *(8 g)*
1 salt shaker
Sprigs of parsley, for garnish

Game Guide

The Legend of Zelda: Breath of the Wild.

Any Vegetable, Herb, or Flower
&
Hylian Rice

Gluten free- Be sure to use gluten free soy sauce!

Veggie Rice Balls

Directions:

1. Prepare rice.
2. To make the mix, lightly oil a pan, preheat to medium high. Add green onions, peas, ginger, soy sauce and brown sugar. Cover and heat for 4 to 5 minutes, checking and stirring occasionally to prevent sticking. Once hot, remove from heat.
3. Pour the mix and any extra sauce from the pan into the rice dish. Fold and mix in the ingredients with a utensil, until evenly spread.
4. Wash your hands, then wet your hands with water, and salt your hands lightly with the salt shaker. Rub your hands until they are wet and salty.
5. Scoop approximately 1/4 of the prepared rice into your hand. Using both hands, firmly shape and smooth the rice ball into a softened triangle, wetting your fingers as needed. Once you have reached the shape you desire, place your finished rice ball on a plate. Repeat approximately 3 more times to make 4 total rice balls, moistening and salting your hands each time.
6. Optional: In The Legend of Zelda: Breath of the Wild, it does not appear as if these onigiri are fried after being assembled, but if you want to fry them, you can do so! Heavily oil a frying pan, and preheat to medium high. Once it is hot, gently and carefully lay your rice balls inside. Cook for approximately 2 minutes, then flip, and cook for 2 additional minutes.
7. Arrange your Veggie Rice Balls on a plate, garnish each with a sprig of parsley, and enjoy!

Seafood Rice Balls

The Seafood Rice Balls in The Legend of Zelda: Breath of the Wild appear to have two different stuffings: salmon or salmon roe! The recipe below makes two of each, but you can make whichever you wish!

4 rice balls	30 minutes	Gluten free

Ingredients:

Prepared Japanese short grain rice, see page 186
4 sheets of dried nori or seaweed
1 salt shaker

Salmon-
1/4 cup cooked salmon flesh *(4 oz or 115 g)*
1 tablespoon soy sauce *(15 ml)*
1/4 teaspoon lemon juice *(1.5 ml)*

Salmon Roe-
1/4 cup cooked salmon roe *(4 oz or 115 g)*
1/2 tablespoon soy sauce *(7.5 ml)*

Game Guide

The Legend of Zelda: Breath of the Wild.

Hylian Rice
&
Any Seafood

Gluten free- Be sure to use gluten free soy sauce!

Seafood Rice Balls

Directions:

1. Prepare rice.
2. Cooked Salmon: In a small bowl, add the salmon, soy sauce and lemon juice. Stir with a fork and separate the salmon into small chunks. Mix until combined.
3. Salmon Roe: In a small bowl, mix salmon roe and soy sauce
4. Wash your hands, then wet your hands with water, and salt your hands lightly with the salt shaker. Rub your hands until they are wet and salty.
5. Scoop approximately 1/4 of the prepared rice into your hand. With the thumb of your other hand, make an indent in the center of the rice. Take a spoonful or so of your stuffing, and place in the indent.
6. Carefully fold the rice in your hand over the indent, keeping the stuffing in the center the whole time. Using both hands, firmly shape and smooth the rice ball into a softened triangle, wetting your fingers as needed. Once you have reached the shape you desire, place your finished rice ball on a plate. Repeat approximately 3 more times to make 4 total rice balls, moistening and salting your hands each time.
7. If necessary, cut your nori into smaller strips, so you can add them to one side of your rice ball. Fold one nori strip around each rice ball.
8. Arrange your Seafood Rice Balls on a plate, and add your leftover ingredients to the tops. Enjoy!

Mushroom Rice Balls

The mushrooms and onions are all mixed through, for a wholesome and delicious meal! The spicy variant is a particular favorite of Pruce, who keeps a recipe poster of it in his general store, East Wind, in Hateno Village! Another poster can be found at Snowfield Stable!

4 rice balls	30 minutes	Vegan	Gluten free

Ingredients:

Prepared Japanese short grain rice, see page 186
1/2 pound of sliced baby portobello mushrooms *(225 g)*
4 reserved whole baby portobello mushrooms
1/2 large yellow onion, diced
1/2 teaspoon minced garlic *(1.5 g)*
1/2 teaspoon vegetable bouillon* *(1.5 g)*
1 teaspoon dried parsley *(2 g)*
1 salt shaker

Game Guide

The Legend of Zelda: Breath of the Wild.

Hylian Rice
&
Any Mushroom

Spicy Mushroom Rice Balls

Rock Salt
Hylian Rice
Sunshroom

*Better Than Bouillon: Seasoned Vegetable Base, or similar.

Mushroom Rice Balls

Directions:

1. Prepare rice.

2. To make the mix, lightly oil a pan, preheat to medium high. Add a splash of water, sliced and whole mushrooms, onion, garlic, vegetable bouillon, and parsley. Cover and heat for 6 to 7 minutes, checking and stirring occasionally to prevent sticking. If necessary, add a little bit more water if mushrooms and onions are sticking, be careful not to burn them. Once mushrooms are shrunken, soft, and cooked, remove from heat.

3. Pick out the 4 whole mushrooms and set aside. Pour the rest of the mushrooms and extra sauce into the rice. Gently mix with a utensil until evenly spread.

4. Wash your hands, then wet your hands with water, and salt your hands lightly with the salt shaker. Rub your hands until they are wet and salty.

5. Scoop approximately 1/4 of the prepared rice into your hand. Using both hands, firmly shape and smooth the rice ball into a softened triangle, wetting your fingers as needed. Once you have reached the shape you desire, place your finished rice ball on a plate. Repeat approximately 3 more times to make 4 total rice balls, moistening and salting your hands each time.

6. Optional: In The Legend of Zelda: Breath of the Wild, it does not appear as if these onigiri are fried after being assembled, but it adds a delicious crunch, and helps keep them together! Heavily oil a frying pan, and preheat to medium high. Once it is hot, gently and carefully lay your rice balls inside. Cook for approximately 2 minutes on each side.

7. Arrange your Mushroom Rice Balls on a plate, and stick a whole mushroom on top of each one. Enjoy!

Monster Rice Balls

These savory vibrant purple rice balls hold a secret Monster Extract hidden inside!
Makes 4 rice balls. The dessert version of this recipe can be found on page 161!

| 4 rice balls | 30 minutes | Vegan | Gluten free |

Ingredients:
Purple* prepared Japanese short grain rice, see page 186
4 umeboshi or dried plums
4 sheets of dried nori or seaweed
1 salt shaker

Purple Color:
2 tablespoons freshly and finely diced beet *(16 g)*
or
Monster Extract, page 173, or purple food coloring, to reach desired color

Game Guide
The Legend of Zelda:
Breath of the Wild.

Hylian Rice
Rock Salt
Monster Extract

Monster Rice Balls

Directions:

1. *Prepare purple rice by mixing in monster extract or purple food coloring or 2 tablespoons of finely diced beet to the rice and water, just before you begin cooking it. Continue cooking as normal.

2. When rice is ready and cooled, wash your hands, then wet your hands with water, and salt your hands lightly with the salt shaker. Rub your hands until they are wet and salty.

3. Scoop approximately 1/4 of the prepared rice into your hand. With the thumb of your other hand, make an indent in the center of the rice. Take 1 umeboshi or dried prune, and place it into the indent.

4. Carefully fold the rice in your hand over the indent, keeping the stuffing in the center the whole time. Using both hands, firmly shape and smooth the rice ball into a softened triangle, wetting your fingers as needed. Once you have reached the shape you desire, place your finished rice ball on a plate. Repeat 3 more times to make 4 total rice balls, moistening and salting your hands each time.

5. Cut your nori into strips, so you can add them to one side of your rice ball. Fold one nori strip around each rice ball.

6. Arrange your Monster Rice Balls on a plate, and enjoy!

Meaty Rice Balls

These rice balls are kept warm and cozy with a thinly sliced beef jacket! They are crispy on the outside with sweet and spicy meat stuffed on the inside! Makes 4 rice balls.

| 4 rice balls | 30 minutes | Gluten free |

Ingredients:

Prepared Japanese short grain rice, see page 186
1/2 pound steak, finely diced, or ground beef *(8 oz or 225 g)*
1 tablespoon honey *(15 ml)*
1 tablespoon soy sauce *(15 ml)*
1 pinch ground cayenne pepper, to taste
1 salt shaker
4 to 8 slices of thinly sliced sandwich beef
Toasted or Black Sesame Seeds

Game Guide

The Legend of Zelda: Breath of the Wild.

Any Meat
&
Hylian Rice

Vegan- This is a great place for me to push avocado filling! Fill your rice balls with ripe avocado, skip the honey, and jacket it with a leaf of lettuce instead. Enjoy!

Gluten free- Be sure to use gluten free soy sauce!

Meaty Rice Balls

Directions:

1. Prepare rice.
2. To make the stuffing, lightly oil a pan and preheat to medium high. Add meat, honey, soy sauce, and cayenne pepper to taste. Cook while stirring until meat is cooked, approximately 5 to 7 minutes. Remove from heat.
3. Wash your hands, then wet your hands with water, and salt your hands lightly with the salt shaker. Rub your hands until they are wet and salty.
4. Scoop approximately 1/4 of the prepared rice into your hand. With the thumb of your other hand, make an indent in the center of the rice. Take a spoonful or so of your stuffing, and place in the indent.
5. Carefully fold the rice in your hand over the indent, keeping the stuffing in the center the whole time. Using both hands, firmly shape and smooth the rice ball into a softened triangle, wetting your fingers as needed. Once you have reached the shape you desire, place your finished rice ball on a plate. Repeat approximately 3 more times to make 4 total rice balls, moistening and salting your hands each time.
6. To wrap your rice balls in meat, lay a circular slice of sandwich beef flat, lay a rice ball in the upper center, with a point sticking out of the top of the circle. Fold the lower half of the beef up over the rice, then fold the right and left sides over as well. Depending on the size of the slice, you may need to use more than one. Repeat for all rice balls.
7. Next, heavily oil a frying pan, and preheat to medium high. Once it is hot, gently and carefully lay your rice balls inside. Cook for approximately 2 minutes on each side, remove when they are lightly browned and toasted.
8. Plate rice balls with the exposed rice up. Sprinkle the tops with sesame seeds. Enjoy!

Rice for Rice Balls

This recipe is for those poor unfortunate souls, like Link, who do not have a rice maker! This recipe will produce 2 cups of cooked rice (~400 g), suitable for any of the recipes in the rice ball section! Make sure to make fresh rice each time, and multiply this recipe if you intend to make multiple recipes!

2 cups	1 hour	Vegan	Gluten free

Ingredients:
1 cup uncooked Japanese short grain rice *(175 g)*
1 1/4 cup water *(300 ml)*

Directions:
1. Pour rice into a large bowl, and place in sink. Add cold water from the faucet until rice is covered. With clean hands, rinse rice in a gentle circular motion, then carefully pour the water out. Repeat this 3 to 4 times.

2. Optional if you have time: Add clean water again from the faucet, covering the rice. Let the rice soak in the water for 30 minutes.

3. Strain any water from the rice, and add the rice to your cooking pot, a heavy pot with a heavy and tight fitting lid is best. Add the water to the pot, cover with the lid, and bring it to a boil.

4. Once it is boiling, reduce heat to low, and cook covered for an additional 12 minutes. Peek in to see if all of the water has been absorbed. If there is still water left, cover and cook for another minute before checking again.

5. Once there is no water left, remove from heat. Keep lid on, and let sit for 10 minutes.

6. Move the rice to a large walled dish or plate to cool. Fluff with a fork or rice scooper. The rice is ready to mold once it cools enough so you can hold it in your hands comfortably.

7. Use immediately! It is important not to let it cool too much before using it, but do be careful. Enjoy!

Curry

This chapter is dedicated to the Goron's most delicious non-geological dish: Curry! Armed with the secret Goron Spice recipe on the next page, you'll be making delicious and nutritious curry in a heartbeat!

Guide to Great Curry

Curry is a dish I did not discover until I was an adult cooking for myself. I had tried curry as a child and found it to be too spicy and unfamiliar. But curry is so easy to throw together, and is as diverse as the people who make it; your curry will be and should be different from everyone else's! Curry is a delicious and easy staple to add to your normal menu.

Here are some secrets and some tricks:

1. Play with the spices, especially at the end. I make these recipes as is, and then when I serve myself a bowl, I sprinkle and stir in another pinch of 'Goron Spice'. Pow! Delicious! It reawakens the spice in the dish.

2. Brown your onions. Don't just wait until they are translucent, really brown them. Release that flavor.

3. Add your spices to HOT oil. Preheat the oil first, then sizzle those spices before continuing.

4. For some added tang, try it with a squeeze of fresh lemon juice, just before eating.

5. Beans! Add more beans. Black beans, lentils, peas, garbanzo beans, add your favorite beans! Drain a can and add the whole thing.

6. Rice! This is so necessary. Serve your curry atop or beside a hefty heaping of freshly cooked and hot rice. What kind? I prefer Hylian rice, or medium grain white rice, but the sky is the limit!

Goron Spice

This secret recipe has been hoarded among the Goron, but now it is in your hands! Make magical curries with this exclusive and aromatic spice blend!*

~4 servings	5 minutes	Vegan	Gluten free

Ingredients:

1/2 teaspoon ground cayenne pepper *(1 g)*
1 teaspoon ground cinnamon *(2.6 g)*
2 tablespoons ground coriander *(3 g)*
2 tablespoons ground cumin *(12 g)*
1/2 teaspoon ground ginger *(1 g)*
1/2 teaspoon ground mustard seed *(1 g)*
2 teaspoons ground turmeric *(6 g)*
3 sticks of cinnamon, for accurate garnish
2 bay leaves, for accurate garnish

Game Guide

The Legend of Zelda: Breath of the Wild.

Goron Spice

Directions:

1. Add all ingredients to a glass spice jar, ideally with a cork top like the Goron Spice bottle in The Legend of Zelda: Breath of the Wild. Close firmly with a cork or lid, and shake ferociously! It is suspected that this spice is traditionally mixed by rolling down a mountain with it!

2. Once the color is even and no longer marbled, add 3 sticks of cinnamon, you may need to cut them to fit the bottle, and the bay leaf. For an even more accurate look, finish the bottle by tying on a Goron Spice label with dark red cord. Use in any of the following recipes, and enjoy!

*This is a simple recipe for mild curry powder! If you already have a premixed bottle of curry powder, or if you have a favorite mix, go ahead and use that in the following recipes!

Curry Pilaf

This comfort food is served piping hot, and is so easy to throw together with fresh rice!

| 2 servings | 15 minutes | Vegan | Gluten free |

Ingredients:

1 tablespoon Goron Spice, page 188, or curry powder *(6.3 g)*
2 to 3 cups cooked rice *(375 g to 550 g)*
1 tablespoon oil *(15 ml)*
1 small yellow onion, finely chopped
1 large carrot, shredded or finely chopped
1 tablespoon soy sauce *(15 ml)*
1 tablespoon garlic, minced *(9 g)*
3/4 cup peas, fresh or frozen *(240 g)*
1 green onion, finely chopped

Game Guide

The Legend of Zelda: Breath of the Wild.

Hylian Rice
Bird Egg
Goat Butter
Goron Spice

Directions:

1. Prepare rice.
2. Oil and preheat cast iron pan to medium high. Add oil, Goron Spice, onion, carrot, and a splash of water. Cook and stir occasionally for 5 minutes, until onions are browned.
3. Add soy sauce, garlic, peas, and rice. Cook on high while stirring and breaking up the rice. The dish is ready when it is steaming hot all the way through, about 6 to 8 minutes. Remove from heat, garnish with green onion, and serve immediately. Enjoy!

Curry Rice

Lester from Rito stable loves this chunky Goron Spiced curry served with a large serving of Hylian rice! This can also be prepared in a slow cooker throughout the day.

4 servings	1 hour	Vegan	Gluten free

Ingredients:

1 tablespoon Goron Spice, page 188, or curry powder *(6.3 g)*

2 to 3 cups cooked rice *(375 g to 550 g)*

1 tablespoon oil *(15 ml)*

1 tablespoon garlic, minced *(9 g)*

1 yellow onion, finely chopped

1/2 teaspoon ginger, minced *(1.5 g)*

1/4 teaspoon thyme *(.75 g)*

1 teaspoon vegetable bouillon* *(2.6 g)*

1 cup water *(240 ml)*

1 large carrot, diced

2 large Yukon gold potatoes, chopped

1 can of garbanzo beans, drained *(15 oz or 425 g)*

1 can of black beans, drained *(15 oz or 425 g)*

1/2 cup peas, frozen is fine *(160 g)*

1/2 cup corn, frozen is fine *(160 g)*

> ## Game Guide
> *The Legend of Zelda: Breath of the Wild.*
> Hylian Rice
> &
> Goron Spice

Directions:

1. Prepare Goron Spice, page 188, and rice. In a large soup pot, add oil, a splash of water, Goron Spice, garlic, and onion. On medium high cook and stir for 4 to 5 minutes until onion is browned.

2. Add ginger, thyme, bouillon, water, carrot, potatoes, garbanzo and black beans, peas, and corn. Mix thoroughly, and bring to a boil. Reduce heat to medium, cover, and cook for an additional 30 to 45 minutes, until potatoes and carrots are cooked through and tender.

3. Once curry is ready, remove from heat, and serve immediately with a serving of hot rice! Enjoy!

*Better Than Bouillon: Seasoned Vegetable Base, or similar.

Monster Curry

Another frighteningly purple recipe, served with a half plate of rice!

| 2 servings | 1 hour | Vegan | Gluten free |

Ingredients:

1 tablespoon Goron Spice, page 188, or curry powder *(6.3 g)*

2 to 3 cups cooked rice *(375 g to 550 g)*

1 tablespoon oil *(15 ml)*

1 yellow onion, finely chopped

1 teaspoon garlic, minced *(9 g)*

1 pound PURPLE potatoes, chopped

1 can of black beans, drained *(15 oz or 425 g)*

1 cup water *(240 ml)*

1 medium beet, very finely diced

1/3 cup chopped fresh cilantro *(17 g)*

Cayenne pepper to taste, about 1/4 teaspoon *(.5 g)*

Monster Extract, page 173, or purple food coloring, to reach desired color

Game Guide

The Legend of Zelda: Breath of the Wild.

Hylian Rice
Goron Spice
Monster Extract

Directions:

1. Prepare rice.

2. In a soup pan, add oil, Goron Spice, and onions and heat to medium high. Cook and stir occasionally for about 5 minutes, until onions are browned.

3. Add the garlic, potatoes, black beans, and 1 cup water *(240 ml)*. Mix thoroughly, and bring to a boil. Reduce heat to medium and continue cooking for 30 minutes, stirring occasionally. Potatoes should be nearly done, soft all the way through, and easy to slice with a knife.

4. Add very finely diced beet, mix thoroughly, and continue cooking for 10 minutes.

5. Remove from heat, stir in cilantro and any desired cayenne pepper or salt. If the curry isn't as monstrously purple as you would prefer, add a little bit of Monster Extract or purple food dye. Serve with rice, and enjoy!

Meat Curry

Three thinly sliced curried steaks served with brown curry sauce and white rice!

| 2 servings | 25 minutes | Gluten free |

Ingredients:

2 tablespoons Goron Spice, page 188, or curry powder *(12.6 g)*
2 to 3 cups cooked rice *(375 g to 550 g)*
1 tablespoon oil *(15 ml)*
1 yellow onion, finely chopped
2 tablespoons lemon juice *(30 ml)*
1 pound beef steak, sliced 1/2" thick, 3 slices per plate *(450 g)*
2 teaspoons garlic, minced *(6 g)*
1 teaspoon ginger, minced *(3 g)*
1 tablespoon tomato paste *(14 g)*
1/2 tablespoon vegetable bouillon* *(4 g)*
1 cup water *(240 ml)*
Corn starch or instant mashed potatoes, to thicken

Garnish:

4 to 5 fresh mint leaves
1 mini red bell pepper, cut into thick rings

Game Guide

The Legend of Zelda: Breath of the Wild.

Raw Meat
Hylian Rice
Goron Spice

Vegan- Substitute mushroom steaks or tempeh! Add 16 ounces *(450 g)* of your favorite large whole mushroom heads, or meat substitute.

*Better Than Bouillon: Seasoned Vegetable Base, or similar.

Meat Curry

Directions:

1. Prepare rice.

2. In a large pan, cast iron works well here, add oil, Goron Spice, lemon juice, onions, and a splash of water. Cook covered, stirring occasionally for 5 minutes until onions are just beginning to brown. Scrape onions to the side, and lay the steaks down flat. Cook for about five minutes on each side, until beef is brown and cooked through.

3. Add garlic, ginger, tomato paste, bouillon, and water. Stir to mix everything together, and bring to a boil uncovered. Reduce heat, stir in either a couple tablespoons of cornstarch, a little at a time to prevent clumping, or instant mashed potatoes, to thicken as desired. Remove from heat.

4. Serve with rice, and garnish with mint leaves a mini red bell pepper ring! Enjoy!

Poultry Curry

The yogurt in this recipe elevates this chicken curry from simple to delectable.

2 servings	30 minutes	Gluten free

Ingredients:

1 tablespoon Goron Spice, page 188, or curry powder *(6.3 g)*

2 to 3 cups cooked yellow* rice *(375 g to 550 g)*

1 tablespoon oil *(15 ml)*

1 pound chicken breasts, cut into long strips *(16 oz or 450 g)*

1 yellow onion, finely chopped

1 tablespoon garlic, minced *(9 g)*

1 tablespoon ginger, minced *(9 g)*

1 teaspoon vegetable bouillon,** or to taste *(3 g)*

1/2 cup water *(120 ml)*

1 tablespoon sugar *(15 g)*

1 cup peas, frozen is fine *(320 g)*

3 tablespoons unsweetened yogurt, unsweetened almond yogurt works too *(45 g)*

1/4 cup fresh cilantro, chopped *(12.5 g)*

Ground black pepper to taste

Game Guide

The Legend of Zelda: Breath of the Wild.

Raw Bird
Goron Spice
Hylian Rice

Vegan- use unsweetened almond yogurt!

*Details matter! In The Legend of Zelda: Breath of the Wild, this curry is served with yellow rice! To make yellow rice, buy yellow rice, or add 1/4 teaspoon turmeric *(.75 g)* to the water when making normal white rice. Easy! Enjoy your accurate creation!

**Better Than Bouillon: Seasoned Vegetable Base, or similar.

Poultry Curry

Directions:

1. Prepare rice.

2. In a soup pan, add oil, chicken breast strips, and a splash of water, and set heat to medium high. Sprinkle Goron Spice on top of chicken, and stir thoroughly to coat their sides. Cook and stir occasionally until chicken is lightly browned and cooked all the way through- about 10 minutes.

3. Add onion, garlic, and ginger. Cook and stir for an additional 5 minutes, until onions are browned, then add bouillon, water, sugar, peas, and yogurt. Stir until well mixed, and bring to a boil. Then reduce heat to medium low, cover, and let simmer for 6 to 8 minutes.

4. Remove from heat, and stir in fresh cilantro and any black pepper if desired. Serve with yellow rice, and enjoy!

Vegetable Curry

Spicy and sweet, this is a favorite of Woodland Stable! The extravagant garnish seen in The Legend of Zelda: Breath of the Wild makes this dish look regal!

2 servings	1 hour	Vegan	Gluten free

Ingredients:

2 tablespoons Goron Spice, page 188, or curry powder *(12.6 g)*
2 to 3 cups cooked rice *(375 g to 550 g)*
1 tablespoon oil *(15 ml)*
1/2 cup water *(120 ml)*
1 large yellow onion, finely chopped
1 large tomato, finely diced
2 medium golden yukon potatoes, diced
1 can of lentils, drained *(15 oz or 425 g)*
1 cup chopped green beans, chopped *(150 g)*
1 cup green peas, frozen *(320 g)*
1/2 tablespoon garlic, minced *(4.5 g)*
1 teaspoon ginger, minced *(3 g)*
1/2 cup coconut milk *(120 ml)*
1 tablespoon cornstarch *(8 g)*
1 tablespoon poppy seeds *(9 g)*

Game Guide

The Legend of Zelda: Breath of the Wild.

Any Carrot or Pumpkin
Hylian Rice
Goron Spice

Garnish:

2 slices of tomato per plate, for garnish
2 thick slices of cucumber per plate, for garnish
2 slices of cantaloupe per plate, for garnish
2 whole green beans per plate, for garnish
Fresh or dried parsley, for garnish

Vegetable Curry

Directions:

1.   Prepare Goron Spice, page 188, and rice. In a large soup pot, add oil, Goron Spice, water, onion, tomato, potatoes, and green beans. Heat to medium high, and cook for 5 to 6 minutes, stirring occasionally.

2.   Add lentils, green beans, peas, garlic, ginger, milk, cornstarch, and poppy seeds. Bring to a boil, and then reduce heat to medium. Cover, and cook for an additional 30 to 45 minutes, until potatoes are cooked through and tender.

3.   Once curry is ready, plate half with rice, half with curry. Then garnish each plate with 2 slices of tomatoes, two slices of cucumber, 2 slices of cantaloupe, and two whole green beans sticking up and crossing. Sprinkle the rice with parsley to finish the look, and serve immediately! Enjoy!

Leaf Steaming

These next few recipes utilize a leaf steaming technique in order to trap moisture inside for succulent meat, fish, mushrooms, and even fruit dishes!

Below you will find an introduction to find out more about what type of leaves to use, where to find them, and how to steam; or you can turn the page to get right to the recipes!

Leaves

The recipe descriptions in Breath of the Wild indicate that 'fragrant leaves' should be used. Most commonly, the banana leaf is used in traditional leaf steaming dishes, and is characterized by its fragrance! Lotus leaves, taro leaves, corn husks and more have also been used in leaf steaming dishes, but I think the accessibility of bananas in The Legend of Zelda: Breath of the Wild makes Link's use of the banana leaf most likely.

Procurement

I was surprised to find out that my usual grocery store stocks them frozen! Check your local grocery store, Asian markets, and if all else fails, you can purchase banana leaves online. Fresh is preferable, but if that is not possible or easy, frozen banana leaves work very well.

Preparation

For pliable leaves, soak in hot water for 5 to 10 minutes while you prepare the other ingredients. Frozen leaves may need to be thawed or soaked for longer, with more hot water. You'll notice the following recipes do not use a steamer! If you have a steamer, go ahead and use that instead. However, for infrequent use, the oven steaming technique is easy! All you need is a baking dish with a lid that fits it. A Dutch oven works well. The trick is making sure there is just enough liquid in the bottom of the dish.

Final Notes

You are not supposed to eat the banana leaves, your attack stat probably won't be boosted. Banana leaves are different from banana peels, do not attempt that.

Steamed Fish

This wrapped fish dish is steamed in a tangy lemonade marinade.

Serves 2	40 minutes	Gluten free

Ingredients:

2 fish fillets*

4 or more banana leaves

3 tablespoons butter, melted *(40 g)*

2 lemons, one thinly sliced, one juiced

1 tablespoon parsley *(5 g)*

1 teaspoon sugar *(5 g)*

1 teaspoon minced garlic *(3 g)*

1/2 teaspoon ground black pepper *(1 g)*

1/2 teaspoon thyme *(1 g)*

Game Guide

The Legend of Zelda: Breath of the Wild.

Any Vegetable, Herb, or Flower
&
Any Seafood

Vegan- Try this recipe with fresh green beans! About 1 cups of green beans as substitute for each fillet- trim the ends.

*Approximately 1/2 to 3/4 pound *(225 g to 350 g)* per fillet! If you buy a 1 pound fillet *(450 g)*, cut it in half for half per person. The best fish for this recipe is a plain white fish; cod, tilapia, or haddock are perfect!

Steamed Fish

Directions:

1. Preheat the oven to 425 degrees Fahrenheit *(220 degrees Celsius)*. Lightly oil a baking dish that has a secure lid.
2. Rinse fillets, and pat them dry. Lay the banana leaves into two X's in the baking dish. Slice one lemon into thin rings, and place about 3 rings splayed in the center of each X. Lay fillets face down on top of the lemon slices in the center of both X's.
3. In a bowl, mix butter, the juice of the other lemon, parsley, sugar, minced garlic, pepper, and thyme. Mix thoroughly.
4. Pour full mixture over both fillets.
5. Wrap the legs of each X over each fillet, making 2 wrapped bundles. Flip each bundle over to keep the folds secure.
6. Add about 1/4 cup *(60 ml)* water to the bottom of the baking dish.
7. Bake for about 20 to 25 minutes. The center of the fish should be opaque- if you want to check, stab a knife directly through the leaf into the filet to see. When they are done, remove from the oven, and let sit for 5 minutes before serving! Enjoy!

Steamed Fruit

Apples and bananas star in this steamed cinnamon and sugared fruit dessert!
This recipe yields about 4 servings.

Serves 4	50 minutes	Vegan

Ingredients:

4 Honeycrisp apples, cored, sliced, then chopped
2 bananas, cut into thick coins
1 cup apple juice, reserve 1/2 for the bottom of pan *(240 ml)*
1 teaspoon ground cinnamon *(2.5 g)*
1/2 teaspoon nutmeg *(1 g)*
1/2 cup rolled oats *(45 g)*
1/3 cup packed brown sugar *(60 g)*
1/4 cup flour *(40 g)*
1/4 cup butter, melted *(55 g)*
8 or more banana leaves

Game Guide

The Legend of Zelda:
Breath of the Wild.

Any Vegetable, Herb, or
Flower
&
Any Fruit

Directions:

1. Preheat the oven to 350 degrees Fahrenheit *(175 degrees Celsius)*. Lightly oil a baking dish that has a secure lid.
2. In a large mixing bowl, combine 1/2 cup *(120 ml)* apple juice, cinnamon, nutmeg, oats, brown sugar, flour and butter, mix until there are few clumps. Add apples, bananas, then gently combine until apples and bananas are coated.
3. Scoop about 1/2 cup *(120 ml)* of mixture into a banana leaf, then fold sides in and roll into a secure bundle. Place bundle into baking dish. Repeat until mixture is gone. Arrange bundles so they are tightly packed on the bottom of your baking dish.
4. Pour an additional 1/2 cup *(120 ml)* apple juice into the baking dish.
5. Cook bundles in the oven for about 40 minutes. Apples should be juicy and pliable. Serve hot, but be careful of the steam when opening the bundles! This goes well with a scoop of ice cream! Enjoy!

Steamed Mushrooms

Create the ultimate Hylian brunch by pairing these garlicky steamed mushrooms with fresh fruit and an omelet from the Breakfast chapter!

Serves 3	35 minutes	Vegan	Gluten free

Ingredients:

6 banana leaves

1 pound small cremini mushrooms, whole *(16 oz or 450 g)*

3 tablespoons olive oil *(45 ml)*

2 cups vegetable broth *(480 ml)*

1/4 cup fresh squeezed lemon juice, about 2 lemons *(60 ml)*

1/2 yellow onion, finely chopped

1 tablespoon minced garlic *(9 g)*

2 teaspoons dried thyme *(3 g)*

1 tablespoon dried parsley *(5 g)*

1/4 cup grated Parmesan, optional *(30 g)*

Game Guide

The Legend of Zelda: Breath of the Wild.

Any Vegetable, Herb, or Flower

&

Any Mushroom

Directions:

1. Preheat oven to 450 degrees Fahrenheit *(230 degrees Celsius)*. Lightly oil a baking dish that has a secure lid.

2. In a large mixing bowl, combine mushrooms, olive oil, lemon juice, onion, garlic, thyme, and parsley.

3. Lay out the banana leaves in X's, and spoon about 1/2 cup *(120 ml)* of the mushroom mixture into the center of each X. Sprinkle a couple pinches of Parmesan cheese over the mushrooms. Carefully wrap the legs of the X around the mushrooms to create a secure bundle, then flip it over to keep the legs in place. Pack each bundle snugly into your baking dish.

4. Pour the vegetable broth over your bundles, then cover with secure lid. Cook in the oven for 20 to 25 minutes, but check every 5 to 10 minutes and add more broth if there's less than 1/2 an inch *(1.25 cm)* at the bottom.

5. When done, the mushrooms should be succulent and aromatic. Enjoy!

Steamed Meat

This recipe draws inspiration from tamales! In tropical Latin American areas, it is common to wrap tamales with banana leaves instead of corn husks. Banana leaves lend a slightly sweet flavor to this dish- so drizzle your favorite hot sauce for a kick! This recipe makes 10 small tamales.

Serves 5	1 hour	Gluten free

Ingredients:

10 banana leaves
3 cups corn masa* *(345 g)*
1/2 cup corn oil *(120 ml)*
1 teaspoon salt *(5 g)*
1/4 teaspoon baking powder *(1.2 g)*
3 cups chicken broth *(720 ml)*
1 cooked chicken,** shredded
1 small yellow onion, chopped
1/2 cup chopped cilantro *(25 g)*
1 cup salsa verde *(240 ml)*
Hot sauce, to taste

Game Guide

The Legend of Zelda: Breath of the Wild.

Any Vegetable, Herb, or Flower (except Pumpkin)
&
Any Meat

Vegan- Replace chicken broth with vegetable broth. Substitute chicken with chopped and briefly sautéed red bell peppers, green bell pepper, 2 teaspoons minced garlic *(10 g)*, 1 can drained black beans *(15 oz or 425 g)*, and 1 can drained pinto beans *(15 oz or 425 g)*. Mix and drain again before adding to banana leaves.

*Not just cornmeal! Red Mills makes some. Vegans, make sure lard is not in the ingredient list.

**You can purchase a rotisserie chicken and shred it by hand, or you can cook chicken of your choosing. Aim for about 2 pounds. *(1 kg)*

Steamed Meat

Directions:

1. Preheat oven to 375 degrees Fahrenheit *(190 degrees Celsius)*. Lightly oil a small baking dish that has tall sides and a secure lid. Tamales stand up next to each other, so small is good! I personally use a stove top pot with a lid, just be sure your pot is okay to use in the oven.
2. In a large mixing bowl, combine corn masa, corn oil, salt, baking powder, and 2 cups *(480 ml)* of chicken broth. Stir vigorously or use a mixer until lumps are gone.
3. In another bowl, stir chicken, onion, cilantro, and salsa verde together.
4. Lay out the banana leaves, and spoon 2 to 3 tablespoons *(30 to 45 ml)* of corn mixture into the widest part of each leaf, then fill the center with a small scoop of chicken; not too much or you won't be able to fold it up securely. Add another table-spoon *(15 ml)* of corn mixture on top.
5. Fold the sides of each leaf in, then fold the end over. One end will be left open. If this is confusing, look up a tamale folding tutorial online!
6. You will stand each tamale upright in your dish, the open top facing up. Pour the final 1 cup *(240 ml)* of chicken broth into the bottom of the dish,*** then fill the pot with tamales so they hold each other up. Cover with a secure lid.
7. Bake for 35 to 40 minutes, check a few times to add broth if necessary. When done, the tamales will be firm, not squishy. Serve hot with optional hot sauce, and enjoy!

***There should be at least 1/2 inch *(1.25 cm)* of broth at the bottom- add more until you reach that point. When you check on the tamales, you may need to add more broth.

Seafood

This chapter is filled with adventurous recipes and foods! From a creamy Salmon Meunière to the real (or fake) escargot, from colorful paellas to the crispy golden fish pie, this chapter covers it all!

Seafood Disclaimer

Please make sure to research, source, clean, and prepare your seafood so that is safe to eat.

Seafood preparation can be a complex task, so many of these recipes include previously prepared or frozen ingredients. If you feel comfortable doing so, feel free to gather and prepare your own from fresh ingredients as Link would have!

Vegan and Vegan Curious Folk

Only one of the recipes in this chapter is vegan, I am sorry. The 'fake' escargot alternative recipe is fully plant based, so I hope you can enjoy it! The Fish Pie recipe also includes a vegan alternative version for a vegetable pie version with a crunchy and delicious pie crust top!

Blueshell and River Snail Escargot

Authentic stuffed escargot, served in giant shells! This recipe includes alternatives for those who would rather it be authentic in appearance, instead of ingredients.

2 servings	30 minutes	Vegan	Gluten free

Ingredients:

2 washed and dried 5 to 6 inch Drill or Trumpet Seashells*
8 ounces of giant snails,** or baby button mushrooms *(225 g)*
1/4 cup butter or vegan butter *(55 g)*
1 small yellow onion, finely diced
1/4 cup celery, finely diced *(80 g)*
1/4 cup fresh parsley, chopped *(15 g)*
1/2 tablespoon fresh rosemary, chopped *(1 g)*
1/2 tablespoon fresh thyme, chopped *(1 g)*
1/4 cup bread crumbs *(30 g)*

Game Guide

The Legend of Zelda: Breath of the Wild.

Hearty Blueshell Snail
or
Sneaky River Snail

*Ideally, you want shells that look like the snails in The Legend of Zelda: Breath of the Wild! Search for drill, trumpet, horn, frog shell, striped fox, and some types of conch shells. Alternatively, you can use giant uncooked pasta shells, make your own croissant shells, or purchase bake safe ceramic shells!

**I was surprised to learn that you can find these canned at almost any grocery store, or you can order them online. If you prefer fresh, you may have to research how to do that in your area.

Gluten free- A bread crumb alternative can be substituted! Toast about 2 to 3 slices of gluten free bread, let it cool, and then crush or blend it!

Blueshell and River Snail Escargot

Directions:

1. Preheat your oven to 350 degrees Fahrenheit *(175 degrees Celsius)*. Oil and pre-heat a small saucepan to medium high, then add the butter and onion. Cook covered for 3 to 4 minutes, until the onions are translucent.

2. Add the snails or mushrooms, then cover and cook for an additional 3 minutes before turning to low. Add the celery, parsley, rosemary, thyme, salt, pepper, and bread crumbs. Mix thoroughly, then cover. Heat for 5 minutes on low.

3. Mixture should be soft and moist, if it is too dry, add a couple of tablespoons of water to the bottom of the pan, and cover for a couple more minutes on low.

4. Stuff each shell with stuffing, making sure that there are similar numbers of snails or mushrooms in each shell. Arrange with the stuffing side up on a baking tray. If necessary, use aluminum foil to make sure the shells stay face up.

5. Bake for 10 minutes. It is done when the stuffing has just begun to crisp. Sprinkle with salt and pepper, serve hot, and enjoy!

Crab Risotto

Rice and crab cooked in spicy vegetable broth until tender, steamy, and utterly delectable.

2 servings	45 minutes	Gluten free

Ingredients:

2 crab claws, optional for accurate garnish
1 tablespoon oil *(15 ml)*
1/2 pound small prepared shrimp *(8 oz or 225 g)*
1/2 pound jumbo lump crab *(8 oz or 225 g)*
2 tablespoons soy sauce *(30 ml)*
1 tablespoon minced garlic *(9 g)*
1 small yellow onion, finely chopped
1 cup Carnaroli or Arborio dry rice *(200 g)*
3 cups vegetable broth *(720 ml)*
A pinch of ground cayenne pepper, optional
1/2 cup fresh or frozen peas *(160 g)*
1/2 cup fresh or frozen corn *(160 g)*
1/4 teaspoon ground ginger *(.5 g)*
2 green onions, finely chopped

Game Guide

The Legend of Zelda: Breath of the Wild.

Hylian Rice
Goat Butter
Rock Salt
Any Crab

Gluten free- Be sure to use gluten free soy sauce!

Crab Risotto

Directions:

1.   Optional: If serving with crab claws, steam them covered in a large pot on a steaming rack over boiling water for 5 to 7 minutes. Claws are done when they turn fully orange or red.

2.   Oil and heat skillet to medium high. Add the oil, shrimp, crab lumps, and soy sauce. Cook covered for 5 to 7 minutes, stirring occasionally to make sure all sides are cooked. With tongs, remove shrimp and crab, leaving the juices behind. Set shrimp and crab aside.

3.   Add garlic and onion. Let simmer on medium, stirring occasionally, for 5 minutes. Onions should be translucent but not browned.

4.   Add dry rice to skillet, sauté for 2 minutes to lightly toast the rice before adding all of the broth, and cayenne pepper. Bring to a boil, then reduce heat to medium low, cover and let simmer for about 12 to 15 minutes, stirring occasionally. The rice should be almost done, with a little broth left. If not, continue cooking until only a little broth is left.

5.   Add the peas, corn, and ginger. Mix thoroughly, then add the set aside shrimp and crab on top. Cover and let simmer on low for about 7 more minutes, stirring to prevent sticking if necessary. The dish is ready when the rice is fully cooked! Serve with the crab claw presented on top of each plate of rice, like in The Legend of Zelda: Breath of the Wild. Enjoy!

Crab Stir Fry

This is Riverside Stable's favorite dish, a delightfully spicy, curried coconut and bell pepper crab stir fry!

| 2 servings | 20 minutes | Gluten free |

Ingredients:

2 king crab legs, cooked*
3 tablespoons oil *(45 ml)*
1 medium red onion, finely chopped
1 medium red bell pepper, finely chopped
4 mini baby bell peppers, whole
3 tablespoons Goron Spice, page 188, or curry powder *(19 g)*
1/2 cup coconut milk *(120 ml)*
2 tablespoons red curry paste, the Maesri brand is good *(32 g)*
2 teaspoons brown sugar *(8 g)*
1 teaspoon salt *(6 g)*
Freshly ground black pepper, to taste
Cornstarch or instant mashed potatoes, optional for thickening
2 sprigs of parsley for garnish

Game Guide

The Legend of Zelda: Breath of the Wild.

Goron Spice
&
Any Crab

*In The Legend of Zelda: Breath of the Wild, this recipe does appear to be a full crab in broth. I have assumed here that crab legs may be a more edible and easier to prepare alternative. Many large stores sell washed and cooked king crab legs, so all you have to do is make sure they are clean, cut them into chunks if you desire, and proceed as normal with the recipe.

Crab Stir Fry

Directions:

1. Add oil, a splash of water, and red onion to your pan on medium heat. Cook covered until onions are translucent, about 3 minutes, then add yellow curry powder, coconut milk, red curry paste, brown sugar, salt, and black pepper. Stir and cook on medium high until it reaches a light boil, about 5 minutes. For thicker sauce, sprinkle and stir in corn starch a little at a time, up to a spoonful or two. Then add the chopped and whole bell peppers, and the crab legs.

2. Stir and cook for an additional 5 minutes, making sure that the crab legs are full coated. It is ready when the crab is fully heated through, and the whole bell peppers should be cooked but still vibrant.

3. Serve with white rice if desired, and garnish each dish with a sprig of parsley and two of the baby bell peppers. Enjoy!

Fish Pie

This fish pie is a beautiful puff pastry fish, filled with soft vegetables and fish fillet, served fresh from the oven! Make several small fish pastries, or one large one with this recipe, and don't forget the canon side of mashed potatoes, page 104!

2 servings	1 hour

Ingredients:

1 tablespoon oil *(15 ml)*

1 small yellow onion, diced

1/2 cup shredded carrots *(55 g)*

1 red pepper, seeds and stem removed, diced

1/2 cup frozen peas *(160 g)*

1/4 teaspoon salt *(1.5 g)*

1/4 teaspoon freshly ground black pepper *(.5 g)*

1 teaspoon garlic, minced *(3 g)*

1 teaspoon vegetable bouillon* *(3 g)*

1 pound white fish fillet, de-boned and skinned *(8 oz or 225 g)*

1/2 teaspoon dill weed *(.5 g)*

1/2 teaspoon Italian seasoning *(.5 g)*

Lemon juice, to taste

Pie or puff pastry dough, there's a pie crust recipe in the Meat and Veggie Pies on page 114

Pastry glaze, 1 tablespoon honey diluted with 2 tablespoons of hot water *(15 ml per tbs)*

Mashed potatoes, page 104, add 1 cup mixed peas, corn, and carrots *(320 g)*

Vegan- I love this with yellow summer squash or zucchini or both instead of fish, and add a can of drained black beans *(15 oz or 425 g)*, and a half cup corn *(160 g)*. You can still make it look like a fish on the outside if you want! Go without the honey glaze or make it with 1 tablespoon maple syrup and 2 tablespoons unsweetened coconut milk! *(15 ml per tbs)*

Gluten free- A gluten free pie crust, especially from King Arthur's Flour, or croissant dough will work here.

*Better Than Bouillon: Seasoned Vegetable Base, or similar.

Fish Pie

Directions:

1. Preheat oven to 400 degrees Fahrenheit *(200 degrees Celsius)*. Oil and set your pan to medium high. Add onion, carrots, diced red pepper, peas, salt, and pepper. Cover and cook for 5 minutes, stirring occasionally.

2. When onions are translucent and beginning to brown, stir in garlic, vegetable bouillon, dill weed, and Italian seasoning to the pan. Clear a spot in the middle, and place the fish fillet there. Cook covered at medium heat for 5 to 7 minutes, flipping the fish fillet once. It's ready when the fish is cooked enough to break easily into pieces.

3. With a fork or masher, mash until chunky but well mixed. If desired, add some lemon juice here.

4. Prepare a baking tray with baking paper.

5. Roll out your pastry dough on a flat, floured surface. Cut fish shapes, 2 per fish you want to bake. You can make a pattern by drawing and cutting out a fish shape on clean cardboard to get accurate shapes each time, or you can just wing it. Place half of the fish carefully on the baking paper tray. Save extra pastry for fish details!

6. Spoon out your fish filling onto each fish, leaving a margin of at least one half inch.

7. Oil the edges of each fish, and then carefully top each one with a second fish shaped pastry. Gently pinch the edges together all the way around the fish. You may wish to use a fork here to make sure the edges won't break apart.

8. Use any extra pastry to add details! The Legend of Zelda: Breath of the Wild Fish Pie has fish lips, a circular eye, crisscrossed scales, and a puffy little fin! After that, you can do additional detailing with a toothpick; scalloped scales on the body, and lots of lines on the tail.

9. Lightly brush on the pastry wash, then bake for 20 minutes. It is done when the pastry has turned a dark golden brown. Cool for at least 15 minutes before serving. Enjoy!

Hearty Salmon Meuniere

Meunière prepared salmon steak with matching sauce! Serve with spinach and halved tomatoes for an authentic Rito Village dish. This is a traditional meunière à la minute, the sauce is made using the remaining oils and flavor from the pan.

2 servings	25 minutes

Ingredients:

2 deboned ~1 inch *(~2.5 cm)* thick Salmon Steaks*

1/4 cup butter *(55 g)*

1/4 teaspoon garlic salt *(1 g)*

1 medium sized lemon, wedged

1 to 1 1/2 cups all purpose wheat flour *(150 g to 225 g)*

1 tablespoon minced garlic *(9 g)*

1/2 cup finely chopped fresh parsley *(30 g)*

1 tablespoon capers, if desired *(9 g)*

1/4 cup milk, unsweetened cashew milk works well *(60 ml)*

Fresh baby spinach, for garnish

Halved medium sized tomatoes, 2 halves per person, for garnish

Dried parsley, for garnish

Game Guide

The Legend of Zelda: Breath of the Wild.

Tabantha Wheat
Goat Butter
Hearty Salmon

*Your grocery store fish department should be able to cut and debone salmon steaks for you, especially if you are able to provide a picture. If not, feel free to use normal fillets for this recipe, or if you are comfortable doing so, cut and debone a salmon steak yourself.

Hearty Salmon Meuniere

Directions:

1. Squeeze 1/4 of the lemon over the salmon steaks, rubbing it into both sides. Sprinkle garlic salt over both sides. Prepare a shallow dish with wheat flour, then dip salmon steaks one at a time into the flour. Make sure each side is coated in flour.
2. Preheat your oven to 200 degrees Fahrenheit *(95 degrees Celsius)*. This will keep the steaks warm while you prepare the sauce.
3. Oil and preheat your cast iron pan to medium high. Add butter, and as soon as it begins to steam, add your salmon steaks face down in the pan. Cook for 4 minutes on medium high, but turn down heat if the butter begins to smoke. Flip, and cook for an additional 4 minutes on the other flat side. The steaks are done when the flesh is an opaque pink all the way through, it will appear golden and crispy.
4. Remove the steaks and place them in the oven for now.
5. Do not clean your pan. Add garlic, parsley, capers, milk, and remaining 3/4 lemon juice directly to it, over medium high heat. Bring to a light boil, and, while stirring continuously, add a small spoonful of flour every minute or so for 5 minutes. Meunière translates to miller's wife, so this dish uses a fair amount of flour!
6. Once the sauce is thick and creamy, turn off the heat and bring the steaks out of the oven. Plate each steak with a side of spinach and halved tomatoes, and carefully pour your Meunière sauce over each steak. Garnish with a sprinkling of parsley, and enjoy!

Glazed Seafood

A buttery, white, skillet-fried fish fillet, with a delicious browned honey glaze.

2 servings	15 minutes	Gluten free

Ingredients:

2 white fish fillets with skin on one side*
2 tablespoons butter *(25 g)*
2 tablespoons honey *(30 ml)*
2 teaspoons minced garlic *(6 g)*
Fresh lemon juice, to taste

Game Guide

The Legend of Zelda: Breath of the Wild.

Courser Bee Honey
&
Any Seafood

Directions:

1. Oil and preheat your cast iron skillet to medium heat. Add butter, and cook for 2 to 3 minutes, stirring constantly, until the butter is just golden brown and fragrant.
2. Add the honey, garlic, and any desired lemon juice. Mix, turn to medium high, and then add the fillets skin side down. Cook for 2 to 3 minutes each on all four sides, while using a spoon to drizzle the skillet sauce over the fish.
3. The fish is done when the flesh is opaque all the way through, and the outside is golden brown and crystallized with honey sauce. Serve hot, and drizzle any extra sauce over each fillet. Enjoy!

*Cod works very well for this simple recipe! Each fillet should weigh at least 1/2 pound *(8 oz or 225 g)*.

Pepper Seafood

A whole roasted fish, encrusted with herbs, served with roast peppers!

| 2 servings | 30 minutes | Gluten free |

Ingredients:
2 small, whole fish, a little over 1 pound each* *(>16 oz each)*
2 and 1 tablespoons oil, avocado oil is great here *(30 and 15 ml)*
1 teaspoon salt *(6 g)*
1 teaspoon freshly ground pepper *(3 g)*
1 tablespoon minced garlic *(9 g)*
1 lemon, peeled and very thinly sliced
1/4 teaspoon thyme *(.5 g)*
1 tablespoon dried parsley *(5 g)*
4 baby red peppers, whole

Game Guide
The Legend of Zelda: Breath of the Wild.

Spicy Pepper
&
Any Seafood

Directions:
1. Preheat the oven to 450 degrees Fahrenheit *(230 degrees Celsius)*. Prepare a baking sheet with baking paper. Mix 2 tablespoons oil *(30 ml)*, salt, and ground pepper together. Rub each fish with the oil mixture, and then place them, and the whole peppers, onto the baking sheet.
2. Deeply slice each fish to the bone 3 times, like this: < \ \ \ <
3. Mix 1 tablespoon oil, garlic, thyme, and parsley together. Stuff each slice with lemon, and this mixture. Drizzle any excess mixture over the rest of the fish and peppers.
4. Roast for about 20 minutes, it is ready when the flesh is opaque all the way through. Serve 1 fish with 2 peppers on each plate, and enjoy!

*The model in The Legend of Zelda: Breath of the Wild appears similar to a red snapper, which would be ideal for this recipe!

Porgy Meuniere

The red striped Porgy could be nothing else but a delicious red snapper! These soft fillets are prepared with flour, rosemary, and oregano, sautéed until delectable, and then topped with a creamy meunière sauce.

2 servings	30 minutes

Ingredients:

2 large deboned fish fillets*
1 medium sized lemon, wedged
1/4 teaspoon garlic salt *(1.5 g)*
Freshly ground black pepper to taste
1 teaspoon dried rosemary *(1 g)*
1 teaspoon dried oregano *(1 g)*
1 to 1 1/2 cup all purpose wheat flour *(150 g to 225 g)*
1/4 cup butter *(55 g)*
1 tablespoon minced garlic *(9 g)*
1/2 cup finely chopped fresh parsley, or 3 tablespoons dried *(30 g or 15 g)*
1/4 cup milk, unsweetened cashew milk works well *(60 ml)*
Fresh baby spinach
Halved medium sized tomatoes, 1 full tomato per person

Game Guide

The Legend of Zelda: Breath of the Wild.

Any Porgy
Goat Butter
Tabantha Wheat

*'Porgy' is an umbrella name for fish of the Sparidae family. However, The Legend of Zelda: Breath of the Wild red striped porgy is the spitting image of a red snapper, which is not a type of porgy, but does happen to be a delicious kind of fish! Use the fish you think will be best, but for an accurate look alike, definitely choose a red snapper! Whatever you decide, keep the skin on one side of the fish fillet for an accurate look.

Porgy Meuniere

Directions:

1. Squeeze 1/4 of the lemon over the fillets, rubbing it into both sides. In a small dish, mix garlic salt, ground black pepper, rosemary, and oregano together. Using your fingers, sprinkle this mixture over both sides of the fillets. Prepare a shallow dish with wheat flour, then dip fillets one at a time into the flour. Make sure each side is coated in flour.

2. Preheat your oven to 200 degrees Fahrenheit *(95 degrees Celsius)*. This is to keep the fillets hot while you prepare the sauce!

3. Oil and preheat your cast iron pan to medium high. Add butter, and as soon as it begins to steam, add your fillets face down in the pan. Cook for 4 minutes on medium high, but turn down heat if the butter begins to smoke. Flip, and cook for an additional 4 minutes on the other flat side. The steaks are done when the flesh is opaque all the way through, it will appear golden and crispy.

4. Remove the steaks and place them in the oven for now.

5. Do not clean your pan, instead, add garlic, parsley, capers, milk, and the remaining 3/4 lemon juice directly into it, and heat at medium high. Bring to a light boil, and, while stirring continuously, add one small spoonful of flour every minute or so for 5 minutes. Meunière translates to miller's wife, so this dish uses a fair amount of flour!

6. Once the sauce is thick and creamy, turn off the heat and bring the fillets out of the oven. Plate with a side of spinach and halved tomatoes, and carefully pour your Meunière sauce over each fillet. Enjoy!

Salmon Risotto

Discover this recipe by snooping in the diary of Ivee, found inside the East Wind store in Hateno Village, or avoid invading her privacy by using the recipe below! Sautéed salmon with lemon and capers, served over a bed of luscious risotto rice!

2 servings	45 minutes	Gluten free

Ingredients:

1 tablespoon oil *(15 ml)*
1 small lemon, juice
1 tablespoon capers, optional *(9 g)*
2 pounds salmon fillet, deskinned, cut into chunks *(900 g)*
2 teaspoons minced garlic *(6 g)*
1 small yellow onion, finely chopped
1 cup Carnaroli or Arborio dry rice *(200 g)*
3 cups vegetable broth *(720 ml)*
1/2 cup shredded carrots *(55 g)*
1/2 cup fresh or frozen peas *(160 g)*
1/4 cup fresh parsley, 1 tablespoon dried *(15 g or 5 g)*

Game Guide

The Legend of Zelda: Breath of the Wild.

Hearty Salmon
Hylian Rice
Goat Butter
Rock Salt

Salmon Risotto

Directions:

1. Oil and heat skillet to medium high. Add the oil, 1/2 of the lemon juice, capers, and salmon chunks. Cook covered for 5 to 7 minutes, stirring occasionally to make sure each side is cooked. It is done when the salmon flesh is opaque all the way through. Remove just the salmon chunks from the skillet and set aside.
2. Keep the salmon oil and remnants in the skillet, and add garlic and onion. Let simmer on medium, stirring occasionally, for 4 minutes. Onions should be translucent but not browned.
3. Add the dry rice to the skillet, and sauté for 2 minutes to lightly toast the rice before adding all of the broth. Bring to a boil, then reduce heat to medium low, cover and let simmer for about 15 minutes, stirring occasionally. The rice should be almost done, with a little broth left.
4. Add the carrots, peas, parsley, and lemon juice. Mix thoroughly, then add the set aside salmon chunks on top. Cover and let simmer on low for about 7 more minutes, stirring to prevent sticking if necessary. The dish is ready when the rice is fully cooked! Serve with the salmon presented on top of each plate of rice, like in The Legend of Zelda: Breath of the Wild. Enjoy!

Seafood Curry

You'll be surprised at how easy and quick this recipe is, and it includes the shrimp, crab, and calamari you see in The Legend of Zelda: Breath of the Wild! If you want to skip the seafood, this is a delicious and filling vegan curry- easy to throw together and eat all day.

3 to 4 servings	15 minutes	Gluten free

Ingredients:

1 crab claw per plate, optional for accurate garnish
1/2 pound cooked medium shrimp, *(8 oz or 225 g)*
1/2 pound king crab legs, cooked and chopped* *(8 oz or 225 g)*
1/2 pound calamari rings** *(8 oz 225 g)*
1 tablespoon oil *(15 ml)*
1 tablespoon minced garlic *(9 g)*
1 can black beans, drained *(15 oz or 425 g)*
1 can lentils, drained *(15 oz or 425 g)*
1/2 cup peas, fresh or frozen *(160 g)*
1/2 cup corn, fresh or frozen *(160 g)*
2 cups water *(480 ml)*
1 1/2 tablespoon vegetable bouillon*** *(12 g)*
1/2 teaspoon thyme *(1 g)*
1/4 teaspoon freshly ground black pepper *(1 g)*
1 tablespoon of Goron Spice, page 188, or mild curry powder *(6 g)*
Freshly cooked white rice
Dried parsley, for garnish

Game Guide

The Legend of Zelda: Breath of the Wild.

Goron Spice
Hylian Rice
Hearty Blueshell Snail
or Any Porgy

*You can find cooked crab legs at large stores for reasonable prices. Chop them straight through the armor into 2 inch long *(5 cm)* chunks.

**You can often find fresh calamari at a nearby luxury food store, or frozen calamari almost anywhere. Both work perfectly here.

***Better Than Bouillon: Seasoned Vegetable Base, or similar.

Seafood Curry

Directions:

1. Prepare white rice.
2. Optional: If serving with crab claws, steam them covered in a large pot on a steaming rack over boiling water for 5 to 7 minutes. Claws are done when they turn fully orange or red.
3. In a large pot, add oil, garlic, black beans, lentils, peas, corn, and water, then add vegetable bouillon, thyme, black pepper, and yellow curry powder. Stir until well mixed, cover, and cook at medium high until boiling.
4. Add shrimp, crab legs, and calamari rings. Mix thoroughly, and heat for 5 minutes on medium, and remove from heat. The seafood should be hot all the way through, try not to overheat. Calamari will become rubbery if cooked for longer than a few minutes.
5. Plate half rice, half curry, and add an optional crab claw to each plate for that final touch of accuracy to The Legend of Zelda: Breath of the Wild. Garnish the rice with a sprinkling of parsley. Enjoy!

Seafood Meunière

Below you will learn how to prepare the official fish of Hyrule, the Hyrule Bass! This is another Meunière recipe, another crispy and flavorful fish dish with cream sauce. Be sure to use a flavorful striped bass for this recipe to shine!

2 servings	30 minutes

Ingredients:

2 large deboned fillets of Striped Bass
2 tablespoons oil *(30 ml)*
1/4 teaspoon garlic salt (1.5 g)
Freshly ground black pepper to taste
1 to 1 1/2 cup all purpose wheat flour *(150 g to 225 g)*
1/4 cup butter *(55 g)*
1 tablespoon minced garlic *(9 g)*
2 tablespoons water *(30 ml)*
1 large yellow onion, finely diced
1/2 cup finely chopped fresh parsley, or 3 tablespoons dried *(30 g or 15 g)*
1/4 cup milk, unsweetened cashew milk works well *(60 ml)*
Lemon juice to taste, optional
Fresh baby spinach
Halved medium sized tomatoes, two halves per person

Game Guide

The Legend of Zelda: Breath of the Wild.

Any Seafood (except Porgy or Salmon)
Tabantha Wheat
Goat Butter

Seafood Meunière

Directions:

1. Rub the oil all over the fillets, and then garlic salt and pepper both sides. Prepare a shallow dish with wheat flour, then dip fillets one at a time into the flour. Make sure every side is coated in flour.

2. Preheat your oven to 200 degrees Fahrenheit *(95 degrees Celsius)*, to keep the fillets hot later.

3. Oil and preheat your cast iron pan to medium high. Add butter, and as soon as it begins to steam, add your fillets face down in the pan. Cook for 4 minutes on medium high, but turn down heat if the butter begins to smoke. Flip, and cook for an additional 4 minutes on the other flat side. The steaks are done when the flesh is opaque all the way through, it will appear golden and crispy.

4. Remove the steaks and place them in the oven for now.

5. Do not clean your pan, instead, add the garlic, water, and yellow onion. Cook covered on medium high for 2 to 3 minutes, until onions are translucent, not caramelized. Then add parsley and milk. Bring to a light boil, and, while stirring continuously, and add a small spoonful of flour every minute or so for 5 minutes. Meunière translates to miller's wife, so this dish uses a fair amount of flour!

6. Once the sauce is thick and creamy, turn off the heat and bring the fillets out of the oven. Plate with a side of spinach and halved tomatoes to resemble The Legend of Zelda: Breath of the Wild dish, and carefully pour your Meunière sauce over each fillet. Enjoy!

Seafood Paella

What's for dinner in Lurelin Village? This traditional spicy rice and seafood dish! It is named after the double handed pan, paella, Link so frequently finds in his travels! This recipe serves 5 to 7 people if you have a large enough pan, but it can be easily halved!

6 servings	45 minutes	Gluten free

Ingredients:

1 pound large shrimp, peeled and deveined *(450 g)*

1 pound mussels, debearded *(450 g)*

1 pound fresh clams *(450 g)*

1/2 pound spanish chorizo or similar, sliced into coins *(225 g)*

1 tablespoon oil *(15 ml)*

1 small yellow onion, reserve 4 rings for garnish, then chop

1 tablespoon minced garlic *(9 g)*

1 green bell pepper, finely diced

3 strands of saffron*

2 cups white short grain rice, uncooked *(300 g)*

4 cups chicken broth *(960 ml)*

1/2 teaspoon freshly ground pepper *(1 g)*

1/4 teaspoon paprika *(.5 g)*

1 chicken breast, cooked and then shredded

1 cup peas, fresh or frozen *(320 g)*

1 red bell pepper, cut into strips for garnish

1 jalapeño, deseeded and cut into coins for garnish

2 lemons, wedged, optional to taste

Game Guide

The Legend of Zelda: Breath of the Wild.

Any Seafood (except Porgy or Salmon)

Tabantha Wheat

Goat Butter

*Saffron is expensive, and a little goes a long way. You can skip it, but this is a traditional style dish, and saffron is a very unique flavor.

Seafood Paella

Directions:

1. Make sure all ingredients are thoroughly cleaned! Oil and preheat your large pan to medium high. Add a little extra oil, onion, garlic, green bell pepper, and chorizo. Sauté and stir until both sides of the chorizo are cooked, about 5 to 7 minutes.

2. Add the saffron and rice, stirring to toast the rice for 1 to 2 minutes. Then add the broth, pepper, and paprika. Stir thoroughly, then cover, reduce heat to medium low, and simmer for 15 minutes, until rice is al dente but nearly done. Keep in mind the rice in this recipe is meant to be slightly crunchy and al dente; if that is not your thing, add another 1/2 cup *(120 ml)* of broth or water now.

3. Remove pan from heat. Add the cooked chicken and peas, then mix thoroughly. Next, arrange the mussels, clams, shrimp, red bell pepper strips, reserved onions, and jalapeños to the top like The Legend of Zelda: Breath of the Wild's beautiful traditional serving style! Cover and cook on medium low for an additional 20 minutes, or until liquid is fully absorbed and mussel and clam shells have opened. Discard any shells that do not open. Serve with optional lemon wedges, and enjoy!

Seafood Fried Rice

Gloriously tender and juicy shrimp sautéed with rice and vegetables, with a kick of ginger and a garnish of freshly chopped green onions.

2 servings	20 minutes	Gluten free

Ingredients:

4 cups freshly cooked rice *(750 g)*
2 tablespoons sesame oil *(30 ml)*
2 tablespoons vegetable oil *(30 ml)*
1 pound small fresh shrimp, shelled and deveined* *(450 g)*
6 jumbo shrimp, shelled and deveined, 3 per person
1 cup peas and diced carrots, frozen *(320 g)*
1/2 cup corn, fresh or frozen *(160 g)*
1 teaspoon minced ginger, or 1/2 tablespoon fresh *(3 g or 6 g)*
1 tablespoon minced garlic *(9 g)*
3 large eggs, beaten
3 tablespoons soy sauce *(45 ml)*
1 to 2 tablespoons ketchup, or Lon Lon Ketchup, page 274 *(30 ml)*
Freshly ground black pepper to taste
2 green onions, chopped for garnish

Game Guide

The Legend of Zelda: Breath of the Wild.

Hylian Rice
Rock Salt
Hearty Blueshell Snail or
Any Porgy

*You can use frozen shrimp or fresh shrimp, fresh will be marginally better. Make sure to wash!

Seafood Fried Rice

Directions:

1. Add oils to a cast iron skillet, and preheat to medium high, add both the small and jumbo shrimp, and cook for about 4 minutes until the shrimp is fully cooked and opaque. Stir often, and cook all the jumbo shrimp on both sides. Remove the shrimp and set aside, leaving the oils and juices behind in the skillet.
2. Add peas, carrots, corn, ginger, and garlic. Mix thoroughly, cover, and cook while stirring occasionally for 5 to 6 minutes. It should all be hot and sizzling.
3. Push everything aside to clear a space in the center of the skillet, and add the eggs there. Scramble them on medium high, and when they are done, mix everything together.
4. Add the shrimp and rice, then evenly add the soy sauce, ketchup, and black pepper. Stir and break up the rice while continuing to heat, until everything is hot and well mixed. Serve with three jumbo shrimp atop each dish, garnish with green onions, and enjoy!

Gooey Tartare

A local specialty of Gooey Swamp, this purple tartar sauce recipe is the finishing touch for so many seafood dishes! Try it with the Salt Grilled Crab Cakes on page 98!

| 8 servings | 10 minutes | Vegetarian | Gluten free |

Ingredients:

1 cup mayonnaise *(235 ml)*
1 cup dill pickles, chopped finely *(150 g)*
2 tablespoons yellow onion, chopped finely *(7 g)*
1 teaspoon dried dill weed *(1 g)*
1 tablespoon fresh parsley, chopped finely *(5 g)*
1 tablespoon sugar *(12.5 g)*
1 teaspoon fresh lemon juice, or much more to taste *(5 ml)*
1/4 teaspoon freshly ground black pepper, or to taste *(.5 g)*
Purple food coloring,* or Monster Extract, page 173,
A glass mason jar with lid, for accuracy

Game Guide

Freshly-Picked Tingle's Rosy Rupeeland

7 Bitter Newts
8 Soft Eggs

Directions:

1. Mix all ingredients, except purple dye, together until well combined.
2. A little bit at a time, add the purple dye and mix until you achieve a nice purple.
3. Transfer to a glass mason jar for accuracy, and serve immediately! It will keep in the refrigerator if sealed tight for a week, but tastes best when freshly made. Enjoy!

*Gooey Tartare is purple! You can add a few drops of dye, or use one of the natural purple Monster Extract dye recipes on page 173. However, the natural dye will affect the taste here. I recommend using normal store bought purple food coloring.

Fire Cooking
Roasted and Toasted

In The Legend of Zelda: Breath of the Wild, Link can cook a variety of one ingredient meals by tossing them near an open fire! This chapter explains the ins and outs of open fire cooking for a variety of different dishes, from apples to mushrooms to fish!

There is an indescribable joy that comes from cooking over a fire, and then sharing good food with friends! You'll notice that the recipes in this chapter are very simple, at times only one or two ingredients, just like in the game. The main goal is to help you properly cook a variety of food over a fire!

Safety

Please obey fire regulations, and check your local government website before lighting a fire.

1) *Wood.* For a clean cooking fire, always use fully dry seasoned wood. Green firewood, or wood freshly stripped from trees, will be smoky and messy. Seasoned wood is simply wood that has been left to dry for a long time, or 'season'.

2) *Location.* Use established fire pits, if possible. Otherwise, try to build on rock, or bare soil. Especially if its a new pit, keep in mind that the soil underneath will retain the heat and fire. It will take more than a bucket of water to put it out, and it could catch fire again even hours later. Also make sure to be at least 10 feet *(3 meters)* away from flammable growth, with no overhanging trees.

3) *Weather.* Avoid wind, which will burn your fire out more quickly, and is difficult to cook with. It is also dangerous; a spark can get away and ignite grass or trees, starting a wildfire.

There is a simple guide to making a cook fire on the next page!

How to Start a Fire

A good cooking fire has a large bed of hot coals, and may take 30 to 45 minutes to prepare. Some of the following recipes may also require a cooking grate, or other special equipment. Please also look over the safety precautions on the previous page!

1) Prepare your fire pit.

If making a new one, arrange rocks in a U shape, with a large upright rock in the curve of the U. It will help direct smoke away. Prepare a bucket of water and a nearby water source.

2) Arrange the kindling.

Fill the U with starter kindling, like tinder or crumpled paper. Then add additional light layers of small dead branches. Layer your kindling over the full inner area of the U, laying it in one direction, and then the other. It should be fairly even and flat, not a pyramid shape.

3) Light the tinder.

Try to light it in more than one spot, so the full area will catch. After the tinder and kindling has caught, add your firewood. Try to select firewood roughly the same size, and distribute it evenly over the pit. Go with small logs at first, and add larger pieces as necessary.

4) Scrape the coals.

The flames will eventually calm, leaving behind a bed of coals. You can scrape these together into a thicker layer for a high heat setting, or spread them out more thinly for a medium heat setting. It's time for cooking! Proceed with your chosen recipe, which may require more wood to be added! If cooking in a cast iron pan, nestle the pan directly on top of the coals, and scrape them around the sides to make sure the pan is stable.

5) After cooking.

Simply add more wood for a normal campfire afterwards. When done, extinguish and soak the area completely with water.

Baked Apple

These cinnamon apples are the perfect dessert for a fireside meal.
You can add them to the coals, and then continue cooking your other dishes!

| 4 apples | 20 minutes | Vegan | Gluten free |

Ingredients:
4 apples, Honeycrisps are best
1/4 cup brown sugar *(50 g)*
1 teaspoon ground cinnamon *(2.6 g)*
Aluminum foil
Leather gloves

Game Guide
The Legend of Zelda:
Breath of the Wild.

Apple

Directions:
1. Prepare your cooking fire, see page 234.
2. Cut out the core of your apples, leaving a hollow space.
3. Mix brown sugar and ground cinnamon together, then fill the hollows of your apples with the mixture. Sprinkle any excess on the outside of the apples.
4. Individually wrap each apple into a large piece of aluminum foil, and twist the extra foil into a long handle. No need to be too tight with this, you don't want to tear the foil.
5. Nestle the apples into the coals of the cook fire. You can gently scrape the coals around the apples for added heat.
6. Cook for at least 10 minutes, maybe a little longer if you prefer softer apples. These can cook for a while before they start to burn.
7. Carefully take them out of the fire, and unwrap them enough that the tops are showing. Allow them to cool for another 10 minutes before eating with spoons. Be careful not to burn yourself with the hot sugar, and enjoy!

Baked Palm Fruit

Papayas are used in this recipe, as they are naturally delicious and look so similar to the Palm Fruit in The Legend of Zelda: Breath of the Wild!

| Serves 6 | 30 minutes | Vegan | Gluten free |

Ingredients:

3 papayas, halved and seeded
1/4 cup brown sugar *(50 g)*
1 teaspoon cinnamon *(2.6 g)*
Honey or agave nectar for drizzle
Aluminum foil
Leather gloves

Game Guide

The Legend of Zelda: Breath of the Wild.

Palm Fruit

Directions:

1. Prepare your cooking fire, see page 234.
2. Mix brown sugar with cinnamon, and sprinkle into the papayas. Follow with a drizzle of honey or agave nectar over each.
3. Stick each papaya half back together, and wrap each whole papaya in a large sheet of aluminum foil. Twist excess foil into a long handle, so you can retrieve them from the fire easily.
4. Nestle your papayas individually into the coals, and scrape the coals to blanket the sides.
5. Cook for 15 to 20 minutes, they are done when they smell divine and are soft all the way through.
6. With your leather gloves, carefully remove from fire, open the aluminum foil, and allow to cool until safe to eat! Enjoy!

Baked Pumpkin

This recipe uses the "Stuffed Pumpkins" recipe on page 122! You can prepare and stuff the pumpkin, or bell peppers, beforehand, and then cook them over the fire later!

Serves 4	1 hour	Vegan	Gluten free

Ingredients:

Unbaked stuffed pumpkins or bell peppers, page 122
Aluminum foil
Optional, fire safe pot with handle, or long handled pan
Leather gloves

Game Guide

The Legend of Zelda: Breath of the Wild.

Fortified Pumpkin

Directions:

1. Prepare your stuffed pumpkins or bell peppers, see page 122. After stuffing, make sure to replace the tops. Prepare your cooking fire, see page 234.
2. Wrap each with aluminum foil, and leave the top exposed. If it is a larger heavy pumpkin, you may want to wrap with several layers of foil.
3. Decide on a reliable way to retrieve them from the fire when they are done. You could cook them in a pot or pan with a suitable handle, if they are small bell peppers you could use a pair of long metal tongs, if it is a large pumpkin you can serve directly from the fire with a long and large ladle or spoon.
4. Nestle the wrapped pumpkins or bell peppers into the coals, and scrape the coals to blanket the sides.
5. For large pumpkins, rotate a quarter turn every 10 to 15 minutes, for around 45 minutes. To check if it is done, remove the top and prod the interior. If the pumpkin flesh is soft all the way through, it's ready!
6. For bell peppers, cook for around 15 to 20 minutes. It's ready when it's soft and hot all the way through!
7. With your leather gloves, remove carefully from the fire, and keep in mind they are very hot and will likely continue cooking for a while. Allow to cool before serving to children, and be careful when starting to eat! Enjoy!

Blackened Crab

This is a perfect beach fire treat! Serves wonderfully when paired with a variety of skewers from the Skewer Adventure Chapter, page 49.

Serves 4	25 minutes	Gluten free

Ingredients:

2 pounds of crab, washed* *(32 ounces or .9 kg)*
1/2 cup butter *(110 g)*
1 teaspoon salt *(5.6 g)*
1 teaspoon minced garlic *(3 g)*
1 teaspoon dried parsley *(1.5 g)*
2 large lemons
A fire safe bowl, for the dipping sauce
A pair of long metal fire tongs
Leather gloves

Game Guide

The Legend of Zelda: Breath of the Wild.

Any Crab

Directions:

1. Prepare your cooking fire, see page 234.
2. Nestle your crab or crab legs directly into the coals, then scrape the coals over to cover them. Don't worry about it being dirty, you'll rinse them later.
3. Cook for 15 to 20 minutes, and if cooking full crabs, flip half way through. You'll know it is done with the shell is bright reddish orange throughout.
4. While the crab is cooking, mix butter, salt, garlic, and parsley into a small fire safe bowl. Don't add the lemon yet, as cooking it will make it less flavorful. Nestle the bowl near the coals, just close enough to melt the butter.
5. When the crab is done, remove with leather gloves and tongs. Wash thoroughly. Juice the lemons into the sauce bowl and mix. Serve with dipping sauce, and enjoy!

*I would recommend purchasing fresh or frozen crab legs from the store. You could also buy them cooked, so there's no need to worry about cooking it all the way through. Depending on where you live, you could also get a live crab. If so, please kill it as humanely as possible, fully gut it, and wash it out. You can then cook the entire crab in the fire, but you will mainly eat the legs.

Campfire Egg

If you don't follow these instructions precisely, it can cause an explosion!
Cooking eggs has never been so exciting!

| 1 egg | 20 minutes | Vegetarian | Gluten free |

Ingredients:

1 egg, or as many eggs as you desire
Black pepper and garlic salt to taste
1 heavy and pointy knife
Leather gloves

Game Guide

The Legend of Zelda:
Breath of the Wild.

Bird Egg

Directions:

1. Prepare your cooking fire, see page 234.
2. With your knife in one hand, and an egg in the other, carefully tap the top of the egg to make a small hole. Continue tapping to make the hole bigger, until it's about 3/4 inches *(2 cm)* wide. Remove any fragments of egg shell, and repeat with the other eggs. Doing this allows the air and pressure to escape during cooking! When you boil an egg, this process happens slowly through the shell itself, but when you cook an egg in coals or near a fire, it happens far too quickly, so eggs explode instead.
3. Using your leather gloves, nestle your eggs in the ashes at the edge of the fire. You do not need to place them in the center of the coals in the direct heat. You can scrape the ashes together around each egg to prevent them from falling over.
4. Cook for 10 to 15 minutes, this really varies depending on the fire and where you placed the egg! You can tell when it is cooked by looking at the top, once it has turned fully opaque, it only needs a few more minutes to finish cooking.
5. With your leather gloves, carefully remove the eggs from the fire, and let them cool for an additional 10 minutes, until you can touch them with your bare hands without burning yourself.
6. Peel away the shell, sprinkle with pepper and salt to taste, and enjoy!

Charred Pepper

These fire roasted peppers pair perfectly with campfire eggs for breakfast after a night in the wild! These instructions use the Spicy Sautéed Pepper recipe from page 124.

Serves 6	20 minutes	Vegan	Gluten free

Ingredients:

12 Uncooked Spicy Sautéed Peppers, from page 124
1 cast iron pan, safe for fires
1 long clean stick
Leather gloves

> ### Game Guide
> *The Legend of Zelda: Breath of the Wild.*
> Spicy Pepper

Directions:

1. Prepare your cooking fire, see page 234. Prepare your peppers and ingredients from page 124, in a well oiled cast iron pan.
2. Place the pan directly onto the hot coals, and cook for about 10 minutes. It will take a few minutes for the pan to warm up, and then the peppers will cook quickly. Keep in mind they will continue cooking on the pan when you remove it from the fire. Poke the peppers with your stick to keep them from burning.
3. Remove from fire when they are softened but still brightly colored, the final result should still have a bit of crunch!
4. Take off the pan to serve, but allow to cool a little before eating! Enjoy!

Roasted Acorn

This is not a recipe for the faint of heart! Keep the fire going for hours to properly prepare fresh acorns, remove any trace of bitterness, and cinnamon roast to perfection!

Serves 4	2+ hours	Vegan	Gluten free

Ingredients:

1 pound acorns, about 2 to 3 cups* *(450 g)*
A hammer or nutcracker
A large fire safe pot, a cast iron dutch oven with lid is ideal
1 teaspoon vanilla extract *(5 ml)*
1/4 cup brown sugar *(110 g)*
1 teaspoon ground cinnamon *(2.6 g)*
1/4 teaspoon salt *(1.5 g)*
2 tablespoons maple syrup *(30 ml)*

Game Guide

The Legend of Zelda: Breath of the Wild.

Acorn

Directions:

1. Prepare your cooking fire, see page 234. Prepare your acorns by removing the caps and washing them throughly.
2. With a hammer or nutcracker, remove the acorns from their shells.
3. Add the acorns to the pot, and fill with water so it covers the acorns by a few inches. Nestle the pot into the coals of the fire, and cover. During the boiling process, keep the fire going on one side, adding logs as necessary, and periodically scrape the coals and ashes from the fire towards the pot.
4. Boil the acorns in water for 15 minutes, toss the water out, and more water, and repeat. Especially the first time you boil them, you may notice a few floating acorns. Toss them, in case they have gone bad. Repeat until the water is no longer brown.
5. Pour the water out. Add vanilla, brown sugar, cinnamon, salt, and maple syrup. Mix thoroughly, cover, and add the pot back to the edge of the fire.
6. Cook for an additional 10 minutes, stirring occasionally. Pour onto a plate, and allow to cool. Break them up as necessary, and enjoy!

*Collect them yourself from underneath mature oak trees in Autumn! This is a fun annual recipe, and can also be prepared indoors on a stove top if you wish.

Roasted Armoranth

Armoranth in The Legend of Zelda: Breath of the Wild look like artichokes! Artichokes bloom into vibrant purple flowers, much the same color, and when harvested for eating, are a lot like this armored bud. Here is a fire roasted artichoke recipe!

Serves 4	20 minutes	Vegan	Gluten free

Ingredients:

2 large artichokes
1 large lemon, juiced
3 tablespoons minced garlic *(27 g)*
2 teaspoons salt *(11 g)*
1/2 teaspoon ground thyme *(.75 g)*
1/2 teaspoon dried oregano *(.5 g)*
1/2 teaspoon dried rosemary *(.6 g)*
Ground black pepper
4 tablespoons oil, optional *(45 ml)*
1 cup water *(240 ml)*
Aluminum foil
Leather gloves

Game Guide

The Legend of Zelda: Breath of the Wild.

Armoranth

Directions:

1. Prepare your cooking fire, see page 234. Prepare your artichokes by cutting off the tops, and slice them in half. Spoon out the center fuzz.

2. Mix lemon juice, garlic, salt, thyme, oregano, and rosemary together. Fill the center cavities of the artichokes with this mixture, and rub the outsides as well. Finish by grinding fresh black pepper over them.

3. Sandwich the halves back together, and wrap each artichoke in a large sheet of aluminum foil, keeping the top open. Drizzle 2 tablespoons of oil *(30 ml)* into each, and shift it around so the oil coats all sides. Then add 1/2 cup water *(120 ml)* to each. Loosely twist the remaining aluminum foil together over the tops to create a long pointy handle.

4. Nestle the artichokes into the coals, and scrape the ashes around the sides. Cook for 15 to 20 minutes, then remove from the fire, and untwist the foil to cool. Pour out any excess water if necessary, and enjoy!

Roasted Bird

This succulent honey and lemon glazed roasted chicken dinner goes so well with Roasted Radishes on page 251! Always take care when handling raw poultry to prevent sickness.

4 servings	1 to 2 hours	Gluten free

Ingredients:

1 small whole chicken, about 5 pounds *(2.25 kg)*
3 sprigs of rosemary
1 tablespoon minced garlic *(9 g)*
2 lemons, 1 juiced, 1 peeled and roughly chopped
1/4 cup honey *(60 ml)*
3 tablespoons soy sauce *(45 ml)*
Aluminum foil
A meat thermometer
Leather gloves

Game Guide

The Legend of Zelda: Breath of the Wild.

Raw Whole Bird
or
Raw Bird Thigh
or
Raw Bird Drumstick

Directions:

1. Prepare your cooking fire, see page 234. Clean and prepare your bird for cooking, if you bought a whole chicken from the store, it should be prepared already.

2. Set the chicken in the center of a large piece of aluminum foil. Stuff with rosemary, garlic, and chopped lemon. Mix the honey, lemon juice from the other lemon, and soy sauce together, and drizzle it all over the chicken.

3. Wrap the chicken securely in aluminum foil. Repeat until you have wrapped it at least 5 layers thick, cinching the edges closed together. This will lock in the moisture, and prevent the skin from burning.

4. Nestle the chicken directly into the coals, and scrape them around the sides. Cook for about 1 hour, and carefully flip it every 15 minutes or so. You can check if it is done by inserting a thermometer directly through the foil and into the chicken, but try to insert it into the thickest part of the thigh. It's done at 165 degrees Fahrenheit *(75 degrees Celsius)*. Depending on your fire, it may take up to 2 hours to cook your chicken.

5. Remove from fire, and cut to verify that it is done all the way through. Allow to cool a bit before eating, and enjoy!

Roasted Carrot

These garlic roasted carrots are so easy, delicious, nutritious, and smell delightful! An ideal vegetable side to any campfire dinner!

Serves 4	20 minutes	Vegan	Gluten free

Ingredients:

12 actual whole baby carrots, with green stems*
2 tablespoons water *(30 ml)*
2 tablespoons basalmic vinegar *(30 ml)*
3 tablespoons minced garlic *(27 g)*
1/2 teaspoon ground thyme *(1 g)*
A small handful of parsley, finely shredded
Aluminum foil

Game Guide

The Legend of Zelda: Breath of the Wild.

Swift Carrot
or
Endura Carrot

Directions:

1. Prepare your cooking fire, see page 234. Trim the green tops of your carrots to 2 inches in length *(5 cm)*.

2. Put your carrots in the center of a large piece of aluminum foil, and pull up the sides to create a small open bowl. Mix water with vinegar, garlic, thyme, and parsley, then drizzle over your carrots. You may have to use your fingers to evenly distribute the garlic.

3. Seal the aluminum up over the carrots, to make a sturdy packet. Wrap it with an additional sheet of aluminum foil.

4. Place the packet directly into the coals, and scrape the coals around the sides.

5. Depending on the fire and carrots, they should be done roasting in about 15 minutes. They should be soft all the way through, a little charred, and succulent! Remove from fire, open the packets carefully as there will be very hot steam, and allow to cool before serving. Enjoy!

*Not the fake baby carrots that come in a bag, but actual whole carrots. If you can't find whole baby carrots, you can use whole adult carrots, but slice them in half lengthwise.

Roasted Durian

This recipe is an adventure in itself.

6 servings	1 hour	Vegan	Gluten free

Ingredients:

1 small ripe durian fruit
Gloves
Aluminum foil
Nose plugs, optional

Game Guide

The Legend of Zelda: Breath of the Wild.

Hearty Durian

Directions:

1. Prepare your cooking fire, see page 234.

2. While wearing your gloves, prepare the durian fruit by cutting off a bit of the top with the stem, and a bit of the bottom. Locate the seams down the sides, and score them with the knife before ripping them apart. Your goal is to separate the durian into its natural wedges.

3. Line the wedges back up to make it whole again. Wrap it in a large sheet of aluminum foil, then wrap again with a new sheet in the opposite direction. If your durian is particularly spiny and pokes through the foil, don't worry about it.

4. Nestle the durian into the coals, and cook for about 45 minutes, flipping every 15 minutes or so. If you haven't noticed a smell up to this point, you may begin to notice one now.

5. Remove from the fire, and carefully unwrap. Allow to cool until you can touch it, and serve the inner fruit. Enjoy!

Roasted Fish

There are so many ways to roast fresh fish over a fire! This recipe includes two methods, skewered whole and roasted on the coals, or filleted and roasted in aluminum packets.

| 2 servings | 20 minutes | Gluten free |

Ingredients:

2 small to medium sized fish,*
Aluminum foil or long and sturdy skewering sticks
Lemon and garlic salt to taste

Directions:

1. Prepare your cooking fire, see page 234.
2. Method 1: Skewered Whole. Prepare fish by cleaning and gutting it, but leave the skin on. Scrape coals into a raised flat area, then poke a skewer through each fish lengthwise. Place fish directly on the coals. Cook for about 5 minutes, flip, and cook for an additional 5 minutes.
3. Method 2: Aluminum foil fillets. Clean, gut, and fillet your fish. Place each fillet in the center of a large piece of foil, then season with lemon and garlic salt. You can slice the lemon thinly and lay on top, or just squeeze juice and pulp over each fillet. Seal up each fish in the foil like a candy wrapper, and twist the extra foil on each side into a spike as a handle. Lay directly on coals, and scrape coals around each fillet. Cook for 5 minutes, then turn and cook for another 5 minutes in the opposite direction.
4. 10 minutes total should be the perfect amount of time to cook the fish, but you can generally do 15 minutes without burning it. You'll know it's done when the flesh is flaky and opaque all the way through. Be careful of any bones, season with additional squeezed lemon and garlic salt if desired, and enjoy!

Game Guide

The Legend of Zelda: Breath of the Wild.

Any Porgy

or

Any Salmon

or

Any Carp

or

Any Bass

or

Any Trout

*I'm leaving the type of fish up to you! See the Game Guide for ideas, or catch what's available, and prepare for the method of cooking you've chosen.

Roasted Hydromelon

Here you will learn how to roast a watermelon over a fire without it ending in an explosion. Why? Because Link said so. Pairs well with the Seared Steak recipe on page 255.

| 6 servings | 25 minutes | Vegan | Gluten free |

Ingredients:
1 small round watermelon

Game Guide
The Legend of Zelda: Breath of the Wild.

Hydromelon

Directions:
1. Prepare your cooking fire, see page 234.
2. Figure out what side of your watermelon sits the most stable, then cut a hole in the opposite side, so that the hole is facing straight up when the watermelon sits. The hole should be at least 3 inches wide *(7 cm)*.
3. Nestle the watermelon directly in the coals, taking care that it will not topple. You can scrape the coals around it to keep it steady.
4. Roast for about 20 minutes, rotating a quarter turn every 5 minutes. It's done when it is hot all the way through.
5. Cut into thin slices and pair it with Seared Steak, enjoy!

Roasted Lotus Seeds

If you've never tried lotus seeds before, they are both nutritious and delicious, and taste almost like chestnuts! Crystallized with Goron Spice, these are an ideal hiking snack.

| 1 cup | 30 minutes | Vegan | Gluten free |

Ingredients:

1 cup dried lotus seeds *(32 g)*
A small fire safe cast iron pan with lid, well oiled
1 teaspoon Goron Spice, page 188, or curry powder *(2 g)*
1 tablespoon sugar *(12.5 g)*

Game Guide
The Legend of Zelda: Breath of the Wild.

Fleet-Lotus Seeds

Directions:

1. Prepare your cooking fire, see page 234.
2. Add your lotus seeds to your pan, cover, and nestle on the edge of your fire for low heat.
3. Roast for 10 to 20 minutes, stirring occasionally to check on their progress. They are done when hot and crispy, not burnt.
4. Remove from the fire, sprinkle in Goron Spice and sugar, then mix thoroughly. Cover and allow the heat from the pan to continue cooking the seeds for about 10 minutes.
5. Remove from the pan, and allow to cool before eating! Enjoy!

Roasted Mighty Bananas

You haven't lived until you've tried a Campfire Banana Boat or Banana Split!
This messy but delicious treat happens when a smore meets a banana!

| 4 servings | 20 minutes | Vegan | Gluten free |

Ingredients:

4 bananas, with peels on
Any or all of the following to taste:
Chocolate chips
Mini marshmallows
Chopped nuts
Shredded coconut
Small or sliced berries
Crushed graham crackers or cookies
Aluminum foil
Leather gloves
Spoons and napkins

Game Guide

The Legend of Zelda: Breath of the Wild.

Mighty Bananas

Directions:

1. Prepare your cooking fire, see page 234.
2. Lay a banana in the center of a large sheet of aluminum foil
3. Cut a lengthwise slit into the banana, from top to bottom, taking care not to go all the way through. Gently open it into a pocket.
4. Add any ingredients you desire into and on top of the banana. It's natural for it to overflow a bit.
5. Wrap the aluminum foil up over the top of the banana, and twist it closed into a spike. You can use this spike as a handle.
6. Repeat for all bananas.
7. Carefully nestle your bananas into the coals of the fire, and be sure to leave space between each banana, if you cook them all in a cluster the center ones won't cook properly. Cook for 8 to 10 minutes.
8. Remove carefully, and twist open the tops. Make sure to cool for a little, especially before giving to children. Eat with spoons, and enjoy!

Roasted Mighty Thistle

When Link gets hungry, even the thistles start to look appetizing.
See the note and guide at the bottom for finding and preparing the proper thistle!

| 2 servings | 10 minutes | Vegan | Gluten free |

Ingredients:
2 to 3 stalks of thistle with unopened flower buds, washed
Garlic salt, optional
Leather gloves

Game Guide
The Legend of Zelda: Breath of the Wild.
Mighty Thistle

Directions:
1. Prepare your cooking fire, see page 234.
2. Roast whole by the fire. You can stick them into the ground on the edge of your fire, not too close or they'll be scorched; or you can carefully hold them, with gloves, near the coals and spin them to cook the stalk and head evenly. Cook for about 3 to 7 minutes, until piping hot but just before it is about to burn.
3. Remove from fire and allow to cool until you can touch it.
4. To eat the stalk, you can break it in half and squeeze out the center core to eat. For the flower bud, sprinkle garlic salt first. It is much like trying to eat the heart of an artichoke, you'll dig through some layers, and then eat the soft parts. Enjoy!

*Particularly, you are looking for *Cirsium horridulum*, but don't worry, true thistles are not poisonous. That said, some people are allergic to thistle, and it can cause contact dermatitis. Please do your own research before cautiously proceeding with this recipe, and wear gloves.

Thistles generally grow in two year cycles, with older perennial plants becoming less edible. Ideally, you want to find a second year plant in the Spring. It will have sent up a flower stalk for the first time, and is at the height of its deliciousness. With spines removed, the leaves and inner core of the stalks are edible, in addition to the closed flower bud bottoms and roots. You can eat them raw or cooked.

Roasted Radish

Fire roasted radish, potato, and onion are the stars in this hearty recipe, which smells divine over a relaxing campfire after a day of adventuring.

Serves 4	20 minutes	Vegan	Gluten free

Ingredients:

1 pound baby radishes, quartered *(450 g)*
1 pound baby golden potatoes, chopped *(450 g)*
1/2 pound peeled pearl onions, halved *(225 g)*
3 tablespoons minced garlic *(27 g)*
1/2 cup fresh parsley, chopped, or 2 tbs dried *(30 g or 10 g)*
1 teaspoon ground thyme *(1.5 g)*
2 teaspoons salt, or to taste *(11 g)*
1 cup water, and more as needed *(240 ml)*
1 long spoon or ladle

Game Guide

The Legend of Zelda: Breath of the Wild.

Big Hearty Radish
or
Hearty Radish

Directions:

1. Prepare your cooking fire, see page 234. In a large fire safe pot with lid and handle, add all ingredients, and mix thoroughly.

2. Cover pot and nestle into the coals. Cook for 30 to 40 minutes, carefully adding more water and stirring as necessary to prevent sticking, until potatoes and radishes are soft all the way through.

3. Remove from fire, remove lid, being careful of steam, and allow to cool a bit before serving. Enjoy!

Roasted Tree Nut

Chestnuts roasting on an open fire! These soft and tender nuts, served still warm from the fire and sprinkled with cinnamon, are an ideal treat as dusk falls.

Serves 4	30 minutes	Vegan	Gluten free

Ingredients:

1 pound chestnuts,* rinsed with water and patted dry *(450 g)*
1 teaspoon cinnamon or pumpkin pie spice *(2.6 g)*
A long handled roaster, or fire safe cast iron pan

Game Guide

The Legend of Zelda: Breath of the Wild.

Chickaloo Tree Nut

Directions:

1. Prepare your cooking fire, see page 234.
2. Prepare your chestnuts by scoring an X into the flat side of each chestnut. Use a sharp knife and take care or wear gloves, it's so easy to slip while doing this. Scoring allows steam to escape the nut while it cooks, and if you do not do this, it will pop like popcorn, but with extreme violence, like an explosion.
3. Add the chestnuts to your roaster or pan. And place into the hottest coals of the fire. You will cook for about 25 minutes, but must flip the chestnuts at least once. With a roaster, this is simple. Just use the handle to shake up the nuts ever few minutes. With a cast iron pan, you can use a long stick to shake up the chestnuts, but you'll need to be more precise about making sure that each chestnut has been flipped.
4. When they are nearly done, you'll start to hear popping, and the shell will be peeling back from your scored X's. They may be slightly charred on the outside.
5. When they are done, pour them out on a flat surface to cool them, and when you can safely touch them, peel them while they are still warm. You'll remove the shell, and the fuzzy part will come off with it. Sprinkle the nuts with cinnamon or pumpkin pie spice, and serve immediately! Enjoy!

*Explosions. I'm writing this twice so you don't forget. Please score the flat sides of each of your chestnuts with a sharp knife, or they will explode. In terms of what kind of chestnuts, the Marroni variety is apparently more sweet and tender, but expensive. The Castagne variety is less expensive and still delicious.

Roasted Voltfruit

This sweet dragonfruit roast is charred from the fire,
sliced in half, and eaten directly out of the shell.

| Serves 4 | 20 minutes | Vegan | Gluten free |

Ingredients:
2 dragon fruit, rinsed and patted dry
Aluminum foil

Game Guide
The Legend of Zelda:
Breath of the Wild.
Voltfruit

Directions:
1. Prepare your cooking fire, see page 234.
2. With a knife, stab each dragon fruit in the side, to allow air to escape while it cooks.
3. Wrap each dragon fruit in aluminum foil, and place directly into the coals. Cook for 10 minutes, flip, and cook for an additional 10 minutes.
4. Remove from fire, and carefully remove from foil. Slice each dragon fruit lengthwise in half, and allow to cool for a few minutes.
5. Once you can hold it in your hands safely, serve with spoons and enjoy!

Roasted Wildberry

Crystallized with sugar and vanilla, these roasted berries go so well on top of the Roasted Mighty Bananas on page 249!

Serves 4	20 minutes	Vegan	Gluten free

Ingredients:

3 cups fresh mixed berries* *(150 g)*
3 tablespoons granulated sugar *(40 g)*
1/4 teaspoon ground dried vanilla or vanilla powder *(1 g)*
A small fire-safe pot, with lid

Game Guide

The Legend of Zelda: Breath of the Wild.

Wildberry

Directions:

1. Prepare your cooking fire, see page 234.
2. Gently mix all ingredients into your fire safe pot, then place in the coals at the edge of the fire, in low heat. Cook for 15 to 20 minutes, turning the pot occasionally. Remove if you smell the sugar burning.
3. Remove from fire, and cool uncovered for a few minutes. Serve on top of Roasted Bananas if desired, and enjoy!

*A mix of blackberries, raspberries, and strawberries is perfect here. The blackberries will stay mostly whole, while the raspberries and strawberries will soften and break apart.

Seared Steak

These simple steaks take on the smoky taste of the wood fire they are cooked on, just season with salt and pepper, and sear them under the open sky.

Serves 2	20 minutes	Gluten free

Ingredients:

2 filet mignon steaks, about 1 pound each *(16 oz each)*
1 teaspoon salt *(5.6 g)*
1/2 teaspoon freshly ground pepper *(.5 g)*
A fire pit cooking grate or grill
Oil and grate brush

Game Guide

The Legend of Zelda: Breath of the Wild.

Raw Gourmet Meat
or
Raw Prime Meat
or
Raw Meat

Directions:

1. Prepare your cooking fire, see page 234. Take your steaks out of the refrigerator and allow them to warm to room temperature for at least half an hour. Sprinkle salt and pepper onto both sides, and massage it in.
2. Scrape your coals together and flatten them, and place the cooking grate on top.
3. Brush your grate with oil, then when it's piping hot, lay the steaks on top. If the coals are good an hot, you should only need about 4 minutes of cook time per side. Cut into your steak to see if it is done to your specifications, 8 minutes total should be about medium or medium rare.
4. Remove from fire, and let rest for 5 minutes on a plate. Serve and enjoy!

Toasty Mushrooms

All kinds of toasty mushrooms can be roasted over an open fire! This guide identifies edible real life mushrooms, though they might be difficult to find, that match the ones found in The Legend of Zelda: Breath of the Wild! Refer to the Skewer Chapter on page 49, for the actual recipe, along with a guide to roasting skewers over an open fire on page 234.

Mushrooms:

Always do your own research, test for allergies, and correctly identify edible mushrooms before eating any!

Indigo Milk Caps, *Lactarius indigo,* as Chillshrooms.

Yellow Wart, *Amanita flavoconia,* as Endura Shrooms.

Black Truffle, *Tuber melanosporum,* as Hearty Truffles.

Grey Knight, *Tricholoma terreum*, as Ironshrooms.

Penny Bun, *Boletus Edulis*, as Razorshrooms.

Mauve Splitting Wax-Cap, *Humidicutis lewellinae,* as Rushrooms.

Werewere-Kokako, *Entoloma hochstetteri*, look exactly like Silent Shrooms, but the edibility is slightly questionable.

Parrot Toadstool, *Gliophorus psittacinus*, as Stamella Shrooms.

American Amanita, *Amanita jacksonii*, as Sunshrooms.

Game Guide

The Legend of Zelda: Breath of the Wild.

Chillshroom
or
Endura Shroom
or
Any Hearty Truffle
or
Ironshroom
or
Razorshroom
or
Rushroom
or
Silent Shroom
or
Stamella Shroom
or
Sunshroom
or
Zapshroom

Zapshroom, do not eat any mushroom that looks like a Zapshroom! I cannot find a variety that is safely edible. Both *Pluteus luteovirens* and *Leucocoprinus birnbaumii* look very similar, but neither are safe for consumption.

Breakfast

In Hyrule, it appears Link has two potential options for a hearty breakfast: omelets or crepes! Savory or Sweet! Most of the recipes in this chapter are for a single large breakfast, so be sure to multiply if you are cooking for more than one!

Crepes and Omelets

The crepe batters in this chapter require at least 1 hour of refrigeration. You can prepare them the night before for breakfast in the morning! There are two types of omelet recipes in this chapter, normal western breakfast omelets, and the Japanese westernized 'Omurice' style meal, which is served over rice!

Vegan or Vegan Curious Folk

For those of you who are vegan or plant based, don't worry! I've developed these recipes to translate easily into plant based fare, and they are just as delicious! You won't just be pushed into another plain tofu scramble recipe either!

There are two different Vegan Omelet Batter recipes included here, which can be used as an alternative for eggs in this chapter. Generally people have a strong preference for one vegan omelet batter over another; so don't worry if you don't like one, the other one might be for you!

Vegan Omelet Batter

Below is one of my two favorite vegan omelet recipes! Use this recipe in any of the omelet recipes in this chapter. They are crispy on the outside, fluffy on the inside!

Tofu Omelet Batter

1 serving	25 minutes	Vegan	Gluten free

Ingredients:
1/2 cup silken tofu, firm and patted dry *(8 oz or 225 g)*
1 tablespoon hummus *(15 ml)*
1/2 teaspoon arrowroot powder *(1.3 g)*
1 tablespoon nutritional yeast *(8.5 g)*
2 tablespoons water *(30 ml)*

Directions:
1. Preheat oven to 375 degrees Fahrenheit *(190 degrees Celsius)*, and oil an oven safe stove top pan.
2. Place all ingredients into a blender, and blend on high until consistent. Scrape down sides, and if necessary, add 1 or 2 tablespoons of water *(15 to 30 ml)* to achieve the consistency of raw eggs. Blend once more.
3. Add any additional ingredients from the other recipes in this chapter, then pour into the hot pan. Swirl to create an even and thin layer, and let cook for 4 minutes, until the edges start to crisp.
4. Transfer to the oven, and bake for 12 minutes, until it is no longer visibly wet. If you prefer a well done omelet, continue for a few more minutes, until it is golden or light brown.
5. Remove from oven, add any additional ingredients or garnishes, and carefully fold. Enjoy!

Vegan Omelet Batter

Below is one of my two favorite vegan omelet recipes! Use this recipe in any of the omelet recipes in this chapter. They are crispy on the outside, fluffy on the inside!

Chickpea Omelet Batter

1 serving	15 minutes	Vegan	Gluten free

Ingredients:

1 tablespoon ground flaxseed *(7 g)*
3 tablespoons boiled hot water *(45 ml)*
1/4 cup Chickpea Flour *(40 g)*
1/4 cup unsweetened vegan milk, almond works well *(60 ml)*
1 tablespoon nutritional yeast, necessary for flavor *(8.5 g)*

Directions:

1. Stir flaxseed and hot water together in a mixing bowl. Let sit for 5 minutes.
2. Add chickpea flour, vegan milk, and nutritional yeast to the mixing bowl with the flaxseed. Thoroughly mix until lumps are gone.
3. Substitute this vegan batter for eggs in the omelet recipes of this chapter. When cooking, make sure to evenly spread the batter into a thin layer. Enjoy!

Crab Omelet with Rice

A Japanese 'Omurice' style recipe, this features crab both within and on top!

1 serving	1 hour	Gluten free

Ingredients:

1 cup cooked rice *(200 g)*

1 tablespoon sesame oil *(15 ml)*

1 teaspoon garlic, minced *(3 g)*

1 tablespoon soy sauce *(15 ml)*

1 tablespoon ketchup, or Lon Lon Ketchup, page 274 *(15 ml)*

1/2 yellow onion, chopped

1/2 cup peas *(160 g)*

1/2 cup carrots, shredded *(110 g)*

2 eggs or vegan omelet batter, page 258

1/2 cup shredded crab

1 cooked crab leg or claw, optional garnish

Game Guide

The Legend of Zelda: Breath of the Wild.

Hylian Rice

Bird Egg

Rock Salt

Any Crab

Vegan- For a vegan version of this recipe, turn to the Omurice recipe on page 270, and for that ocean flavor, add a tablespoon of your favorite dried seaweed or nori.

Crab Omelet with Rice

Directions:

1. Prepare rice.
2. Oil your pan and preheat to medium high. Add garlic, sesame oil, soy sauce, ketchup, and onion. Cover and cook for 5 minutes, until onions are translucent.
3. Add peas, carrots, and shredded crab. Beat vigorously, then mix in rice, cover, and cook for 7 to 10 minutes, stirring occasionally to prevent sticking. Remove from heat.
4. Oil an omelet pan and preheat to medium high or high. In a mixing cup, beat two eggs. Once the pan is hot, pour the eggs into the pan. Let it sit for 30 seconds, then stir everything with a spatula to break it all up, before swiveling the pan so the raw egg batter settles evenly to cover the pan again. Wait for around 2 minutes, monitoring for when the bottom is firm enough to flip. Slip a spatula under the edges of the omelet, separating any parts that have stuck. When it is ready to flip, place the spatula underneath in the center of the omelet, raise, and flip the omelet back into the pan. Allow to cook for another minute or two, check to make sure that all of the egg has been cooked, and then remove from heat.
5. Arrange fried rice in a small hill on a plate, and slide omelet on top to cover the rice.
6. Garnish with a cooked crab claw or leg, and enjoy!

Mushroom Omelet

A mushroom stuffed omelet with a delectable creamy sauce! Serves one.

1 serving	20 minutes	Vegan	Gluten free

Ingredients:

Mushroom Stuffing and Sauce:

1 tablespoon oil *(15 ml)*

1/2 pound finely diced baby portobello mushrooms *(225 g)*

1 handful of tiny whole mushrooms

1/2 teaspoon basil, ground *(.5 g)*

1/2 teaspoon rosemary, ground *(.5 g)*

1/3 cup milk *(80 ml)*

1 teaspoon vegetable bouillon* *(3 g)*

1 teaspoon garlic, minced *(3 g)*

1 tablespoon all purpose flour *(10 g)*

Omelet:

2 eggs or vegan omelet batter, page 258

1 tablespoon water *(15 ml)*

1 teaspoon minced garlic *(3 g)*

1/4 cup your favorite cheese, grated, optional *(30 g)*

Garnish:

1 large mushroom, whole

Fresh spinach

Dried parsley

Game Guide

The Legend of Zelda: Breath of the Wild.

Any Mushroom
Bird Egg
Goat Butter
Rock Salt

Vegan- Use a milk alternative! Cashew or almond work well here.

*Better Than Bouillon: Seasoned Vegetable Base, or similar.

Mushroom Omelet

Directions:

1. Preheat a small saucepan to medium high, and add 1 tablespoon oil *(15 ml)*, a splash of water, chopped mushrooms, tiny whole mushrooms and 1 large garnish mushroom. Cover and cook for about 5 minutes, until mushrooms begin to wilt. Add basil, rosemary, milk, vegetable bouillon, garlic, and flour. Bring to a boil, cover, and cook for 10 minutes, stirring occasionally. If thickening is necessary, sprinkle more flour and continue cooking for a few more minutes, until desired thickness is reached. Decrease heat to very low.

2. Oil your omelet pan, and preheat to medium high. In a mixing bowl, beat eggs, water, and minced garlic together.

3. Oil an omelet pan and preheat to medium high or high. In a mixing cup, beat two eggs. Once the pan is hot, pour the eggs into the pan. Let it sit for 30 seconds, then stir everything with a spatula to break it all up, before swiveling the pan so the raw egg batter settles evenly to cover the pan again. Wait for around 2 minutes, monitoring for when the bottom is firm enough to flip. Slip a spatula under the edges of the omelet, separating any parts that have stuck. When it is ready to flip, place the spatula underneath in the center of the omelet, raise, and flip the omelet back into the pan.

4. Sprinkle cheese, if desired, onto the omelet, and allow to cook for another minute or two. Check to make sure that all of the egg has been cooked, and then slide flat onto a plate.

5. Pour most of your mushroom stuffing inside, then fold the omelet closed, and drizzle the rest of the mushroom sauce with tiny whole mushrooms on top.

6. Garnish with large mushroom and spinach on the side, with a sprinkling of parsley on top. Enjoy!

Omelet

The fabulous flip and fold, no frills omelet! As depicted in The Legend of Zelda: Breath of the Wild, it is optionally served with a side of tomatoes and spinach.

| 1 serving | 15 minutes | Vegan | Gluten free |

Ingredients:

1 tablespoon oil *(15 ml)*
2 eggs or vegan omelet batter, page 258
1 tablespoon water *(15 ml)*
1 teaspoon garlic, minced *(3 g)*
1/4 cup of your favorite cheese, grated, optional *(30 g)*

Game Guide

The Legend of Zelda: Breath of the Wild.

Bird Egg

Garnish:

1 tomato
1 cup spinach *(30 g)*
Freshly ground black pepper, to taste

Directions:

1. Oil your omelet pan, and preheat to medium high. In a mixing bowl, beat eggs, water, and minced garlic together.

2. Once your pan is hot, pour the mixture into the pan. Let it sit for 30 seconds, then stir quickly and swivel the pan so raw egg fluid is settled evenly to cover the pan again. Wait for around 2 minutes, monitoring for when the bottom is firm. Slip a spatula under the edges of the omelet, separating any parts that have stuck. After, place the spatula underneath in the center of the omelet, raise, and flip the omelet back into the pan.

3. Sprinkle the cheese if desired onto the omelet, and allow to cook for another minute or two. Check to make sure that all of the egg has been cooked, and then fold one side onto the other before sliding onto a plate.

4. Adorn your plate with the sliced tomato and spinach. Sprinkle black pepper on top if desired. Enjoy!

Vegetable Omelet

This omelet topped with hot salsa will jump start your day of questing!

1 serving	15 minutes	Vegan	Gluten free

Ingredients:

1 tablespoon oil *(15 ml)*
2 eggs or vegan omelet batter, page 258
1 tablespoon water *(15 ml)*
1 teaspoon garlic, minced *(3 g)*
1/4 yellow onion, finely chopped
1/4 red or yellow bell pepper, finely chopped
1/4 cup finely chopped green onion *(25 g)*
1/4 cup your favorite cheese, grated, optional *(30 g)*

Garnish:

1 tomato, sliced
1 cup spinach (30 g)
Salsa, hot sauce, or ketchup, Lon Lon Ketchup, page 274, to taste

Game Guide

*The Legend of Zelda:
Breath of the Wild.*

Any Vegetable, Herb, or
Flower
Bird Egg
Goat Butter
Rock Salt

Directions:

1. Oil your omelet pan, and preheat to medium high. In a mixing bowl, beat eggs, water, minced garlic, yellow onion, bell pepper, and green onion together.
2. Once your pan is hot, pour the mixture into the pan. Let it sit for 30 seconds, then stir quickly and swivel the pan so raw egg batter is settled evenly to cover the pan again. Wait for around 2 minutes, monitoring for when the bottom is firm. Slip a spatula under the edges of the omelet, separating any parts that have stuck. After, place the spatula underneath in the center of the omelet, raise, and flip the omelet back into the pan.
3. Sprinkle cheese, if desired, onto the omelet, and allow to cook for another minute or two. Check to make sure that all of the egg has been cooked, and then fold one side onto the other before sliding it onto a plate.
4. Adorn with sliced tomato and spinach, and top with salsa, hot sauce, or ketchup like The Legend of Zelda: Breath of the Wild model! Enjoy!

Plain Crepe

Topped with powdered sugar, fluffy and light, this crepe is a delight! Makes 2 to 3 crepes.

| ~2 servings | 15 minutes | Vegan | Gluten free |

Ingredients:

1/4 cup cold water *(60 ml)*
1/4 cup milk, vanilla almond milk works well *(60 ml)*
2 tablespoons butter or vegan butter, melted *(30 g)*
1/2 tablespoon brown sugar *(6 g)*
1 tablespoon maple syrup or Desma syrup, page 273 *(15 ml)*
1/2 cup all purpose flour *(75 g)*
1/4 teaspoon salt *(1.5 g)*

Game Guide

The Legend of Zelda: Breath of the Wild.

Fresh Milk
Cane Sugar
Tabantha Wheat
Bird Egg
Goat Butter

Garnish:

Powdered sugar
1 pad of butter
Optional Desma Syrup, page 273

Directions:

1. In a mixing bowl, combine all ingredients. Beat vigorously until a smooth texture is reached, then chill in the refrigerator for at least 30 minutes for fluffier crepes.
2. Oil and preheat a large pan to medium high, and add approximately 1/4 cup batter *(60 ml)* to the pan. Swirl to create a thin and even layer. Cook for 2 to 4 minutes, until top has bubbled and is dry, and then flip. Cook for an additional 2 minutes, check the bottom with your spatula, and remove when golden.
3. Garnish with a pad of butter, and a sprinkling of powdered sugar. Enjoy!

Honey Crepe

This energizing crepe, topped with coconut whip cream,
is a mainstay dish at both Outskirt Stable and Tarrey Town!

~2 servings   20 minutes   Vegetarian   Gluten free

Ingredients:

1/4 cup water *(60 ml)*
1/4 cup milk *(60 ml)*
2 tablespoons butter, melted *(30 g)*
1/2 tablespoon brown sugar *(6 g)*
1 tablespoon honey, or Desma syrup, page 273 *(15 ml)*
1/2 cup all purpose flour *(75 g)*
1/4 teaspoon salt *(1.5 g)*

Garnish:

Honey, or Desma Syrup, page 273 to taste
Coconut whip cream, page 172
Mint leaves
Powdered sugar

Game Guide

The Legend of Zelda: Breath of the Wild.

Fresh Milk
Bird Egg
Tabantha Wheat
Cane Sugar
Courser Bee Honey

Directions:

1. In a mixing bowl, combine all ingredients. Beat vigorously until a smooth texture is reached, then cover and refrigerate for at least 1 hour.
2. Oil and preheat a large pan to medium high.
3. Add approximately 1/4 cup *(60 ml)* batter to the pan. Swirl the pan to create a thin and even layer. Cook for 2 to 4 minutes, until top has bubbled and is dry, and then flip. Cook for an additional 2 minutes, check the bottom with your spatula, and remove when golden. Repeat this step until batter is gone.
4. Plate by folding each in half, and roll one side in toward the center to make a triangle shape. Garnish each with a drizzle of honey, a dollop of whipped cream, a sprinkle of powdered sugar, and a sprig of mint. Enjoy!

Vegan- Use vegan milk, soy creates good fluff, but sweetened almond milk is good too! Use your favorite vegan butter, and maple syrup instead of honey!

Wildberry Crepe

Wildberries appear to be a hybrid between raspberries and strawberries, so this recipe uses a mix! Makes 2 to 3 crepes.

~2 servings	1 hour	Vegan	Gluten free

Ingredients:

1/4 cup water *(60 ml)*
1/4 cup milk, vanilla almond milk works well *(60 ml)*
2 tablespoons butter or vegan butter, melted *(30 g)*
1/2 tablespoon brown sugar *(6 g)*
1 tablespoon maple syrup or Desma syrup, page 273 *(15 ml)*
1/2 cup all purpose flour *(75 g)*
1/4 teaspoon salt *(1.5 g)*

Game Guide

The Legend of Zelda: Breath of the Wild.

Wildberry
Fresh Milk
Cane Sugar
Tabantha Wheat
Bird Egg

Filling:

1/2 cup mixed small strawberries and large raspberries *(75 g)*
1 tablespoon sugar *(12.5 g)*
2 tablespoons water *(30 ml)*

Garnish:

Coconut whip cream, page 172, or similar
Powdered sugar
Optional Desma Syrup, page 273

Wildberry Crepe

Directions:

1. In a mixing bowl, combine all ingredients. Beat vigorously until a smooth texture is reached, then cover and refrigerate for at least 30 minutes for a fluffier crepe.
2. Clean and cut the tops off the strawberries. Then add berries, sugar, and water to the small saucepan. Increase heat to medium high, stir until brought to a boil, and then remove from heat when the berries are softened and hot, about 5 to 7 minutes.
3. Oil and preheat a large pan to medium high, and add approximately 1/4 cup batter *(60 ml)* to the pan. Swirl to create a thin and even layer. Cook for 2 to 4 minutes, until top has bubbled and is dry, and then flip. Cook for an additional 2 minutes, check the bottom with your spatula, and remove when golden. Fold in half, and plate with one side rolled up.
4. Garnish with an alternating pattern of whipped cream, strawberries, and raspberries, then drizzle with left over sauce! Enjoy!

Omurice

Fried rice with an omelet blanket on top, garnished with a cute ketchup design.
Adapted from the Fried Egg and Rice recipe on page 272,
this is Japan's favorite 'western' food, Omurice!

1 serving	1 hour	Vegan	Gluten free

Ingredients:

1 cup cooked rice *(200 g)*
1 tablespoon sesame oil *(15 ml)*
1 teaspoon garlic, minced *(3 g)*
1 tablespoon soy sauce *(15 ml)*
1 tablespoon ketchup *(15 ml)*
1/2 yellow onion, chopped
1/2 cup peas *(160 g)*
1/2 cup carrots, shredded *(55 g)*
3 eggs or vegan omelet batter, page 258
1 green onion, chopped
Ketchup, or Lon Lon Ketchup, page 274, for garnish

Gluten free- make sure that the soy sauce is gluten free!

Omurice

Directions:

1. Prepare rice.
2. Oil your pan and preheat to medium high. Add garlic, sesame oil, soy sauce, ketchup, and onion. Cover and cook for 5 minutes, until onions are translucent.
3. Add peas, carrots, one egg if desired. Beat vigorously to scramble, then add rice. Break up the rice, mix, cover, and cook for 7 to10 minutes, stirring occasionally to prevent sticking. Remove from heat, but keep it covered.
4. Oil your omelet pan and preheat to medium high. In a mixing cup, beat two eggs. Once the pan is hot, pour eggs into pan. Let sit for 30 seconds, then stir quickly and swivel the pan so the raw egg batter is settled evenly to cover the pan again. Wait for around 2 minutes, monitoring for when the bottom is firm. Slip a spatula under the edges of the omelet, separating any parts that have stuck. After, place the spatula underneath in the center of the omelet, raise, and flip the omelet back into the pan. Allow to cook for another minute or two, check to make sure that all of the egg has been cooked, and then remove from heat.
5. Arrange fried rice in a small hill on a plate, and slide the omelet flat on top to cover the rice.
6. With ketchup, draw a cute design, like a heart piece or Triforce, on top of the omelet! Enjoy!

Fried Egg and Rice

This dish is quick and delicious, best served steaming hot.

| 2 servings | 20 minutes | Gluten free |

Ingredients:

3 cups cooked rice *(550 g)*
1 tablespoon peanut oil* *(15 ml)*
1 teaspoon minced garlic *(3 g)*
2 teaspoons sesame oil *(10 ml)*
3 tablespoons soy sauce *(45 ml)*
1 yellow onion, chopped
3 eggs
2 tablespoons sesame seeds *(16 g)*
Fresh spinach, for garnish
Dried parsley, for garnish

Game Guide

The Legend of Zelda: Breath of the Wild.

Hylian Rice
&
Bird Egg

Directions:

1. Prepare rice.
2. Oil your pan with peanut and sesame oil, then preheat your pan to medium, cast iron works well here. Add garlic, soy sauce, and onion. Cover and cook for 5 minutes, until onions are translucent.
3. Add one egg and sesame seeds. Stir vigorously to lightly scramble, then add rice, mix again, cover and cook for 7 minutes.
4. In a separate pan, fry two eggs. The depiction in The Legend of Zelda: Breath of the Wild is over easy, but cook to your own preference.
5. Serve eggs atop beds of rice, garnish with a tuft of spinach on the side, and a sprinkle parsley on top. Enjoy!

Vegan- Replace the egg with fried tofu, or Vegan Omelet Batter on page 258. Or remove entirely for a simple side of fried rice, and top with stir fried vegetables!
Gluten free- Be sure to use gluten free soy sauce!

*Vegetable oil is fine if peanut oil isn't possible.

Desma Syrup

A peachy light syrup with a hint of cinnamon, ideal for drizzling over desserts or crepes!

| 2 cups | 20 minutes | Vegan | Gluten free |

Ingredients:

1 pound prepared peaches* *(16 oz or 450 g)*
1 1/2 cups water *(360 ml)*
1/4 cup confection sugar** *(40 g)*
1/8 teaspoon ground cinnamon *(.3 g)*
1 tablespoon cornstarch, optional for thickening *(8 g)*
2 tablespoons cold water, optional for thickening *(30 ml)*

Game Guide

Freshly-Picked Tingle's Rosy Rupeeland

10 Bum Peaches
5 Super Sweetcorn

Directions:

1. In a blender, combine peaches, water, sugar, and cinnamon until smooth.
2. Transfer to a large saucepan, and bring to a boil. Turn heat to low, and let simmer for 15 minutes, stirring occasionally to prevent sticking.
3. For a thin syrup for drizzling, you're done! Skip to step 5. If it looks too thin, follow the step 4 to thicken.
4. Combine 1 tablespoon *(15 ml)* cornstarch with a couple tablespoons of cold water, and mix until dissolved. A little at a time, pour into the peach syrup, and stir to combine. Bring to a boil once more, stirring until the syrup has thickened in a couple minutes!
5. Drizzle on top of crepes, desserts, or even savory dishes! Refrigerate in a sealed jar, but use within a couple weeks. Enjoy!

*Peaches should be skinned, pitted, and chopped. Alternatively, you can use frozen chopped peaches, as they will already be skinned!

**Taste and add more if you prefer a sweeter syrup!

Lon Lon Ketchup

This thick homemade ketchup is exactly what you want it to be. Customize it to be sweeter, spicier or saltier by mixing up your own unique Lon Lon blend!

1 cup	10 minutes	Vegan	Gluten free

Ingredients:

12 ounces of tomato paste, two 6 ounce cans *(350 ml total)*

1/3 cup of white vinegar *(80 ml)*

1 tablespoon of sugar *(12.5 g)*

1/2 teaspoon salt *(3 g)*

1/4 teaspoon black pepper *(.5 g)*

1/2 teaspoon mustard powder *(.5 g)*

1/2 teaspoon dried oregano *(.5 g)*

1/2 teaspoon onion powder *(1 g)*

1/2 teaspoon garlic powder *(1.5 g)*

1/4 teaspoon celery salt *(1.0 g)*

1/8 teaspoon ground all spice *(.25 g)*

A pinch of ground cayenne pepper, optional

Game Guide

Freshly-Picked Tingle's Rosy Rupeeland

2 Aroma Toadstools
5 Crisp Tomatoes
7 Sweet Potatoes

Directions:

1. Mix all ingredients into a bowl and mix until uniform.
2. Taste test. A little at a time, add additional spices, mix, and taste, until it's yours.
3. Serve or use in a recipe immediately, or store in a sealed container in the refrigerator, but use within a month. Enjoy!

The Introduction to Hyrulian Alchemy and Bartending

The following recipes are here due to the wild support of over 1500 Zelda and cooking fans from all over the world. Those who wished to be are named at the end of this cookbook! You made this entire book possible. The next chapter is for you. Thank you.

With and Without Alcohol

Every recipe in this chapter has a standard version, without alcohol, and some also include an alcoholic version. The alcoholic versions should be clearly marked, especially when children are present. When served in potion bottles, these drinks are very fun looking and tempting, so please keep them out of reach if necessary!

Hyrulian versus Hylian

Why is this titled Hyrulian and not Hylian? Hylian is a specific race of pointy eared people, whereas Hyrulian is a nationality and refers to all of the people living in Hyrule!

The Unofficial Legend of Zelda Drinkbook: The Guide to Hyrulian Alchemy and Bartending

You might notice this is just an 'Introduction', not a full compendium. One day, I hope to expand this 30 recipe drink chapter into a full Legend of Zelda themed drinkbook! I want to include aromatic loose leaf tea blends, more regional and seasonal drinks, milkshakes, cocktails, smoothies, chu jelly shots, boba teas, and more!

It would be a matching hardcover drinkbook, with much requested illustrations and color! If you enjoyed this cookbook and are in for another adventure, please look forward to a campaign launch date once the book is finished. You can sign up for a notification at theunofficiallegendofzeldacookbook.com if you want to!

Blue Potion

Celebrate a day of adventuring with this sweet, blue, and bubbly concoction, and restore your health and magic! Serve in potion bottles for authenticity.

1 serving	8 oz glass	Vegan	Gluten free

Standard:

1 tablespoon violet syrup* *(.5 oz or 15 ml)*
2 tablespoons blue curaçao syrup* *(1 oz or 30 ml)*
3/4 cup lemon lime soda *(6 oz or 180 ml)*
1 lemon wedge, squeezed
Ice, if you intend to drink immediately
A cocktail shaker and strainer
A funnel, if using potion bottles

Alcoholic:

1 tablespoon crème de violette *(.5 oz or 15 ml)*
2 tablespoons blue curaçao *(1 oz or 30 ml)*
3/4 cup champagne *(6 oz or 180 ml)*
1 lemon wedge per drink
Ice, if you intend to drink immediately

Game Guide

The Legend of Zelda
A Link to the Past
Ocarina of Time
Majora's Mask
The Wind Waker
Twilight Princess
A Link Between Worlds

Directions:

1. Add all liquid ingredients and lemon wedge juice to the shaker, and if you are drinking immediately, then fill the shaker with ice.
2. Shake to mix, then check the color in a clear glass. To darken, add more violet, for more blue, add more Curaçao, and shake again. Strain into your potion bottle.
3. Chill to serve later, or serve immediately and enjoy!

*For syrups, both alcoholic and non-alcoholic, I prefer the Monin brand flavored syrups! They have all sorts of lovely flavors and colors, and are both vegan and gluten-free!

Red Potion

Replenish your health with this classic cherry red and bubbly potion!
Serve in potion bottles for authenticity.

1 serving	8 oz glass	Vegan	Gluten free

Standard:

2 tablespoons grenadine syrup *(1 oz or 15 ml)*

~3/4 cup ginger ale *(7 oz or 210 ml)*

1 lime wedge, squeezed

Ice, if you intend to drink immediately

A cocktail shaker and strainer

A funnel, if serving in potion bottles

Alcoholic:

2 tablespoons grenadine syrup *(1 oz or 15 ml)*

2 tablespoons cherry vodka *(1 oz or 15 ml)*

3/4 cup ginger ale *(6 oz or 180 ml)*

1 lime wedge, squeezed

Ice, if you intend to drink immediately

Game Guide

The Legend of Zelda:
A Link to the Past
Ocarina of Time
Majora's Mask
The Wind Waker
The Minish Cap
Twilight Princess
Phantom Hourglass
Spirit Tracks
Skyward Sword
Hyrule Warriors

Directions:

1. Add all liquid ingredients and lemon wedge juice to the shaker, and if you are drinking immediately, then fill the shaker with ice.
2. Shake to mix, then check the color in a clear glass. For a brighter red, add more grenadine and shake again. Strain into your potion bottle.
3. Chill to serve later, or serve immediately and enjoy!

Green Potion

This sour green apple lemonade will surely recharge your magic meter!
Serve in potion bottles for authenticity.

| 1 serving | 8 oz glass | Vegan | Gluten free |

Standard:

2 tablespoons sweet and sour drink mix *(1 oz or 30 ml)*

2 tablespoons granny smith apple syrup *(1 oz or 30 ml)*

3/4 cup lemonade *(6 oz or 180 ml)*

A cocktail shaker and strainer

A funnel, if using potion bottles

Alcoholic:

2 tablespoon vodka *(1 oz or 30 ml)*

1 tablespoon sweet and sour drink mix *(.5 oz or 15 ml)*

1 tablespoon granny smith apple syrup *(.5 oz or 15 ml)*

3/4 cup lemonade *(6 oz or 180 ml)*

A cocktail shaker and strainer

A funnel, if using potion bottles

Game Guide

The Legend of Zelda:
A Link to the Past
Ocarina of Time
Majora's Mask
The Wind Waker
Hyrule Warriors
Cadence of Hyrule

Directions:

1. If drinking immediately, chill all ingredients beforehand.
2. Add all liquid ingredients to the shaker.
3. Shake to mix, then quickly check the color in a clear glass. For a greener color, add more granny smith apple syrup, and mix again. Strain into your potion bottle.
4. Chill to serve later, or serve immediately and enjoy!

Lon Lon Milkshake

This brown sugar and banana sweetened milkshake will have you whistling a nostalgic tune from the Ranch! Best served in Lon Lon Ranch milk bottles with a straw.

| 1 serving* | 12 oz glass | Vegan | Gluten free |

Standard:
2 tablespoons brown sugar *(25 g)*
1 ripe banana
1/2 cup milk, sweetened almond works well *(4 oz or 120 ml)*
1 cup vanilla ice cream, almond works well *(6 oz or ~240 ml)*

Alcoholic:
Add before blending:
2 tablespoons bourbon *(1 oz or 30 ml)*

Game Guide

The Legend of Zelda:
Ocarina of Time
Four Swords Adventures
The Minish Cap

This milkshake is inspired by Lon Lon Ranch, which makes an appearance in the above games!

Directions:
1. Add all ingredients to a blender. Blend on high until smooth and frothy. You may need to stop and push down the banana.
2. Pour into milk bottles, add a straw, and serve immediately! Enjoy!

*This is a large serving, but most blenders can still do two of these milkshakes at a time, if you want to double this recipe!

The Water of Life

You can choose between red cranberry or blue raspberry for this refreshing fruit infusion!
Make a pitcher, chill overnight, and serve in round potion bottles!

8 servings	64 oz pitcher	Vegan	Gluten free

Ingredients:

Red Water of Life:
8 cups cold water *(64 oz or 1920 ml)*
1 cup fresh cranberries *(120 g)*
1 small orange, sliced
2 tablespoons cranberry syrup, or to taste *(1 oz or 30 ml)*

Blue Water of Life:
8 cups cold water *(64 oz or 1920 ml)*
1 cup fresh raspberries *(120 g)*
1 small lemon, sliced
2 tablespoons blue raspberry syrup, or to taste *(1 oz or 30 ml)*

Game Guide
Zelda II: The Adventure of Link

The Legend of Zelda Game Watch

The Legend of Zelda: Valiant Comics

Link: The Faces of Evil

Zelda: The Wand of Gamelon

Directions:
1. Combine water and fruit in a large pitcher. Cover and chill overnight.
2. Check the color, and add syrup until desired red or blue color is achieved. Generally 2 tablespoons *(1 oz or 30 ml)* is enough, but for a sweeter or more vibrant water, add more!
3. Serve in round potion bottles, or in tall glasses over ice! Enjoy!

The Vodka of Life

Use these fruity vodka infusions to make spiked red orange cranberry or lemon blue raspberry Water of Life potions! You'll need a large sealable jar, strainer, and funnel.

| 25 servings | 32 oz jar | Vegan | Gluten free |

Alcoholic Ingredients:

Red Vodka of Life Infusion:
1 bottle of vodka *(25 oz or 750 ml)*
1 cup fresh cranberries, washed *(120 g)*
1 small washed orange, sliced

Blue Vodka of Life Infusion:
1 bottle of vodka *(25 oz or 750 ml)*
1 cup fresh raspberries, washed *(120 g)*
1 small washed lemon, sliced

Potion bottles:
Lemon lime soda
Cranberry syrup, to taste
Blue raspberry syrup, to taste

Directions:
1. In a clean 32 oz jar, add vodka and fruit. Seal tightly, and set in a room temperature cabinet, away from sunlight. Allow to infuse for 4 to 5 days.
2. Strain the infused vodka, and pour it into a newly clean jar. Store in the refrigerator. Use within 6 months. The blue water of life might look red, that's okay!
3. Add one shot of infused vodka to each potion bottle, then almost fill with icy chilled lemon lime soda.
4. Add either cranberry syrup, for red, or blue raspberry syrup, for blue, until desired color is achieved. Careful not to shake to mix, just swivel to combine.
5. Serve immediately, and enjoy!

The Fireproof Elixir

This black cherry and blackberry elixir will help you withstand heat like a Goron!
Serve in elixir bottles with small red tags for authenticity.

| 1 serving | 8 oz glass | Vegan | Gluten free |

Standard:

2 tablespoons blackberry syrup *(1 oz or 30 ml)*
3/4+ cup chilled black cherry soda *(7 oz or 210 ml)*
A pinch of edible shimmer dust per elixir
A funnel, if using potion bottles

Alcoholic:

2 tablespoons black vodka *(1 oz or 30 ml)*
2 tablespoons blackberry syrup *(1 oz or 30 ml)*
3/4 cup chilled black cherry soda *(6 oz or 180 ml)*
A pinch of edible shimmer dust per elixir
A funnel, if using potion bottles

Game Guide

The Legend of Zelda: Breath of the Wild.

Flame Guard Effect:

Fireproof Critter
Monster Part

Directions:

1. Add shimmer dust to each elixir bottle first.
2. Add all ingredients, except dust, to a large glass measuring cup, and stir gently.
3. Pour into elixir bottles, gently swivel to mix with shimmer dust.
4. Serve immediately, and enjoy!

Chateau Romani

This vintage milk is inspired by royal milk dessert teas! Combine fresh caramelized sugar with a dash of black tea and milk for a steamy cuppa, that also grants unlimited magic! Serve in Chateau Romani milk jars for an authentic Milk Bar look!

2 servings	8 oz mugs	Vegan	Gluten free

Standard:
1 tablespoon water *(.5 oz or 15 ml)*
1/4 cup white granulated sugar *(50 g)*
2 cups milk, sweetened almond milk works well *(475 ml)**
2 teabags of simple black tea**

Game Guide

The Legend of Zelda: Majora's Mask

Hyrule Warriors Legends

Alcoholic:
Add before blending:
2 tablespoons Baileys Irish Cream or Baileys Almande Almondmilk liqueur *(1 oz or 30 ml)*

Directions:
1. Add water and sugar to sauce pan on medium to medium high heat. Monitor for 4 to 6 minutes as it melts, bubbles, then caramelizes. Do not stir, simply wait for the sugar to melt, and swivel the pan if absolutely necessary. Wait until it is brown, thick, and syrupy, and stay with it the whole time. If it begins to burn, take it off the heat immediately.
2. Add milk and tea bags directly to the sauce pan, stay on medium to medium high heat. Now you can stir to fully dissolve the caramelized sugar. Do not boil, lower the heat if necessary to keep it just below boiling for 2 to 3 minutes, stirring the whole time. Boiling it can make the milk taste different, and can bitter the tea.
3. Serve immediately in heat safe Chateau Romani labeled milk jars, and enjoy!

*If you prefer less sweet, use unsweetened milk or 3 cups *(700 ml)* instead.
**You can also prepare this using loose leaf black tea, just use a tea strainer ball.
Vegan- make sure to use both almond milk and Baileys Almande Almondmilk liqueur.

The Chilly Elixir

This icy blue coconut blended lemonade is exactly what you need to trek across the desert! This slushie is a bit difficult to funnel into potion bottles, but do it anyway and add a white tag and a blue cork for an authentic Chilly Elixir!

| 1 serving | 8 oz glass | Vegan | Gluten free |

Standard:

1/4 cup lemonade *(2 oz or 60 ml)*

1/4 cup puréed coconut* *(60 ml)*

2 tablespoons fresh lime juice *(1 oz or 30 ml)*

2 tablespoons Blue Curaçao syrup *(1 oz or 30 ml)*

2 cups cubed ice *(480 ml)*

A funnel, if serving in potion bottles

Game Guide

The Legend of Zelda: Breath of the Wild.

Heat Resistance Effect:

Chilly Critter
Monster Part

Alcoholic:

Add before blending:

2 tablespoons white coconut rum *(1 oz or 30 ml)*

Directions:

1. Blend everything together until the slush is smooth. You can spoon a little at a time through a funnel to serve in potion bottles, or simply pour into a glass!

2. Serve with a straw, and enjoy!

*You can generally find this in the frozen aisle, or you can make it yourself by blending the milk and flesh of a coconut together with a dash of sugar!

Noble Pursuit

This tropical piña colada style blend will keep you cool while you bask at The Noble Canteen! Be sure to use ice fresh from the Northern Icehouse.

2 servings	10 oz glasses	Vegan	Gluten free

Standard:

1 cup cream of coconut *(8 oz or 240 ml)*
1 1/2 cups fresh ripe chopped pineapple *(250 g)*
1 teaspoon vanilla extract *(5 ml)*
2 to 3 cups cubed ice *(480 ml to 720 ml)*
2 wedges of pineapple, for garnish
2 maraschino cherries, for garnish
2 bendy straws and umbrellas, for garnish

Alcoholic:

Add before blending:
2 tablespoons white rum *(1 oz or 30 ml)*

Directions:

1. Blend coconut cream, pineapple, vanilla extract, and ice together until creamy and smooth. Stop to push down pineapple chunks if necessary.
2. Pour into two fancy glasses.
3. Garnish with a wedge of pineapple on the rim of each glass, a maraschino cherry, and an umbrella. Serve with a bendy straw, and enjoy!

Game Guide

The Legend of Zelda: Breath of the Wild.

A Noble Pursuit from The Noble Canteen is the heart of the The Perfect Drink quest, for the Misae Suma Shrine in the East Barrens.

*For a Yiga Clan spin on this drink, turn to page 15 for the Yiga Pursuit.

The Guardian Potion

This light pink, shimmering, and opalescent concoction could help shield you from damage, but don't count on it. Serve in cylindrical potion bottles for authenticity!

| 1 serving | 8 oz glass | Vegan | Gluten free |

Standard:

2 tablespoons rose syrup *(1 oz or 30 ml)*
1 tablespoon fresh lemon juice *(.5 oz or 15 ml)*
3/4+ cup white grape juice *(7 oz or 210 ml)*
A pinch of light pink or white edible glitter
A funnel, if serving in potion bottles

Game Guide

The Legend of Zelda: Skyward Sword.

Alcoholic:

3/4+ cup rosé wine, instead of white grape juice *(7 oz or 180 ml)*

Directions:

1. If you are going to serve right away, chill your potion bottles and ingredients.
2. Add everything but the white grape juice and glitter directly to your potion bottle.
3. Add a small pinch of glitter to the potion bottle. It's easier to do this without the funnel.
4. Fill the bottle nearly full with white grape fruit juice. You want to leave a little air at the top so you can mix the contents more easily. Cork your bottle firmly, and keeping your thumb over the cork, gently shake and swivel to mix.
5. Serve immediately, or keep chilled. The glitter will settle over time, so just gently shake it up again to get that lovely shimmer effect again! Enjoy!

The Electro Elixir

This tangy, sweet, and blended icy concoction is electrifying on a hot summer day!
Serve in an elixir bottle with a gold tag and mud green cork for authenticity!

1 serving	8 oz glass	Vegan	Gluten free

Standard:

1 tablespoon granny smith apple syrup *(.5 oz or 15 ml)*
1 tablespoon fresh lime juice *(.5 oz or 15 ml)*
1/4 cup sweet and sour drink mix *(2 oz or 60 ml)*
1 cup cubed ice *(240 ml)*

Alcoholic:

Add before blending:
2 tablespoons tequila *(1 oz or 30 ml)*

Game Guide

The Legend of Zelda: Breath of the Wild.

Electricity Resistance Effect:

Electro Critter
Monster Part

Directions:

1. Add ingredients in order to a blender, and blend until smooth.
2. Patiently funnel into potion bottles, or pour into a glass. Tapping is helpful with the potion bottles.
3. Serve with a straw, and enjoy!

The Gold Potion

This sparkling metallic gold drink will awe your party of adventurers!
Serve in mini cauldrons or mortar and pestle vessels for authenticity.*

1 serving	8 oz glass	Vegan	Gluten free

Standard:

2 tablespoons butter pecan syrup *(1 oz or 30 ml)*
3/4 to 1 cup apple cider** *(7 oz or 210 ml)*
A pinch of gold edible glitter

Game Guide
BS The Legend of Zelda:
Ancient Stone Tablets.

Alcoholic:

Add before mixing:
1 tablespoon straight bourbon whiskey *(.5 oz or 15 ml)*
1 tablespoon cinnamon flavored whiskey *(.5 oz or 15 ml)*

Directions:

1. Add all ingredients to your chosen vessel, and simply stir to mix! Stir 7 times clockwise, and 1 time counterclockwise, repeat until glitter and syrup are consistent throughout.
2. Serve immediately, and enjoy!

*First, you can buy cauldron shaped mugs, and I think that is ideal for this recipe! Second, while serving in a cauldron is more authentic, you won't get the full effect of this beautiful shimmering potion, which is best admired through a clear glass that you can shake up! I serve it in spherical potion bottles instead. Since this is inspired from an older entry in the series, not many know what it is supposed to look like anyway!

**First, you can serve this drink hot or cold! Heat the apple cider up on the stove top first for hot, or chill it for a few hours for cold. I love this served hot in the late fall! Second, this drink is a bit sweet for some people! If you find that is the case, I think the best solution is adding a shot of espresso, or you can water it down a little bit while adding a pinch of cinnamon!

The Spicy Elixir

This spicy habanero, lime, orange, and tomato elixir will help you brave the cold!
Serve in an elixir bottle with a brown tag and a dark red cork for authenticity!

| 1 serving | 8 oz glass | Vegan | Gluten free |

Standard:

2 tablespoons habanero lime syrup *(1 oz or 30 ml)*
2 tablespoons orange juice *(1 oz or 30 ml)*
1/2 cup bloody mary mix *(4 oz or 120 ml)*
Celery salt
Black pepper
Tabasco, to taste
Ice, small enough to fit into your potion bottles, or crushed
Funnel, if serving in potion bottles

Alcoholic:

Add before mixing:
2 tablespoons vodka *(1 oz or 30 ml)*

Directions:

1. If serving immediately, chill all ingredients and potion bottles beforehand.
2. Fill 8 oz potion bottles less than half way with ice, then add habanero lime syrup, orange juice, and bloody mary mix. Then add a small pinch of celery salt and black pepper, and Tabasco if you want a kick!
3. Cork, and with your thumb over the cork, shake to mix.
4. Serve with a straw immediately, and enjoy!

Game Guide

The Legend of Zelda:
Breath of the Wild.

Cold Resistance Effect:

Spicy Critter
Monster Part

Secret Medicine

This mysterious blood orange and ginger iced black tea is sure to pep you up! Unlike the game, please drink this potion instead of rubbing it on your body, as Crazy Tracy advises. Serve in a long necked volumetric flask for authenticity!

| 1 servings | 8 oz glass | Vegan | Gluten free |

Standard:

Blood orange purée*
1 pinch of ground ginger or less**
1 lemon wedge, squeezed
3/4+ cup fresh brewed black tea, sweetened to taste *(7 oz or 210 ml)*
Ice
A funnel, if serving in potion bottles

Alcoholic:

Add before mixing:
2 tablespoons whiskey *(1 oz or 30 ml)*

Directions:

1. Fill a large pitcher with ice, then add all ingredients. Stir rigorously to combine for a minute or two.
2. When the drink is icy cold, pour into your volumetric flask.
3. Serve immediately, and enjoy!

Game Guide

The Legend of Zelda: Link's Awakening.

*If using the Monin brand purée add 1 or 2 tablespoons *(.5-1 oz or 15-30 ml)*. If fresh, squeeze a ripe blood orange, and add 2 to 3 strained tablespoons *(1-1.5 oz or 30-45 ml)*.

**This is the secret ingredient of Secret Medicine! Add only a little bit at a time. Ground ginger varies widely in concentration, and can be too powerful for some.

Fairy Tonic

This delightfully pink and sparkling potion is the perfect pick me up!
If possible, serve in fairy wing adorned potion bottles for authenticity!

| 1 serving | 8 oz glass | Vegan | Gluten free |

Standard:

2 tablespoons Monin Black Raspberry Syrup *(1 oz or 30 ml)*
3/4 to 1 cup lemon lime soda *(7 oz or 210 ml)*
A pinch of light pink edible glitter
A funnel, if serving in potion bottles

Game Guide

The Legend of Zelda: Breath of the Wild.

Restore Hearts Effect:

Fairy*

Alcoholic:

3/4 to 1 cup sparkling champagne, instead of soda *(7 oz or 210 ml)*

Directions:

1. If serving immediately, chill ingredients and potion bottle beforehand.
2. Add ingredients in order to potion bottle, and swirl to mix.
3. Serve immediately or chill until serving, and enjoy!

*While it appears that fairy is an ingredient for this particular potion, fear not! No fairies are harmed in the creation of Fairy Tonics! They are simply using their power to help you create a potion, not being consumed.

The Enduring Elixir

A new double recipe, definitely made from frog legs and monster parts!
Serve in an elixir bottle with orange tag for authenticity!

1 serving	8 oz glass	Vegan	Gluten free

Standard:

1/2 ripe kiwi, scooped out of the peel
3/4+ cup lemon lime soda *(7 oz or 210 ml)*
A couple ice cubes
A funnel, if serving in potion bottles

Alcoholic:

Add before mixing:
Use chardonnay instead of soda
1 tablespoon white sangria mix *(.5 oz or 15 ml)*

Game Guide

The Legend of Zelda: Breath of the Wild.

Extra Stamina Effect:

Enduring Critter
Monster Part

Directions:

1. If serving immediately, chill all ingredients before hand.
2. Add all ingredients, except soda, to blender. Blend until smooth.
3. Add soda and stir until well incorporated.
4. Pour into potion bottles, serve with a straw, and enjoy!
5. Serve immediately, and enjoy!

The Revitalizing Potion

This magically color changing and shimmering potion changes from dark blue to purple to pink, right before your eyes! No bugs! Serve in cylindrical potion bottles for authenticity!

| 1 serving | 8 oz glass | Vegan | Gluten free |

Standard:

2 flowers of butterfly pea tea*
1/2 cup boiling water *(4 oz or 120 ml)*
Ice cube tray
1 tablespoon freshly squeezed lemon juice *(.5 oz or 15 ml)*
1 tablespoon white granulated sugar *(.5 oz or 15 ml)*
A pinch of light pink edible glitter
1/3 cup club soda *(2.7 oz or 80 ml)*
A funnel, if serving in potion bottles

Game Guide
The Legend of Zelda: Skyward Sword.

Alcoholic:

Add before mixing:
2 tablespoons gin *(1 oz or 30 ml)*

Directions:

1. Prepare magic ice cubes before hand by pouring boiling water over butterfly pea tea, stirring, and allowing to steep for 4 minutes. Pluck out or strain out the flowers, then pour the tea into your ice cube tray and freeze.
2. Add lemon juice, sugar, and pink glitter into potion bottle, then gently add club soda, and swivel to mix.
3. Retrieve your ice cubes, and crush so you fit them into your potion bottle. You can lightly blend to crush, place in a bag and use a hammer, or add to a cocktail shaker and crush with a cocktail muddler.
4. Add the ice to the potion bottle, and serve immediately! The color changing will begin right away, and will continue as the ice melts! You can shake the bottles for a magically shimmering and colorful effect! Enjoy!

*This is where our naturally vibrant and color changing magic comes from!

Great Fairy's Tears

Toast the great fairies with this desert pear flavored and rejuvenating drink!
Serve in a decorative great fairy bottle with cork for authenticity!

| 1 serving | 8 oz glass | Vegan | Gluten free |

Standard:
2 tablespoons desert pear syrup *(1 oz or 30 ml)*
1/2 cup fresh lemonade *(4 oz or 120 ml)*
1/3 cup sparkling water *(3 oz or 80 ml)*
A funnel, if serving in potion bottles

Game Guide
The Legend of Zelda:
Twilight Princess
Hyrule Warriors Legends

Alcoholic:
Use sparkling white wine instead of sparkling water.

Directions:
1. If serving immediately, chill all ingredients before hand.
2. Pour all ingredients into potion bottle, and swivel to mix.
3. Serve immediately and enjoy!

The Hasty Elixir

This blue raspberry and vanilla cream elixir is sparkling with glitter, and exactly what you need to go fast! Serve in an elixir bottle with a yellow tag for authenticity.

1 serving	8 oz glass	Vegan	Gluten free

Standard:

2 tablespoons blue raspberry syrup *(1 oz or 30 ml)*

A pinch of white edible glitter

3/4+ cup vanilla cream soda* *(7 oz or 210 ml)*

A funnel, if serving in potion bottles

Alcoholic:

2 tablespoons blue raspberry syrup *(1 oz or 30 ml)*

2 tablespoons vanilla vodka *(1 oz or 30 ml)*

A pinch of white edible glitter

3/4 cup vanilla cream soda *(6 oz or 180 ml)*

Game Guide

The Legend of Zelda: Breath of the Wild.

Speed Up Effect:

Hasty Critter
Monster Part

Directions:

1. If serving immediately, chill ingredients before hand.
2. Pour ingredients into your serving container, and swivel to mix.
3. Serve immediately, and enjoy!

*Try to find one that is clear, not yellow, for a more vibrant blue!

Death Mountain Muddy Milkshakes

These Goron inspired chunky, chocolaty, rocky road milkshakes will really get you rolling! Best served with a spoon.

| 1 serving | 12 oz glass | Vegan | Gluten free |

Standard:

Mini marshmallows
Mini chocolate chips
Chopped walnuts or almonds*
Crushed cookies**
1 cup chocolate ice cream, coconut is great here *(240 ml)*
1/2 cup milk*** *(120 ml)*

Game Guide

Death Mountain is an iconic part of The Legend of Zelda series, and features in a majority of its games!

Optional:

Add a shot of espresso for a coffee twist on this milkshake!

Directions:

1. The secret to a true muddy milkshake is to blend by hand! If you use a real blender, the chunks are too uniform! Use about 1 cup of ice cream (240 ml) and 1/2 cup milk (120 ml) per milkshake, and add additional ingredients to taste!
2. Add all ingredients except milk into a large bowl, and with a wooden spoon, begin mixing them together. Add the milk, and espresso if you desire, a little at a time while you mix, if you add it all at once, it's easy to splash it everywhere while you're mixing. It's done when the chunks are pretty evenly distributed, and the milk is mixed through.
3. Spoon the milkshakes into glasses, and serve immediately with a spoon. Enjoy!

*In case neither of these work due to allergies, this recipe is still wonderful without.
**Oreos are great, traditional chocolate chip cookies or wafers work too!
***My recommendation is to go with whatever milk your ice cream is made out of. Coconut ice cream, coconut milk. Almond ice cream, almond milk.

The Hearty Elixir

This stone fruit black tea is so delicious served over ice,
but is more authentic when served from elixir bottles with light brown tags!

| 1 serving | 8 oz glass | Vegan | Gluten free |

Standard:
2 tablespoons stone fruit syrup* *(1 oz or 30 ml)*
2 tablespoons orange juice *(1 oz or 30 ml)*
3/4 cup chilled black tea *(6 oz or 180 ml)*
Ice
A funnel, if served in potion bottles
A cocktail shaker and strainer

Alcoholic:
Add before mixing:
2 tablespoons white rum *(1 oz or 30 ml)*

Directions:
1. If serving in a potion bottle, add syrup, juice, tea, and ice to a cocktail shaker. Shake rigorously, then strain into potion bottle.
2. If serving over ice, fill a glass with ice, add just syrup, juice, and tea to a cocktail shaker. Shake rigorously, then pour into the glass filled with ice.
3. Serve immediately with a straw, and enjoy!

Game Guide

The Legend of Zelda:
Breath of the Wild.

Extra Hearts Effect:

Hearty Critter
Monster Part

*Stone fruit meaning fruit that contain stone pits, like peaches! You can use peach, apricot, or dark cherry syrup in this recipe, or purchase stone fruit syrup itself, which is often a mix of all three.

Monster Extract

This Monster Extract, unlike the dye recipes on page 173, is a smoothie!
Violently purple, lumpy, and delicious!

| 1 serving | 8 oz glass | Vegan | Gluten free |

Standard:

3/4 cup frozen blueberries *(100 g or 180 ml)*
1 sliced banana, frozen
1/3 cup frozen pineapple chunks *(45 g or 80 ml)*
1/2 cup sweetened vanilla almond milk *(4 oz or 120 ml)*

Game Guide

The Legend of Zelda: Breath of the Wild.

Monster Extract

Alcoholic:

Add before mixing:
2 tablespoons rum *(1 oz or 30 ml)*

Directions:

1. Add all ingredients to a blender, and blend just until purple color is uniform! Leaving some chunks behind is preferable.
2. Serve immediately with a thick straw, and enjoy!

The Mighty Elixir

A new double recipe, this orange drink might up your attack and also tastes delicious!
Serve in elixir bottles with yellow tags for authenticity!

1 serving	8 oz glass	Vegan	Gluten free

Standard:

1/2 cup sparkling white grape juice *(4 oz or 120 ml)*
1/4 cup fresh pressed carrot juice *(2 oz or 60 ml)*
3 tablespoons orange tangerine syrup *(1.5 oz or 45 ml)*
A funnel, if serving in potion bottles

Alcoholic:

Replace grape juice with champagne
Add 1 tablespoon triple sec before mixing *(.5 oz or 15 ml)*

Game Guide

The Legend of Zelda:
Breath of the Wild.

Attack Up Effect:

Mighty Critter
Monster Part

Directions:

1. Add sparkling grape juice to your glass first, then stir in carrot juice and orange tangerine syrup. Swivel and stir until the liquid is uniform.
2. Serve immediately, and enjoy!

Tingly Power Up Potion

This raspberry mint concoction will give you tingles, what more can I say?
Serve in a tingly potion bottle for authenticity.

| 1 serving | 8 oz glass | Vegan | Gluten free |

Standard:

4 fresh raspberries
4 fresh mint leaves
2 tablespoons grenadine syrup *(1 oz or 30 ml)*
1 tablespoon fresh lemon juice *(.5 oz or 15 ml)*
3/4 cup ginger ale *(6 oz or 180 ml)*
A cocktail shaker, with a muddler
A funnel, if serving in potion bottles

Game Guide

Freshly-Picked Tingle's Rosy Rupeeland

3 Minced Meat
2 Ground Shell*

Alcoholic:

Add when you add the grenadine syrup:
2 tablespoons dry gin *(1 oz or 30 ml)*

Directions:

1. Add raspberries and mint leaves to the cocktail shaker, and muddle them. Simply mash them a few times with the muddler.
2. Add the grenadine syrup and lemon juice, muddle again.
3. Pour in the ginger ale, cap, and overturn a few times to combine.
4. Strain into potion bottle, serve immediately, and enjoy!

*You'll notice a lack of minced meat and ground shells in this recipe, I am terribly sorry. You are welcome to add them.

Moka Chai's Mocha Chai

Inspired by Chai or Moka, depending on the translation, a character in Mama's cafe in The Legend of Zelda: The Minish Cap! Here is a recipe for loose leaf chai tea! This recipe makes about 12 cups of tea at 2 teaspoons per cup!

12 servings	8 oz mug	Vegan	Gluten free

Ingredients:

3/4 tablespoon cacao husks *(~12ml)*
1/4 tablespoon ground cloves *(.5 g)*
1 stick of cinnamon
1/2 teaspoon ground black peppercorn *(1 g)*
1 teaspoon dried ginger *(1 g)*
1/4 cup loose leaf black tea* *(60 ml)*
Honey or agave for sweetener**

Game Guide

The Legend of Zelda: The Minish Cap.

Chai, in the English version, and Moka, in the Japanese version, inspired this Mocha Chai recipe!

Directions:

1. Add all spices, without the tea, to a blender or coffee grinder, and coarsely grind. Ideally, you want a good mix of chunky and fine, not a consistent powder. I recommend blending for a second or two, stopping to sift and see if you like it, and repeating until you reach a balance.
2. Pour spices into a bowl, and then add your loose leaf black tea. Sift it together until well mixed.
3. Store in a sealed container.
4. To make tea, use freshly boiled water *(212 degrees Fahrenheit or 100 degrees Celsius)*, and steep 2 teaspoons of your loose leaf Mocha Chai for every cup *(8 oz or 240 ml)* of water. Steep for 5 minutes, then remove loose leaf. Stir in sweetener if desired, then enjoy!

*Use a simple loose leaf black tea, with no additives.
**Just a little bit of sweet can help make this spicy tea pop!

Red Chu Jelly

This strawberry and jalapeño red blended smoothie is as explosive as you want it to be! The jelly preserve version can be found on page 132!

| 1 serving | 12 oz glass | Vegan | Gluten free |

Ingredients:
1/2 cup cranberry juice* *(4 oz or 120 ml)*
2 cups frozen strawberries *(300 g)*
1/2 an avocado
1 lemon wedge, squeezed
1 small red jalapeño**
Agave drizzle, to taste
Jalapeño top, for garnish

Game Guide
The Legend of Zelda Series.

Drops from Red Chus or Chuchus, and Fire Chuchus. Can also be made in The Legend of Zelda: Breath of the Wild by exposing Chuchu Jelly to fire.

Directions:
1. Add all ingredients except agave to a blender, and blend on high until smooth. Taste test, if it's a bit too sour, add a drizzle of agave and blend again until it's sweetened to your liking!
2. Garnish with jalapeño top and serve with a straw. Enjoy!

*I use unsweetened, but as a heads up, it is pretty sour.

**I cut off a good portion of the top, to use as a garnish, then toss the whole thing in. If you want a smaller kick, split it and take out all of the seeds before tossing it in. If the idea of putting a jalapeño in a smoothie frightens you, maybe don't do it.

Yellow Chu Jelly

This lemon yellow smoothie is electrifying, and high in citrus!
The jelly preserve version can be found on page 133!

1 serving	12 oz glass	Vegan	Gluten free

Ingredients:

1 orange, peeled and cut up into chunks
1/2 a lemon, peeled
1 frozen banana
1/2 cup orange juice *(4 oz or 120 ml)*
1/2 cup sweetened almond milk *(4 oz or 120 ml)*
1/2 cup of cubed ice *(120 ml)*
Lemon wedge, for garnish

Game Guide

The Legend of Zelda Series.

Drops from Yellow Chus or Electric Chuchus. Can also be made in The Legend of Zelda: Breath of the Wild by exposing Chuchu Jelly to electricity. In The Legend of Zelda: Twilight Princess, it can be used as Lantern Oil.

Directions:

1. Add all ingredients to a blender, and blend on high until smooth. Taste test, and if it's a bit too sour, add a bit more almond milk and blend again until it's sweetened to your liking!
2. Garnish with lemon wedge and serve with a straw. Enjoy!

Green Chu Jelly

This granny smith apple green blend is the perfect good morning smoothie!
The jelly preserve version can be found on page 134!

1 serving	12 oz glass	Vegan	Gluten free

Ingredients:

2 cups spinach *(60 g)*
1 small granny smith apple, wedged*
1 frozen banana
1 cup milk** *(8 oz or 240 ml)*
1 tablespoon ground flaxseed *(7 g)*
1/2 cup cubed ice *(120 ml)*
Thin slice of apple, for garnish

Game Guide

The Legend of Zelda: The Wind Waker,
and Twilight Princess.

Drops from Green Chus or Chuchus, but in Twilight Princess these can only be found in the Wii and HD version after a Blue and Yellow Chu merge, and the resultant Green Chu Jelly has no effect.

Directions:

1. Add all ingredients to a blender, and blend on high until smooth.
2. Garnish with apple slice and serve with a straw. Enjoy!

*Reserve a thin slice for the garnish!
**I prefer sweetened almond milk here!

Blue Chu Jelly

This dazzling cool blue blend is sweet as peaches, tangy as pineapple, and simply delicious. The jelly preserve version can be found on page 135!

1 serving	12 oz glass	Vegan	Gluten free

Ingredients:

2 teaspoons blue spirulina powder* *(8 g or 10 ml)*
1 peach, cored and wedged
1 frozen banana
1/4 cup fresh or frozen pineapple *(60 g)*
1 cup sweetened almond milk *(8 oz or 240 ml)*
1/2 cup cubed ice *(120 ml)*
Mini umbrella, for garnish

Game Guide

The Legend of Zelda Series.

Drops from Blue Chus or Chuchus. In The Legend of Zelda: Breath of the Wild, Chuchu Jelly is neutral, and can be changed into any other Chuchu Jelly with elemental exposure.

Directions:

1. Add all ingredients to a blender, and blend on high until smooth.
2. Garnish with a mini umbrella and serve with a straw. Enjoy!

*Spirulina is blue-green algae, and you can pick up the powder at your local grocery store, health food store, or online! It gives this drink the brilliant blue color!

Black Chu Jelly

This mystifyingly dark smoothie is devoid of light but full of deep flavor.
The jelly preserve version can be found on page 128!

1 serving	12 oz glass	Vegan	Gluten free

Ingredients:

1 cup fresh blackberries *(150 g)*
2 tablespoons cocoa powder *(15 g)*
2 pitted dates
1/2 cup baby kale *(15 g)*
1 cup sweetened coconut milk *(8 oz or 240 ml)*
1/2 cup cubed ice *(120 ml)*
2 fresh blackberries, for garnish

Game Guide

The Legend of Zelda:
Twilight Princess.

Consuming forbidden Black Chu Jelly results in the loss of one heart. That's thankfully not the case in real life.

Directions:

1. Add all ingredients to a blender, and blend on high until smooth.
2. Garnish with black berries on top and serve with a straw. Enjoy!

*This drink results in a pretty dark smoothie in general, but if you want this drink to be inky dark, you can add 1 to 2 teaspoons of activated charcoal *(5 to 10 ml)*. However, there is mixed information regarding the benefits of eating activated charcoal, please do your own research or consult a health care provider before ingesting! It can be used here to create an inky black color, and doesn't noticeably affect the flavor.

Ice Chu Jelly

This pear blended and frosted drink will keep you cool while you're saving princesses!
The jelly preserve version can be found on page 137!

| 1 serving | 12 oz glass | Vegan | Gluten free |

Ingredients:

1 ripe pear, halved, reserve one slice for garnish
2 frozen bananas
~2 tablespoons almonds, optional *(20 g)*
1 tablespoon chia seeds *(10 g)*
3/4 cup sweetened almond milk *(6 oz or 180 ml)*
1/2 cup cubed ice *(120 ml)*
Honey or agave drizzle, to taste
1 slice of pear, for garnish

Game Guide

The Legend of Zelda:
Breath of the Wild.

White Chu Jelly is dropped by Ice Chuchu, or can be made by exposing Chuchu Jelly to ice.

Directions:

1. Add all ingredients except honey or agave to a blender, and blend on high until smooth. Taste test, and add a drizzle of honey or agave to sweeten if necessary! Blend again.
2. Garnish with a slice of pear and serve with a straw. Enjoy!

This recipe was inspired by a backer of this cookbook.
Taylor Robey, we can't forget Ice Chu Jelly! Thank you!

Acknowledgments

To the makers of a little video game series called The Legend of Zelda,
Your glorious world of Hyrule has enhanced so many lives, you have changed the world.
Thank you.

I must start by thanking the immense support this little fan-made cookbook found online. 1511 people discovered it, and decided this was a cooking adventure they wanted to taste test. You made this happen! Those who wished it are named on the next page, the champions of this cookbook. Thank you.

To my love, Walter; my muse, my partner, my favorite. Your supply of food kept me going while I wrote about making it. Thank you.

To my friends, you kept me on track when I was about to let it all go half way through. You believed in me, especially when I was unsure of myself. Thank you.

To my parents and brother, you showed me the incredibly imprecise art of every day cooking, that experimentation is part of growth, and that no matter what is in the house we always have ingredients for soup. Thank you.

To my grandparents on both sides, you instilled in me a love of family cooking and family meals. Those memories of making cheese cakes, lasagna, and graham cracker balls will stay with me forever. Thank you.

To all of my new friends on The Unofficial Legend of Zelda Cookbook discord server,* your well wishes, dank memes, cat pictures, and around the clock community got me through it. I hope this cookbook keeps you happy and well fed. Thank you.

And to *you!* Whether you're one of the 1511, or you just joined the quest. It was dangerous to cook alone, but you aren't alone anymore! I hope you'll make good food and share it with good people! Thank you!

*You are still welcome to join our server to share in the joys of Zelda and Cooking!
You'll find the link on aimeewoodworks.com, I can't wait to meet you!

Thank you

This wonderful community came together to taste test and kick start a cooking adventure. You are all heroes of this cookbook! Those who wished to be are named here.

♥ ♡ ♥ ♡ ♥ ♡ ♥ ♡ ♥ ♡ ♥ ♡ ♥ ♡ ♥ ♡ ♥ ♡ ♥ ♡ ♥ ♡ ♥

♥ Champions ♥

These four champions went above and beyond to support this cookbook, and helped to make it better for everyone. Thank you so very much.

♥ Michael K. Sretenović ♥

♥ Pindar Draconia ♥

♥ Mur Wheaton ♥

♥ Joey Dunning ♥

Anthony ♡
Lukas Brayfield ☆
The Silveira
Family ☆
Nana Silveira ☆
James O'Shea IV ☆
Andrew Nobilette
Bug Catcher Sam ☆
Stetson Lee ♥♥♥♥♥
Aka. StattorZ
Erika R. Broadway
♥♥♥♥♥♥♡
Nhi Ngo ☆
Sarah Pineapple Mother ☆
Kerry Honan ☆
Cody Tripp ☆
Chris "BetaChris" Poir-
ier
Sarah Dingman ♡ ☆
Scott Sesko ♥ ☆
Ella A
Victoria J. McNully
Colby Whitlow
Alley Kinder
Gary Dingman ☆
Róisín Alexander
♥♥♥♡♡♡♡♡♡♡
The Junto Team
Nathan Lueth
Liz
ZachJNL
Jarome
Doctor Binary
Tyrant Chimera ♥♥♥
Morgan L'Fey
Evan :) ☆
Plex
Norbert Zahn ☆
Nina Miller
Emily B Skrodzki ☆
Spensah L. Hill ☆
Michael
Amanda De Busk
Tina-Marie Faunce ☆
Noel Baterna ☆
Allie ☆
Dark_Cthulhu554
Melissa Mulliss
TeeJay Meisterheim ☆
Kyle Quick
Aubry

Olivia
Melanie Rodriguez ☆
Barry Lucero ☆
Chelsea Welch ☆
Chandler G. Melby ☆
Heather ♥♥♥
Kirby
TreeNostalgia
KC Shadow
Xan Brown
Cadence Alvarez
Dominic Young
Richö Butts
Nick Stankovich
Robert Zollo
Emily Smit ♥♡
Elizabeth
Pam Wood, mom ☆
Bruce Wood, dad ☆
David Wood, brother ☆
Marcia McIvor, grams ☆
Mort Gitelman, grandpa ☆
Nancy Garner, grandma ☆
Frances & Henry Leonhardt,
grandmommy & granddaddy ☆
Larry and Nancy Wood,
papa and grandmom ☆
Rosy and Daisy ☆
Alicia J. Dugan
Paige Lovejoy ♡
J-Dubz Avedisian II
Chromaticorn ♥♡♡
Chantal P.
Nicholas Eng
Raegan
Michael Paul
Jennifer Koniges
Cody Kerr
Jen
Rilee
Lauren Moore
Cody 'WhiteKnight' Baldree
♥♥♥♥♥♥♡♡ ☆
Yennefer Ayala ♡
Erika Zetterlund ♥ ☆
Scott Wieland
Brielle Munsch
Fiddlesticks ♥♥♥♡♡♡
Matthew Lin
Milen Spasov
Solocien

Mike K
Gillian Donnelly
Minden Dice
Kate Asher
Dan Asher
Martha Anderson
Kaja Foglio
Kiefer Shenk
Devin Strehle
Beronica and Seth
Goaler
ShadyDevil
Alan Insley
Eric Whittaker
Kaitlyn Ryan
Derek McEwen
Maia F
Robin
Shawn Prater
Catherine Donovan
Birdie & Oreo
Hailey Allen
G0ldenEye5
Ezra Wittwer
Jack Anderson
Hooke
Zach Grubbs
Michelle Fernandez
Mike Mayer
Abby Schepens
Grayson Holland
Matthew Welch
Dr. Suma George Cardwell
Melody Hawkins ♥♡♡♡♡♡
Carly Stewart
Drew Mangold
The Scratch Doktor
Pinball Wave
S. Mcgee
Eric C
Ben Wong
Esther Kollhoff
Andrew Martin
Christina Martin
Ben LeClair
Mads George
Andrew Souza ☆
Alice TinTinFin Woods
Mama & Papa Sasquatch
Katherine Dubsky
Kassandra Larson ☆

Ava Goodale ♥♡♡
Ian
Ember Wolfe ♥♥
Fiammetta Wolfe
Vinnette Monette
Daniel Primich
Amanda
Stefanie Foreman ♥♥♥♥
Alexandra Wells
Nathan Kunkel
Ashley Dusenbery
Kaleb Oechsli
Jeffrey Asai
Aki Lin
Matthew Nohr
Briana C.
Erinn
Kile M.
Herbert West
Jillian Chase
Alice Bentley
Stevie Choe
J. Andrichak
Ethan M
Kayla Lima
Joshua H
Yasmin Zellipour and Felix
Baarz
Samantha
Taylor North
Zhane McRae
teacuplaura ♥
coffeemugtom
Andrew Aschenbrenner
Albert Shih
Dakota Hirst
Donna Buenaventura
Riley Andrews
Taylor Robey ♥♥♥♥♡
James Trevillian
Allie A
Elora ♡
Parker Swayze ♡♡
Danny Farrell
Dan0
Rebecca Northcutt
Christian Brungart ♥♥♥♥♡
Longdead
Rick "Alith" Harvey
ZombieFeynman
Andrew

Phil
Liam David
Katie Samaniego
Josh McCarthy
Nick Andert
Doug Dorman
Ethan and Grace
Angus Skipper ♥♡♡
Megan Even
Jackie Nemeth
Brianna Kooshian
Dru Andrew
Trey Hechlik
Holli Dyer
Andy Mills ♥♥♥♥♥
Taylor Webb
Michael K. Sretenović ♥
Claudia Fox
Terracotta Pie
Anthony Gutierrez
Stacy P.
Jenny Warriner
Stanford J Warner Jr
Lizzie Penman
llearch n'n'daCorna
Aaron Pok
Morgan Lyle
Scott Bradley
Stephanie Markham ♥♥♡♡
Amber
Kozio_ ♥♥♥♡♡♡♡♡
Andrew
Manov
Kenneth Buchanan
Jenni Slinn
Nicole Garand
Hadassah Baum
Anika Freimuth
Damien, Maximus, & Kamilla
Steve & Katie C
Michal Khan
The_Spooky_Cat
Taylor A Swift ♥
Caleb Graham
Sean Prosch
Daniel Henderson
Sesilee
Dajah Renee
Giff
Matthew Meling
Cameron Flores

Peter Kanan
Loren McCoy
Bahamuttone
Franziska Schnellmann
Alexandros Papadopoulos
–238–
Jeff Healy
Ares807
Beto!
Daniel Myhre ♥
Anjay Schedaynjay
Anabear ♥♥♥♥♡
Ola Czajkowski
Squirrel Ivan
HyperFrosting
Tor Karlsson
Geo & Lynn
Anthony Luebke
Grace S ♡
Issaiah White
Julian Rose
Melanie Leland
Jaz Thornton
Janusz Lawniczak ♥
Brittani
Michael W. ♥
Shelby & Joshua Fortenberry
Sean Mabe
Jessica Joy Smith
John Kelso
Andrew Crittenden ♥
Finn Silva
Sorcha Dubhsioc
Benjamin Hazelip
Lauren Nick
Mark Shabunia
Dana Neigel & Steve Rogers
♥♥♥♡♡♡
Patrick
Kathleen Smith
Matt & Lizzie Tetrick
Daniel Keach
Candice Womack
Liana Taylor ♥♡♡
Eliza "HazardousLiquid"
Taylor Volk
Riley Bailiff
John Michael
Daniel J Garcia
Harrison
Daniel LeBlanc

Kristie Erikson ♥
Steven Miller
David Glover-Aoki
S. Paul
Jon Bockelman
Hannah Bolen
Rebekah Peschong
Andrew & Anita
Pindar Draconia ♥
Trish Bradford ♥
Pindar ♥
E. Weier
J. Slack
Tyler Ross Edwards
Dana Shep
Shauna McAllister
Jayden Phillips ♥
Emma Roberts ♡
Raul
GingerAle86
Ryan
Michaela Hlatky
Taeryn
Corey Boudreault
Rob
Devon "Surferdevon" Taylor
JadeTheurgist
Alyssa & Brendan ♡
Russell Dawes
Donna Turcotte ♥♥♥
Puugu ♥
Danny Menikheim ♥
Kara Roncin ♥♥♥
Katrina "Mommy" Roncin
Micheal Roncin
Ethan Roncin
Kenadi Roncin
Douglas Lee
Team Janus
Gabe and Rachel ♥♡♡
Ethan W ♡
Kyle
Thomas Moore
Sarah Ricciadi
Madi
Viki
Gabs
Sasha Wood
Josiah
William Self
Ivan Cunningham

Linda Carter
Kwamanda
Link Josef ♥
Ty R.
Jessie Campbell ♥
Sarai Porretta
The Brownell Family ♥
Mike Kelleher ♥
David K. Hildebrandt
LittleDove
Miranda
Justin C
Kari Wooten
Alanna
Tamas Neltz
Kita Gonzalez
Sarah Hiatt
Josh (sohjsolwin) Wilson ♥
Kevin Lam
Lauren
Benjamin Infosino
Matt Kalafut ♥
Daniel ♥♡♡
Motrax
Jessamy
Anna Coons
For my Lindsey ♥
Caitlin White
Andrew Coffey
Ryan Allen
Sasha Dillman
Rosemary Forst
Brad
Ark & Ayri ♥♥♡
Mary-Claire Graham
Erin Greenslade
Alex Lee Cheng
Ashley Schlegel
Moose "Bubba" Mitchell
Annie
Michael Hagen
Matthew Gregory Serianni
StephiStu
Francesca
Trent Fewkes
Evan Wever
Herbert R Castillo Flores ♥♥♥♡
Idalys & Thomas
Derek Hutchinson ♥♡
Cynthia Jennings

Kat W ♥
Steven Baker
Matthew Carter
Kaden Karras
Jordan Trant
Neva & Nick Hutchinson
William Hopp ♥
Johnathan
Salvatore Puma
Matt, Jaci, & Amanda ♥
Daniel Arvidsson
Betsy
Trisha (Kayru)
Linnea Nilsson
Vincent GERMAIN ♥
Julia Janssen
Sapphire ♥♥♥♡
Susan Ridgway
Jeffrey Sims
Carmen Huff
Derek "tachyon" Reese
Danika Molnar ♥♡♡♡
Weegee ♥
Jordan M (LordZophar) ♥ ☆
Pamela Buzzetta
David Bloemer
Alexandra Buzzetta
Mark Blanton
Kyle Martin
Iris R. Stanley
Stephen Furois ♥ ☆
Morgan Darrow
Bradley Greager ☆
Peter Joseph Love ♥
Andri Ferguson
Chestnut ♡
Virginia Riches
Alison Briggs ♥
Joseph McCoy
Jade ♥
Sgt Skittles
Jordan Peters ☆
Jay Secord
Nick Hawkinson ♥♥♡
Gemma
Juliana, Alex & Caroline C.
Laura G
Emma Jean Hill
Alexander
Julian R.
Joey Kendrick

Prowln Jazz
Dr. Thomas A. Bea
Wellesandra ♥
Katherine Swanson
Shane Daugherty
Sara Pearson ☆
Chris Withers
Kyle Withers
Nathaniel Withers ♥
Kristen Linroth ♥♥♥ ☆
AnneMarie
Martin Nixon
Gabi B.
Eddy Super
Ibelyias
Mathias S L
Tyler "Crayola" Willett
♥♥♥♡
Karen Hampe
Robert T Case II
Lyx Fuge ♥
Jesse Kearns
Ryan Black
Angelica Marciano
Robin B
Sayosien
Larsia
Rhel ná DecVandé
Zelda Williams
Veronica Gartland
Baron von Muffinbeard III ♥
Lady Echo
Kathleen Rose
Michael Davis
Samantha Hodson
Geoohki
Melissa
Robyn Armstrong ♥
Chelsey Kirkland ♥♡♡♡
Sergio Gonzalez
Kristina May Aarek Kidd
♥♥♥
Allison Long
Julie Pilon
Ashley
Kaitlyn McLaughlin ♥
Kathleen Shipley
Rhema and Frank Taylor
Femke Davis ♥
Janina Savio
Kimberly Calderon

Trinity Parker
Steffan Cole
Jocelyn *Cabbit* Gorman
Antoine Olivier ♥♥♥♡
Kara Belcher
Kati ♥
Jennifer Brown
Suzanne Taylor
How2Texan
Han Nguyen
Matt Cochran
Rachael Perkins
Brittany S
Briana C
Henry Hoverton
Monja Elisa Johnsen
♥♥♥♥♥♥
Beck & Sam
Joshua Huffman ♥♡
Erin Cormick
Ryan Morris
Ian
Animedrgn ♥♥
Melissa Plate
Crystal and Ryan Young ♥
Britni and Todd Arnold
Kate Hansen
Mr. Dr. Pib
Sarah M. Gaertner
Donna—Maryse
Amanda Lindsey
Nick Czerew
Baptiste Brylak ♥
Teegan ♥♡
Oliver Mawson—Martin ♥
Kayleigh Skar
Jeremie Lariviere
Loriana
Flavio
Dylan Jacobson & Cathryn
Carney ♥
Katey
LKH
Matthew
Cory Bob
Anthony & Moki ♥♥♡
Lukas Klapatch
Wes Bisheff
Weezel
Jessica Dawn
Brennan Keller ♥

Bryce Keller
Laura Martin
Jeanette Volintine
Timothy Bialecki Jr
Shaistra Narie Narishka ♥
Colin Topping
Jason and Fiona G
Amy B
Michelle
Andreas "Skaw" Maurer ♥
Stephany Rosa ♥♡♡♡♡
Kathleen McFatridge
Graham Mackie
Drew + Natalie
Daniel Albert ♥♡
Tim Szaroleta
Sean Chambers
Wyatt Wagner
John
HumblePhi
Kaitlyn
SageVega
Sadie Bayless
Myrrh Winston
Chris Markham
Stephen Finegan
Colin Rogers
Douglas Adams
johnfrederic1
Stephen Press
Daniel J. Parson
Bill Rhoda
Captain Dibbzy
Vincent Nativi
Jenna Downie
Alexander Sheets ♥
GallantChaos
Drigan
Deku Tony & Midna Chris
Sellheim ♥
Bright Chen
Liz Olhsson ♥
Dean Windemuller
Frances & Logan
Richard & Amy
LesleyDawn Robertson
Ricky Mooney
Chibi Okamiko
Quinton McEachern
Shellese Cannonier
Cyri Thompspn ♥

Kassie M ♥
Kurt
Staff12 ♥
safireblade
Kai ♥
Shaun Fletcher
Vita ♥♡♡
Sarah Margaret Barber ♥♥♥
Kris Kannel
Katelyn Kannel
Jeremy Kannel
Jane Cradic
Harry Cradic
Nathaniel Klein ♥
Tsz Ying Cindy Tang
Douglas Burgman
Christian Burgman
Olivia Steck ♥♥♥♥♡
Mike Kline
hugo
Walid Bendris
Litamaco ♡
Aunt Patty (Liz)
Nephew Kai
Neyko Neykov ♥
Meg Reichert ♥
BounciestVanity & Kailous
Elisha Mariah
Zeniate
Naomi C. Thompson
M. Piedad Camus G.
Michelle Kooi ♥
Mr. Weisner
Kelley Winship
Mrs. Qtini
Grant Bathe
John Woo
Caitlin & Minh-anh ♥
Cam Fowler
Jason Rodgers
Jaquilyn Mackey
Kaleb Jones ♥
Nicki
Daniel Quintero
Bala Ramanujam
Yann Luyet
Laura García Otero ♥♥♥♥♥
Eugenio Bianchi
Geist ♡
John Sweetnam
Jessica Simons

Cairan and Amber ♥
Blizz
Amanda Jennings
Lawjick
RainbowSprink1e
Sergeant H Bear
Cora Anderson
Marian & Lauren
Jennifer Raidt ♥♥♡
Adrienne (Niserie) ♥♡♡
K.E. Clausen
Katherine Hempel
David Clowers
Samantha Nagott
Eric Krul ♡♡
Daniel Ryne Lucio
♥♥♥♥♥♥♡♡♡♡♡♡
David Armando Lucio
Derek Robert Lucio
Dario Miguel Lucio
Duran Arturo Lucio
Parker Boyles
Will Smith ♥
Harriet Sedgwick
Michelle Rokki
Austin Kunze
Corey
Audrey Sulkanen
Leo Williams
Ashli Tingle
KLBL
Hanna Stewart
Kameron Chausse ♥
mestor ♥
Dan Hallock
Zannalov & Kaynary
Jetzsia :) ♥
Emily Betzen
pixya factory
Deren Dang
Julia "RheaKat" Kent
Petrov Neutrino
Edna "DiscoKittii" Rouse
Braden
Christopher
David "Zankabo" Kohler
Benjamin Plotsky
Percival Bunner ♥
Alex and Brenda Fellman
Heather Turnor
Jean-Michel St-Pierre

Lapierre ♥
Stefan
Monica B
Sophie Godin
Matthew Pilgreen
Lonk ♥
The Great & Mysterious Cat
Goeddey
Sir Sandwich Spread
Michael & Evelyn Platt
David Beasley
Danielle Schoen
Hai-Yue Han ♥
Nhonami
Careen Ingle
Tim Gallen
David Eliahou
SerperiorSnivy
J. Rika Simon ♥♥♡
Kevin S.C. Decker
Bobby Driggs
Austin Ponder
Aurora Smith ♥
Kat Smith ♥
B__n___ K__e__
GrandMama ♥♥♥♥♥
GrandDaddy ♥♥♥♥♥
Colin Brown ♥
Will Farley
Jordan Fredriksz
Jacob Evers
Michael Kohl
Juston
Emji Amsdaughter
Travus
James Dickerson
Paul y cod asyn Jarman
Mack Moore
Kevin Zdanowski ♥♥♥
Jon Peard
Zander
Uri Shomroni ♥
Alon Shomroni
Melissa D
Hikari
Merlijn Frikken
Simjuillian Tolero
Molly Shebek (Mek Night)
AwesomeKidKid
Nick Walsh
Brady Williams

Jeffrey [Maho]
Lotus Drop
AzureIceFlare
Simon Ovesen
Stan He
Kenny White
OtakuMike78
Daniel Solis
William Austin Davis
Stephen Hyde
Colin F
Hugo Tremblay
Orian Young
Helen Schneider
Francisco
Esai Morales ♥
Jesse Marie MacDougall ♥
Ben Pollock
Daniel Kitchen ♥♥♥♡♡
Sarah Nihart and Malachi Rademaker
Ian Bobiwash
Athina Agelopoulos
Jenna Myers
Mich Walter
Benjamin Moore
Amanda Maceda
Jack "Klutz" Boyd ♥
Marcela Rivest
Jennifer Chun
Liana Abbott ♥
Brian P. Lewis
Kirsten Doering
Chiyuki
Ashton Dodge ♥♥♡♡
Nina Cerda Montez ♥
JJFox
Belinda Carmona
Serenity Grace
Ryan MacDonald
Jesse P.
Ronic IV
Leslie
Becky Rivera
Pixl
Bradly Garcia
Conor Michael O'Sullivan
Rofia
Zachary
Olli Petäjoki
Tyson Stone

Nicholas Yeager
Brandon M
Brandon
Morgan Glass
Seaile17
ChefWombat ♥♡
Cynthia Leslie Steenvoorden
Diego Garcia
Triforceoflink
Isa
Mary Kenneally
Ralle
SongbirdZingara
Calvin Chiang
Vladimir Govorkov ♥
Heath McArdle
Wilde J
Samantha "Kitty" Carrie
Edward ♥♥♥
Vincent Brignoni
Keara Shae
Andy Pham
BudderGoldenfur ♥
Dani
Alexander Stull
Whitney Stull
Scarlette Starr ♥
Altana
Magda Edith Rodriguez
Ericko
Sara Chandler
Galdon454 ♥
Ulysses
LeJea Williams ♥
Courageous Champion
Rob, Emily & Sean ♥
Courtney Voorhees
Ash
Mur Wheaton ♥♥♥
Bandit Roland
CurlyFries
Drew J
Rachael Goodman ♥♥♥
PoisonJammer ♥
Colby C
Yumeihan
Jordan Sasiela
Katie P.
Jessica Chamberlain
KptnMoewe
Dusk Mirage

Elliott R
Shawna Lee
Guillaume G
Andi Bonde
Gus and Ray Lindgren
Randy Geraads
Pichetchai Jongjiramongkonchai
Victoria A. Jones-Ford ♥
StinaDragon
Bjørnar Lindland
Sawyer Busse
Andrew F
Courtney Storm
Steve Wolf
Ella Parrington
Linzi Knight
Harrison 'Shadow' Lovell
Beathe
Sandra Vos
Mikyn De La Torre
Hillary
James Holloway
Alec Harris
Tom Britland
Marena Montera
Kenneth Sloane
Zan
Paige Ariana Thomas ♥♡
Tara Nicole Thomas
Luca
Steven Beres
Phoebe Brown ♥
Genesis E. Alvarez
Aretsuya
Deborah A. Flores
Yuzuki Blake
Dakota Grundner (Sunshine) ♥♥♥♥♡♡
Derek Purpura
Derek Baker
Koalabulldog
Danette Schardt-Cordova ♥♥♥♥
Kerri Haidys
Michelle Priya Rust
Kyle Denna
Evan Ogden
The Dashing Adrian
Rose
Danielle ♥♥♥♥♥

The concept of cats
as friends.
Taylor and Zach
Nick Rohovie
Marcus Rohovie
Shannon and Brett Janis
Anton Arutunov ♥
Sami Österholm
Claire Dickey
Kelly Gregory ♥
FullyStuffedGeek
IJsbrand
Marion LALANNE-COUCHOT
James "MysticFox" Cole
Jason B. Boig
Michael Halloween Custer
86 Paul
Marcus Shepherd
Aninok ♥♥♥♥♥
Mark Sztainbok
Bobby Luckel ♥♥♥♡♡
Zach Gulden
Christer Håkansson
David Schneider
Marten Schulz
Matthew and Rosie Wessel ♥
Kayla Suppapong & Jeremy
Johnson
Robert & Virginia Locas
Shane Fae ♥
Maddie Fallin
Kipling Rose
Sean Lowther
Ash & James Heitman ♥
Alan Mata
Simon Robinson
Allison Bandel
SpeedForce
Molly King
Bethany Stewart
Emily Stewart
Marmaduke
Dean Ward
Aden S.
Stu & Jo
Barba2
Blue And Ethan
Danny Everett
Jennifer Grzankowski
Laura Rose ♥
Thomas Eldredge ♥

Jill A.
Anthony Barker
Ben Walker
Cinquedia
Jayme Tutor
Jacob Camarillo
Kimea
Prateek SIngh
Zeerion ♥♥♡
Margaret T
Meraligne
Jordan Garrett
Allen Garrett
Nadine Liggett
Denise
Stephanie Kay Aikens ♥
Ross Davis
Michelle Forget
Mackenzie Waldeck
Alex Smith
Paul Evans
Kara
Frank
Sydney Eduardo Aprea
Vallejo
I am Error
Timothy D. McLendon
Daniel O. McLendon
Luke Tammadge
Heather
Riley Herring
Robert Rauch
Bernadette Breeze
Alex Sonnenberg
Kathryn Hemmann
John Ewalt
Michael Graf
Andrew Schroettner
James Smith ♥
Chris Matte
Shawn Burlew
Ashley & Jamie Perry
Iratxe Lizame
Daniel Troncoso
Cristovao Oblad
Sarah Guelbert and Erika
Bradshaw
Timmy Nolan
Kimberly Dillon
Ken TM Wong
Stanley Pieda

Mark Dickman ♥
Erika McEntee
Chevaliers
Chris Laverty
Keith Laverty
Sarah Pagan (Deathless
Goddess) ♥
Kyle McDermid
Antonio Xavier Valdez
Jon Nebenfuhr ♥
Bethan Rimmer ♥♥♡♡
Clarissa Light
John Sharvin &
Dana Laskowski
Michael Kanell
Sita Williams
Lana Barker
Bryson Family ♥
Sarah Linn
Katarzyna Dzilinska ♥
Jennifer Weishaar ♥♥♥♥♥
Jacklynn Imel
Suzilla
Beth Fisher
Tim Suter
Jacob Converset
David Werling
Alexander Lipka
Mamu143
Lizzie!
Anthony Parascando ♥
Kristy Bahr
Ilsa Gordon
Kelsey Morgan
Kaeleigh Morgan
Rachele ♥
Logan Boerm
Dmitry Molkov ♥♥♥♡♡
Elizabeth Lorenzo
Ryu247
Alex, Alison, Lexi and
Summer
Kurtle
Sasha Farore Green ♥
Brooke
AJ & Sara Guilford
Artemios Blanas
Michael Saccucci
Joel Dragon Sword
Jeff Kent
Julia Rither

Aurora Holland ♥
Natalie
Tyler Abbotoni
Andreas "Infinitras"
Schicho
A. M. Imre
Aaron "Ganaron" Gean
Chris
Sara Nelson ♥
Jenny
Heidi Hagen
Jeffrey Boeck
Alex Saltzman
Gabriel Barcenas ♥
Lige Counce
Brad Elders
Barry Wade ♥♥
Abram Wade ♥♥
Maia Fee
Bones
Captain J.
Xiraka
Elisa Conforti
Rebecca McGrath
Mason Douglas Fritz
Joseph R. Toro
Jon Slaco ♥
@EatMoreWorkLess
Ryan Ming Chu
The Spaniers, Westside
Trent Crowe
The Caseys
AZL ♥
Jacqueline Cook
Bechtel Family
Dis McCarthy
The Beselers
Craig and Jamie Thompson
Jonathan Ritacco
Tori Wilson
Andrew Hacker
Shae Moloney ♥
Kyle Keller ♥
Ari Dunning
Andrew Ciocco
Aaron Ciocco
Thom Goodnow
Mallory
Dione Basseri
Briona Warden
Brandon Cheong

Henry Bo Benry
Mathieu Tétreault ♥
Neil + Christena
Sally Rogers
Nora & Grant
Samantha Gardner
Joshua B Freeman
Hannah Coffey
Wrenna Ptak
Dominic Portmann ♥
Sander Roest
Tom Murphy
Troyford Cannell ♥
Andy1210 ♥
Bastien Montassier ♥♥♥
Steven A Murphy
Kalani Anderson ♥
Chris & Kimmi ♥
Mason VanGorkom ♥
Samuel & Raegan Rohmer
Julie Spencer
Rachel Netzband
Gemma Davis
Michael Joseph Dichiera
Lee
Jeff Madicus Ellis
Farfarello ♥
Ta-Lee Shue
Jessica P
Lorna Lavallee
Aiesha Baldry ♥♥♡♡
David Springer
Kaila Kim
Emily Picciotto
Alex Curtis
Katie Blanchard
Riley (Metroid1) ♥
Chloe Rain Booth
Sarah Zdanowski
Steven Wren
Matthew Hohisel ♥
Laurie Hohisel ♥
Urgel Paquin
The Fontaines
flightbypony
Adrian ♥
Nana probata
Pollydolilloló ♡♡♡
Taleb Fernandes
Delrin ♥♥♡♡♡♡♡♡♡♡♡♡♡
E. Sword ♥♥♡♡♡♡♡♡♡♡♡♡♡♡

Zita Orban
Audrey L
Thomee Wright
Jennifer Johnson
Kelsey Ernst
Michael Shumate
Joshua and Mayra Gomez
Mardi, Stanley, and Frankie
Alpha and Beta
Elise Foster
Ziva
Fidel
Cheyanne
André Arko
Dave Scheppler
Kris Francis
Haleigh Vierra
Oliver Guernsey
Ivy Olalla Hughes
Van Hughes Family
Derek McNeill ♥
Devante McLeod ♥
Joshua Bobilin
H & A Priest
B & D Priest
Kenneth Clanton
Christina McGuire ♥
Michael Pulling
Jay Rooney
Jameelah!
Rudy Family
Barthlow Family
Brooklyn (pookierawrz)
Cally Deppen Neely
Alan Grey
Michael Schearf
Moira Lynch
Ben Lord
Brooke & Emily Latimer
The Fichthorn Family
Jennifer L. Birmingham
Brian Mattucci
Samantha Joy Williams
Stephanie
Taylor Ransom
Brittney
Kat Riddler
Cy Butler
Regina Hocke ♥
Trent J.L. Douglas ♥

Matthew
Maryse Keyser
Desirée Carrillo
Guzmán ♥
Joey Civin
Andrew Bennett ♥
Cody Johnston
Natalie Tham
Ohako
Thomas Mueller
Maura Covino
Kat Dalton ♥♥♥♡♡
KitsuneKinomi
Peter Pietrantoni
Hank Wiggins
Chris VandenHeuvel
Christina Lapiccirella ♥
Danny Clark
Adina Kroll
Jack Graves
Peter G Athey
Matthew Delaney
EKela Autry ♥
Craig DeForge
Tim Jacobs
Alba "Naalsi"
Francisco L
Team Mudgett!
Fabrizio & Virginia ♥
Paolo
Benjamin Aldridge
Janie Larson
Jérémy Lopez ♥
Jacob Harper
Amanda Fly
Bryce Combs
Philippe Boisvert
Ratralsis
Sophia & Dani Rodriguez ♥
Kat HP
Monty Montgomery
Katie Diamond
The Rawsons ♥
resspopv
Nicholas Hager
The Dennehys
KillerPit
Tama! ♥♥
Megan McCauley
TheH3ro0fT1me49
Raven

Erika Kapalay
Christina Kurland
Dominic Nelson
Katherine Ventura
Jimin Shim
Russell
Alex Gaub &
Kathleen Karlson
Noah Sheppard ♥
Jenny Herriot
John Cmar
Cedric Christensen
Claire Shaw
Caitlin O'Loughlin
Miguel Jesus
Aqqie
Devon Benco
Cindy Garris
Mikail Paquette
Conor Cooke
Kelsea Rose ♥
Luxi Charlemane
Spud Pie
Drew Stewart
Justus Hertel
Alan and Hannah
Mason Lantz
Aldo & Adriel
Dominic
Christian Anderson ♥
Oscar ♥
Felix ♥
Lyra ♥
Archer ♥
Parley ♥
Ollie ♥
Staci Ardison ♥
Christopher Cromartie
Ruby Laski
Rizu ♥
Taylor Mears
Cody Lund
Kristian Handberg
Tyler Fake ♥
Oliver Maximilian Seidel
Brittany and Joe Strazz ♥
Kristoffer Sørheim
Reesha Rajen ♥
Lisa Kuenzel
The Harrington Family
Caden Potter

Alexis Chernish –
Unknowen
Jesse Brooks ♥
Erin Casteel
Louise Johansson ♥♡
Kristen Roberts
Alison Yih ♥ ☆
Courtney Boddy
Quinn
Indie Contreras
CJ Raulli
Drew Chrisman ♥
Ryan and Sarah Grill
Hannah B
Carter D ♥
Tess and Frances Schmucker
Franklin Liu
halee roberts ♥
Mary "MarMar" Stewart
skdomino
Joseph Smay, II
Robbie, Luke, Aiden, &
Kieron Hobbs
Mary K. Williams
George Pudding & Pie
Daniel Longenbaker
Daniel Lin
Christopher Ramirez
Anthony Melluzzo ♥
Lucas Breckenridge
Tabi, Matilda, and Aviva
Alexander H
Jonathan Ginther
Crystal McCarty
Katie Scandozza
The Tobias Family
Becca H. ♥
Joshua Levitt
Jan Joseph Kruit
samurguybri
Joakim
Robert Ewans
Brian Jones
Muhammed Ali Keskin
Nina Dietterle
Tiffany Despina Patronas
Alexander Beech ♥
Lord Buick aka,
King Vegeta ♥
Rob in AUS ♥
Finnian Nordenberg

David Ruskin
Joshua Wiffen
Lakshman
Andrew Hainline
E. Woj
In Memory of Éowyn Maynes
♥♥♥
Tracy Fraser
Justin & Stacey Burghardt
RainbowDragoon
Kristin
Alessandro Caffari ♥
Megan Greene ♥
TheKevann
Sunshine
Andrew Parsons
Bruce H Webster Jr
John Suckbut
Michelle Steele
Corbzor
The Rogers Family
(Liz, Bill, Link, and Nox)
Zac & Jill
Carter Lien
Erich M Staehling ♥
Hanna Julie
Steven x Davis
Ryan Benson
Jason Bolton
R A Van Epps & Jannus
Blackseed
Radmüller Stefan
Meredith Wood
CookieyedGamer
Jon Ballew
Micah Dawson
Ed Clark
Maya
Cat Zarate
Scott Loper
Jeff & Isaac Hopkins
Roger Adams
Team Kram
The Mysterious Backer "X"
Alaura
Erik Connor
JeNai Dalton
Maurice Schlagheck
Bruno San Agustín
Hunter Kunzler
Chelsea Slevin

Chris Lewis-Brown
Amber & Jeff Ruthford
Ari Miller
IdleArene
Isadora Fonseca
Justin LaChance
James N.H. Baxter
Noah S. ♥
Aubri E. ♥
Caitlyn D. ♥
Jesse S
Emily Van Etten
Brian & Helene McLaughlin
Daddy ♥
Brandon JK
Isaac Ramos
Madison Howell ♥♥♡
BlueBow501
Christopher Jackson
Kyle
Katie
Fllipy
Nathaniel Hacker
Minerva
The Spaulding Family
Donovan R. Mobley ♥
Chevy Williams
JJ Castillo
Sascha Völkering
Jennifer Schmidt
Florian Schmolke
Sasux3
Eblis
Abigail Awad
James Canny
Tyler Brown
Lauren A. Kruesi
Alex Formato
Krysta ♥
The Amanteas
Michael & Amanda
Andrew Thomas (CyanBlob)
Jillian Cox
Edward Miller
Finn Lee Binkley
Marissa G.
Amanda Lonsdorf
Lily Islas
Alexander Cruz
Kimberly Rigler
Christina Woods

Tyler
Kramer Walz
Maddi and AJ
Kiri & Gwen
Jarod Lewis
Olivia Staciwa
Liz Glavich ♥
JoodallyJoo
Shon M
Jack Spaulding ♥
Akahoshisenjo
Ian Jones
Rafal Frelas
Kali Pohle ♥
David Vessels ♥
Inga Anita Fischer
Natalie Eichler
Crystal Muse
Irene Caru
Sergey Borisov
Christoffer Heine Haugsdal
Tonje Lenore Reitan
Edward Alm
Jessie Compton
Jennie Huynh
Sharon Byerly
Kim Stanford and Wei Sung
Fermin Serena Hortas
Rebekah Jordan
Hayley Chan
Mina S
E.T. Siblings
Becky Kirk
James JJP
Chris Jones
Jacob "Wolfman"
Damian
Nathan Jones
Melody Lindsay
Caitlin Jane Hughes
Ethan Warwick
The Gills
Landen Stricklin
Taylor Tschida
Eddie Forstoffer IV
Sophia Bromwell
Osco
dkn2
Jesse McArdle ♥
Joshua Lake
Jessica S

Michael Panchaud
Cameron Monk
Bonitoflakes
Samantha Yigdal
Matt Westlund
ConnorStJimmy
Logan Crecraft
Jessica Stanton
Joey Dunning ♥
Dmitriy Kozlovskiy
Emanuel Guadarrama (Emmy) ♥
Traye
Wan
Paul Morano
The Scotteth
Hannah Gibson
Blake Myrddin
Hale217
ShiaSurprise
Dirk Ritzel Grebenstein
Germany
Silje Eide
Steven DeBirk
Nick Biggs
David Lundberg ♥♥♥
Jacqueline Sergent ♥
LinksAwokening
YaBoiLink
Kimberly ♥
Kendall Myers
Lukasz Pawlus
Kaitlin VanderPryt
Karlee VanderPryt
Philips Clarke
Gweemz
Katsumaa
Sean
Adam Hagel
David McCallister
Kimberly Sampson
Leander Temüjin Tiffany
Aisling and Saoirse Baker
Hendren
Casey/Nat Grebe
Jared Krinsky
Casayndra Basarab
Renee A. Rosales ♥
Charles C.
Brad McNay ♥
Getty Family
Agata Soler Vives

Joshua Hecker
Megan D.
Bobby Keller
Douglas Truong
Dicentra
Deirdre McLeod
Benjamin Herman
Celeste Lauren
Chloe Roop
Melissa
Lee Redmond
Aimee Wood ♥
S, you know who you are.
Michael Sexton
William C. Roe ♥
The Saligas
Max Marcello
Austin & Brooke Carpenter
Michael Lory
Lia & Jukes
Arthur
Isaac Smith
Musogato ♥
Hannah Rasmussen
Ryan Kent
Bubba
Sean Rachford ♥
Keidy A. Cortés Padilla
Thomas Ellis
Chef Marcus Godwin
Chef Isabelle Vernon
Magnificent Mike Castro
Kristin Houchin
Jeff and Sarah
Agmenine Malincar
Christian Kim
Lee Lovato-Kralovec
Jacob Smith
Heroic Hylian
Kevin and Ivana ♥
Matthew Bonnema
Nick Ahlers ♥
JL & MP ♥
Robert Warner
Khav
High King Walter ♥♥♥ ☆
Happy House ☆
Happy Colorado
Nerd Club ☆
The Discord ☆
The #cat-tax-channel ☆

Everyone who sent me an encouraging private message, thank you.
♥♥♥♥♥♥♥♥

Those who successfully completed quests have been listed with heart containers, thank you for your help and dedication!

And thank you to all of those not listed here. I am so sorry if I misspelled anyone's name, if I forgot a heart, or if, by my own error or by survey deadline, I missed you here entirely. Thank you!

Recipe Index

Vegan = V, Vegetarian = v, Gluten free = GF. Menus are not marked.
(V) or (GF) indicate recipes that include alterations for those diets.

Recipe Index

Vegan = V, Vegetarian = v, Gluten free = GF.
(V) or (GF) indicate recipes that include alterations for those diets.

Recipe Index

Vegan = V, Vegetarian = v, Gluten free = GF. Alchemy Chapter is fully V and GF.
(V) or (GF) indicate recipes that include alterations for those diets.

The Author

I'm Aimee!* I'm going to take this moment to encourage you all as best as I can. I am fiercely proud of the people I have found during this project, and I want to reflect your support right back at you.

Ingredients:
3 perspectives on modern life:
Lost Connections, by Johann Hari
Digital Minimalism by Cal Newport
How Not to Die, by Michael Gregor
2 books on stoic philosophy:
Guide to the Good Life, by William Irvine
Letters by Seneca

Directions:
1. Spend time reflecting on what your values are, then build a lifestyle where you can live in accordance with them. Focus on how you can, not on why you can't.
2. Memento mori, and amor fati. Your time is finite, and you must abide by the trichotomy of control. If your time is so valuable, how much of it are you actually willing to sell? Start viewing prices as time sold, not money spent.
3. Conquer your risk aversion and learn to take calculated leaps. You've got this!
4. Relearn how to focus your attention for long periods of time, it's the only way you'll complete long projects and stay motivated longterm. For this, and when you feel like you don't have enough time, read Digital Minimalism by Cal Newport. Reading in general can help your brain learn how to do this again.
5. You are your own limiting factor. Anyone can have ideas or talk about them, we need to go and do and be. Be like Link, very little talking, a lot more doing!
6. It's dangerous to go alone. Please, surround yourself with close, true friends; put time and effort into making new ones. They will save you as often as you save them.

*Aimee Wood or @AimeeWoodWorks is me! aimeewoodworks.com is my online home, you can email me or join my email list there. Thank you!!!

The Drinkbook

If you loved this cooking adventure, I hope you'll join me for the companion book and drinking adventure! Introducing, The Unofficial Legend of Zelda Drinkbook: A Complete Guide to Hyrulian Alchemy and Bartending!

Ingredients:

1 Hardcover Drinkbook, to match this Cookbook

Watercolor Illustrations and Color Printing

100+ Recipes, including more:

Potions and Elixirs

Cocktails and Mixed Drinks

Milkshakes and Smoothies

Loose Leaf Tea Blends and Boba Teas

Chu Jelly Shots and Themed Specials

Seasonal and Regional Drinks

Directions:

1. Set a timer for 1 to 2 years. I started the Drinkbook when I started the Cookbook in 2017, but food quickly took over. I'll need time to expand and perfect it! In the mean time, I hope you'll enjoy the introduction chapter, included on page 275.

2. Take care of yourselves! Continue exploring the world of cooking, and make new friends to share with!

3. Optional: Join the Discord* to keep updated, and to taste test some early drink recipes while they are finished!

4. Optional: Join my Newsletter* so you won't miss the campaign announcement!

5. Once everything is done, the project will be posted on Kickstarter. 2021 is my hope, and, as a thank you to those who have been supporting this from the start, if you join on the first day, there will be a special early cucco bonus for you!

6. Another heart-container-felt thank you to all of you. Keep going! ♥

You can join on theunofficiallegendofzeldacookbook.com ! Thank you!

Eat Skewers Raw

>You've skewered your skewer on page 62, and have now chosen to forgo the hassle of cooking it! You have decided to eat your skewer raw!

>You proceed to eat your raw skewer!
It is delicious, but a little hard to chew through.

>Four days later...

YOU HAVE DIED OF DYSENTERY.

GAME OVER

Continue playing ?

Yes   No

Quick!

Grab the ocarina! Play the Song of Time! Travel back to change your fate and cook your skewers! With your acquired knowledge of the future, you decide to:

>**Bake in an oven,** turn to page 63
>**Grill on a grill,** turn to page 64
>**Roast on an open fire,** turn to page 65

*It was vegan you say? Too bad you have already died, the mystery will never be solved.